I Gotta Rock

Twenty Years of Tales 1965-1985

Cowboy Mach Bell

Panther Rock Books

Marshfield Hills Massachusetts

Panther Rock Books

I Gotta Rock / Cowboy Mach Bell

COLLECTOR'S EDITION

ISBN Paperback 978-1-7334712-4-4

Every effort has been made to trace the copyright holders of the photographs in this book, but some were unreachable. The publisher would be very grateful if the photographers concerned would contact Panther Rock Books.

Negative scanning and archiving by Denise Geddes.

For more about Mach Bell,
the Joe Perry Project, Thundertrain & the rest, please visit
oncearocker.com

For my mother Paddy Bell
and in loving memory to
Bobby Edwards

Get down and Get with it.

– NODDY HOLDER

I GOTTA ROCK

CONTENTS

Mach Bell '75 Photo by Lynn Ciulla

{ 1 }

Jimi Hendrix and the Mechanical Onions

Jimi Hendrix is coming to town. Well, not my town exactly, the next town over. I have a ticket for his Sunday, August 25th show. My former bandmate, Dave, is a year older than me, he has a license and a Karmann Ghia and he's the one who managed to snag the tickets.

It's 1968 and the first two Jimi Hendrix Experience albums are starting to get pretty popular. Right now the Experience is transitioning from being a warm-up band on big shows like the Mamas and the Papas, the Association and the Monkees, to being a headline act.

I first heard about the Experience from articles written in London. They got reprinted here in a free tabloid rock mag called GO. I find it freshly stacked every week, near the back entrance to my old man's store, the Music Box in Wellesley.

The early publicity photos and articles about Jimi's Experience portray the group in a savage, dark, scary way. That initial UK press campaign for Hendrix was way over the top.

Onward to Monterey '67, Jimi's splashy photo appearance in Life Magazine and finally, the long delayed USA release of "Are You Experienced?"

I buy the first Hendrix album a few weeks after it comes out. I buy Vanilla Fudge that same day.

On first listen "Are You Experienced?" sounds confusing.

I put on the Vanilla Fudge album.

After hearing the Fudge's heavy versions of "Ticket to Ride" and "You Keep Me Hanging On" - that's *all* I want to hear.

I spin Vanilla Fudge non-stop for a couple weeks.

Eventually I put Jimi back on the turntable. This time I'm finally prepared to be Experienced.

Foxey Lady and Hey Joe are already getting some play on the brand new underground FM station in Boston, WBCN.

Hendrix is popular here in Framingham too.

But for a different song.

"Fire" has taken off at local school dances.

Girls like to bounce around to it.

Local groups like to play it.

Leading up to the concert the music grapevine is buzzing that Jimi might lose his temper onstage.

According to the gossip, Jimi Hendrix can be a dangerous and outrageous person to deal with.

"Jimi beat up one of the guys in his band during the show."

I dig Noel and Mitch, so these fistfight rumors make me a bit apprehensive.

Jimi is ten years older than me. He'll be turning 26 later this year, in November.

The Experience are performing two shows tonight at 7 pm and 9:30 pm inside a round canvas tent. It's called the Carousel. I have the expensive $5.50 ticket for the early show. This is my first time stepping inside the Carousel. "The Music Man" just closed a five-day run here and I've ridden past this blue, canvas venue a million times.
Other acts booked for the tent this summer are grown-up things like Liberace, Danny Kaye and a Burlesque Night with Ann Corio.
But lately, Carousel owner Frank Connelly is booking rock groups for us kids. Usually the rock & soul shows only happen on Sunday nights. Vanilla Fudge and The Association headlined the first two Sundays of August. The Young Rascals are booked here for tomorrow - right after Hendrix - a rare Monday engagement at the tent.

Entering the Carousel we quickly get ushered past several dozen other young patrons to our seats. Dave turns to me, stunned. They're leading us to Jimi's side of the stage, house left, only five rows back from the circular plywood stage. Two 100 watt Marshall stacks. Black, scuffed-up speaker boxes piled two-high with an amp head on each grace Jimi's side of the platform. What a beautiful sight.

The lights dim and Eire Apparent, a group produced by Hendrix, warm up the teen crowd with a fast-paced set, offered at ear splitting volume. I can't decipher their tunes but the Irish quartet dress flash, and they move around a lot.

A Hammond organ is rolled into place and after a few adjustments the second band begins noodling. Soft Machine dispense psychedelic sludge served with minimal stage action. Very low energy. The longest thirty minutes this 15 year-old has ever endured.

The trio races center stage with instruments in hand. Jimi, decked out in black silk shirt, V cut at the neck, ruffled at the front, a silver necklace worn high on a short chain, black velvet pants, flared from the knee, drape over short-heeled boots. Embroidered vines growing up the outer seams of his trouser legs. A colorful scarf and a round-linked, silver chain drape around his hips. No hat. His afro mane is full and riding high. Jimi has oversized eyes and hands but the rest of him is compact and taut but graceful. Using a coiled guitar cord, Hendrix quickly plugs his white Fender Stratocaster into the dual stack of Marshalls.
The Experience opens with Johnny B. Goode.
I'm surprised. I play this same song with my band, The Cynics. Jimi's version is a lot better, and faster, than ours.

The Experience slam into Are You Experienced? From the first album. My ears tingle. It really does sound just like the record. The parts I thought were overdubbed or backwards tape...they're recreating every nuance, doing it right in front of my eyes. Noel is on the other side of the stage from me. His bass is Fender too, a Jazz bass I think. His amplifiers are Sunn and his pile of speakers might be even larger than Jimi's. Redding is wearing cool-looking hippy glasses with an even huger afro-style haircut than the boss.

Mitch Mitchell is set-up on the floor, no riser. There's a boom stand in front of his Ludwig bass drum. Mic'ing the kick I guess. He's got a four piece kit with an oversized bass drum. Mitch doesn't have an afro like I saw on the album covers. Just a long, wavy British rockstar cut. Like John Mayall or Ray Davies would wear. It's a hot August night and Mitchell hasn't got a shirt on, just a small scarf tied around his throat.

Jimi twangs out the familiar opening cascade of notes and The Experience drop into a dramatic version of Hey Joe. Jimi is such a great vocalist. Some lyrics he wrings-out soulfully, others he tosses aside with a wink and a grin. Every word he mutters feels personal and real. Finishing the number, Hendrix flicks back the volume knob on his Strat and addresses us for the first time. He mentions another British power trio, a band still charting with a song they released last year.

"But they're breaking up, and that's a drag."

Jimi kicks into a double-time, instrumental-only version of Cream's "Sunshine of Your Love." Wow. That's another song my band likes to jam on for hours on end. At least half the kids in the tent are begging for "Fire." The audience looks to be divided between a few long-haired rock musicians like myself and lots of oiled-up jocks with their girlfriends. Some of my friends call those kids "greasers." Foxey Lady is next but even this song can't shut up the gang of kids who seem to only want to hear one song.

"Play Fire!"

On Foxey Lady the Experience do it just like the record. Hendrix has two foot pedals. A rectangular, see-sawing wah-wah effect and a round-shaped fuzz box. Jimi punctuates his sexy lyrics by darting his tongue in-and-out at some awestruck girls in the front row. He throws the Strat behind his back, blazing through the outro licks while teasing the crowd, mixing lewd faces and gestures with winks and nods. Jimi is glowing, smiling right at us... and we'll never forget it.

Hendrix complains that something isn't right with his amplifiers. Then, gently rocking his wah-wah, he solos a brief, beautiful theme I've never heard. A few months later I'll discover that same melody, on his soon to be released Electric Ladyland album. Burning of the Midnight Lamp.

The jocks and greasers won't shut up, so finally Jimi saunters to the mic and mutters,

"Okay, okay then... Here it is. Here's you're cookie-shit little song..."

Spinning round, flaming into action with "Fire." Joyful howls from the crowd, this particular song is obviously the reason a lot of these people came out tonight. Jimi plays most of it with his teeth. Fire gets the biggest, longest ovation of the evening.

Mitch Mitchell hammers straight into the opening of
"I Don't Live Today" but something must be wrong.
Hendrix won't play the opening guitar riff. He just stands
there, glaring at his drummer. Bassist Noel, backs away
nervously as Mitch continues stomping quarter notes on
the kick with double-flams on the snare followed by a dual
cymbal crash. Round and round he goes... Instead of
joining in, Jimi shakes his head impatiently. He slowly
approaches the drummer. Oh, no. Mitch looks scared.
Noel Redding ducks behind the speaker cabinets.

Shit. What's going to happen now?

Running in from the side with a spare snare drum comes a
guy. Mitch keeps right on playing while the helper swaps
in the substitute drum. Mitch continues knocking-out the
same first bars. To my ears it doesn't sound any different
with the new snare drum. But the leader is apparently
pleased. Potential fistfight averted, Noel emerges from his
hiding place and "I Don't Live Today" springs to life before
our bugged-out eyes.

Song finished, Jimi reaches into his back pocket and whips
out a handkerchief emblazoned with the rebel colors of ol'
Dixie. He wipes his brow and blows his nose on the little
Confederate flag to hoots of approval. Another great bit of
business from this masterful showman.

The Experience close their first show of the evening with their first USA hit "Purple Haze" which sees the young star unleashing his wildest gyrations yet, amid a torrent of beautiful noise. I'm taken aback when, during the second verse, Jimi changes the word "sky" to "scuse me... while I kiss this *guy*" lunging comically in the direction of bass player Noel Redding.

As the last refrain and cheering dies down, Jimi announces our "National Anthem" which turns out to be "Wild Thing." The side-stage guy takes away the white Stratocaster, trading it for a baby-blue model.

Jimi bangs into the song.

His lighter fluid-doused version of The Troggs #1 smash was the talk of the Monterey Festival last year.

Promoter Frank Connelly doesn't allow fires inside his tent - so instead - Jimi closes this show by repeatedly bashing the Strat against the upper speaker box of his Marshall stack. Before his attack begins, the speaker cabinet and the blue Fender are already covered with scorch marks and dents. Scarred from recent dates on the Monkees Tour and at New York's Singer Bowl. What's left of the grille cloth is shredded and blackened. Hendrix violently swings the Fender around his head, ramming it straight through the speaker box and leaves it hanging.

The shouts of the crowd nearly drown out the roar of the feedback. Exuberant kids are ushered out of the tent.

A line for the second show forms as heat lightning cracks the sky. Waiting for their turn to be Experienced.

Head spinning, shell-shocked.

I just saw my first rock concert.

As babies, music is one of the first things that fascinates us. Most of us anyway. Me, definitely. I loved those magical sounds but as a tot I didn't know or care where they came from or what they were.

My mother has a clear, pretty voice. She's a good melody and harmony singer. As a youngster during WWII, she sang with a teenage trio out of the Bristol Vermont area, appearing on local radio and at live events.

A decade later - after I was born - Mother tried-on an accordion for a day or two before settling on a guitar instead. A Silvertone six string, sunburst finish acoustic guitar from the Sears catalog.

Records by the Kingston Trio played a lot at our house. The Bell's had all their albums.

Tom Dooley was one of the Trio's top songs. One day I suddenly hear my mother strumming the opening chords to that very song. Steel strings resonating, buzzing, zinging, carving a path into thin air. "Hang down your head Tom Dooley..." Mother begins to sing, perfectly in time to the rhythm her fingers draw from the guitar.

I started out as a cellist when I was ten. But turning 13 in 1966 - right when the fuzz-tone guitar pedal got invented - I hear the Stones' I Can't Get No Satisfaction and Heart Full of Soul by the Yardbirds. The distorted lead guitar tones set me ablaze. I ditch my cello and save up for an electric guitar. And a fuzz box. It's all I ever think about.

I get my first guitar at Mammoth Mart for $27.99.

A ZimGar. White solid-body with one pickup mounted on it. It has brutally high-action and whatever heavy gauge strings came with it. I hardly notice, because the cello has fat strings and even higher action. My solid-body guitar has metal bumps (frets) built-into the fingerboard. Cellos don't have those. Just a smooth, blank neck. So my cheap electric guitar is a step up, in a weird way, from the expensive concert instrument I've been studying for the past four years.

It takes awhile but I begin figuring out how to tune my ZimGar. Chords will be next. The day soon arrives when I can team up with the other 13 year-old rockers on my block. Right here in my own neighborhood there's another kid with a Japanese-made, electric guitar like mine and another kid who plays the drums. We put together a whole rock group right on the street.

The Mechanical Onions. We have everything except a bass player. Nobody we know has a real bass guitar. Or an electric organ...that would be cool...

(Pause...rewind tape a couple years.)

I missed the boat when The Beatles first hit the USA.

Back then I was 11 years old, the eldest of the Bell kids.

If I'd had older siblings, it might have been different.

At our regular table in the sixth grade lunchroom, me and the boys are busy trading Famous Monsters of Filmland cards and talking about the upcoming Cassius Clay vs. Sonny Liston heavyweight bout.

Over at the next table the girls are all giggling and gasping about Ringo and Paul, while swapping well-worn teen

magazines back and forth. Weird zines with names like
Teen Talk, Flip, Teen Scrapbook, 16 and *Tiger Beat.*
The front covers of these things are covered with colorful
pics of the two overnight-sensation British rock groups,
the Dave Clark Five and The Beatles. The cover art usually
features the Dave Clark musicians engaged in some sort of
battle scene against the Fab Four. The art department
pastes an actual photo of John Lennon's smirking mug
onto a small cartoon body of the mop top, astride a
galloping stallion or maybe firing a cannon at the noggin
of Mike Smith of the Dave Clark Five. Dave Clark is
chasing George Harrison up a tree while Ringo peeks up
from a foxhole. The girls collect all the DC5 and Beatles
trading cards too. Hearing all the squealing, gushing and
cooing "he's *so* cute" coming from the lady's lunch table
convinces me that The Beatles is mostly a girl thing.

It's 1964 (the Jimi Hendrix Experience won't show up for
another three years) and my eleven year-old friend, Bean,
is a trumpet player. A girl named Linda is planning her
backyard birthday party. Bean convinces her to hire his
band to play the party. Contract in hand, Bean sets out to
find players for his group. Since I'm Bean's best friend, he
asks me to join his combo on cello. Our other friend, Dave,
doesn't have an instrument. I remove the neck from an old
banjo I find in the attic, hang the banjo body from the base
of a music stand and create a makeshift drum that Dave
can bang on while Bean and I handle the melodies.

I find it hard keeping up with the volume of the trumpet so
I go electric. There's an old intercom setup in our house.

Records like "Who Wears Short Shorts?" by the Royal Teens, Sheb Wooley's "The Purple People Eater" and "Surfin' Bird" by the Trashmen.

Once the stack of records goes back to the dentist's daughter, I begin saving up for my own albums.
I keep it on the semi-down-low. I'm a bit confused by this new obsession and a little bit ashamed, afraid that my parents will look down on me, a (former) classically trained cello player for gosh sakes.

Schoodic Point, Maine 1966. The author at 13.

Once I save up a penny, I send it to the Columbia House
Record Club and they send me 12 albums in return. Soon I
have my own Out of Our Heads, Big Hits (High Tide and
Green Grass) and Aftermath. I find a crazy looking James
Brown record, the Ventures, Lulu, The Kinks and the
newly released (Feb. 11, 1967) Between the Buttons.
My favorite is "Having a Rave Up with the Yardbirds," on
the Epic label. I love looking at all my album covers so
much that, using strips of wood, I construct a wall display
on my bedroom wall where I can show-off a half-dozen LP
covers at a time.

Here I am with my growing record collection and my
Mammoth Mart axe, bashing around on Satisfaction,
Midnight Hour, Wild Thing, Miss Amanda Jones, Hang
On Sloopy, Dirty Water and Sam and Dave's "Hold On I'm
Coming." My band, The Mechanical Onions, has it all.
Except for a gig.
But when we change our name to "The Effective" things
start to happen.

{ 2 }

Jeff Beck and The Effective
The Effective beat the Militia Men and the Sonic Needle to win the $10 first prize at the 1967 Holliston 7th-Grade Battle of the Bands, held in the Flagg School cafeteria.

"Murph" is our lead singer. He wears a funny little cap. I play guitar and sing the back-ups. My friend Dave, the banjo basher from my first trio, can't play his electric guitar yet so he just pretends. Mainly, Dave is here to balance out the group's look onstage. Our secret weapon is Joey Hamwey on drums. Nobody plays dance beats like Joey. Nobody sits still when he plays them either.

Murph and I write a forgettable song with a great title, "The Paisley Hangman."

My father brings home a surprise for me. An Aria Diamond electric guitar with two pick-ups and a whammy bar. He bought it from Chuck, at Wellesley Music Center, a few doors down from the Music Box. Secretly, I wish it had a solid body. This guitar is semi-hollow with F holes, like the electric guitar Chuck Berry plays.

The whammy comes in useful when we perform the brand new Animals hit "When I Was Young" at the Battle. The song opens with a pluck of the low E string, detuned and then brought back up to pitch. Our version of the song is okay but my opening whammy bar note is top shelf.

16

The Effective are getting popular. We're hired to play two
songs at the local church hall Variety Show. We open with
the classic three-chord-wonder. *Gloria.*
But I'm still pretty shaky with my chords, so I just plonk
the three main notes on a single string.
On the opposite end of the stage, Dave sways his guitar
back'n'forth silently.
Murph shouts the melody and mashes potatoes all over the
stage while drummer Joey produces a massive teen-beat.
The crowd gobbles it up and gives us a monstrous ovation.
The Variety Show continues with a piano solo, some tap
dancers and an accordion player.
The Effective hang around in the wings, waiting for our
cue. The director chose us to close the show - after hearing
the other great song we've rehearsed.

I'll never forget it.
I'm standing here in front of a packed house. The junior
high girls are all pushing into the first section.
Murph steps up to the mic, wags his eyebrows, rolls his
eyes, and coughs out the strange, garbled syllables that
announce the surfin' classic. *Wipe Out.*
Joey unleashes a pounding tidal wave on his mounted
tom. I hot-dog to the very edge of the stage, releasing the
gnarly opening riff.
Notes shoot from my fleet fingers, zig-zagging through the
awe-struck audience. Silent Dave strums along silently.
Murph struts Malibu-style across the stage.
Gnarly tones from my Aria Diamond ricochet off the
gyrating bodies of awestruck teenieboppers.
We've got 'em in the palm of our hands.

First big drum break, Joey lets loose. Oh, man. The girls
will be chasing us all over Holliston after this show.
I toss back my blonde bangs, curling into the second verse
- which is exactly the same as the first verse.
But wait... What are those girls pointing at?
How come their mouths aren't hanging open anymore?

We sound outta-sight, I know that for a fact.
So why are the fans grinning and beginning to laugh?
Joey thunders into the second drum break as I glance over
my shoulder... something's going on behind his drum set.
What the hell? Who let those people in here?
What the...?
A conga-line of Hawaiian-dancers swishes onto the stage
from the wings.
They're lining-up, behind my band. There's like twenty of
them. Doing the hula in unison to Joey's beat.
Wearing grass skirts and jiggly coconut shell bikini tops.
But these hula dancers are...hairy.
Really hairy. Underneath the dumb wigs it's just a bunch
of old guys. Paunchy dads of the church group sponsoring
this talent show. Swinging their hips, bouncing their
coconuts up and down. *Stealing our spotlight*.
Making a big joke out of The Effective and our heroic
version of Wipe Out.

Following this public humiliation we change our name to
The Cynics.
Not because we've become distrustful and jaded about
show business and adults.

No, I think Dave and I just thumbed through a dictionary looking for weird, cool words that might work as a new group name. Joey doesn't care what I call the band, he just wants to play his drums.

In 1967, switching my group's name to The Cynics isn't the only big change in rock music.
Hullabaloo, Shindig, Shivaree, Lloyd Thaxton, Wing Ding (from Rhode Island), New Hampshire Bandstand, The Real Don Steele, Upbeat, Where the Action Is and all the other go-go TV dance shows begin to vanish.
The Young Rascals become the Rascals. Paul Revere and the Raiders become the Raiders. Micky Dolenz lets his hair go naturally frizzy on his Monkees TV show.
Debut albums by The Doors, Sly and the Family Stone, Electric Flag, Cream and the Jimi Hendrix Experience keep me and the other local rockers busy. Soaking up the more mature lyrics and increasingly complex chord changes. I'm digging the psychedelic album covers and fashions.
I try to absorb the revolutionary notion of rock events being treated like concerts instead of dances.

On September 11th Cream arrive in Boston. Booked for 7 consecutive nights, two shows a night at the Psychedelic Supermarket. It's the Summer of Love and nobody's looking to hire me or The Cynics. My lead singer Murph splits. Dave gets a part-time job, working for my dad at the Music Box. Dave's saving up to buy a Karmann Ghia.
So now, it's mostly just Joey and me.

We rehearse in Joe's finished basement where he keeps his brand new, purple-sparkle Trixon drum kit. The shells are round, not those Dali-esque, melted-bass drums that Trixon is famous for.

Joe has a gorgeous sister too, a year older than us.

Sue totally ignores The Cynics.

Joey and I spend our afternoons bashing through a two-man songfest that includes Smokestack Lightning, I Feel Free, Little Latin Lupe Lu, Purple Haze, Just Like Me, Spider and the Fly, I Can't Control Myself, Little Girl, Foxey Lady, Rari, All Over Now, We Gotta Get Out of This Place, Little Bit o' Soul, Mustang Sally, Hey Joe and I Feel Good. Since we don't have a lead singer, I sing.

Still no bass. We don't have a PA system either. Maybe a vocal mic plugged into a guitar amp, or maybe no mic at all. I don't know if my singing is any good but my voice becomes more powerful by the day.

The year ends on a high note when my role models, the Rolling Stones, release the psychedelic "Their Satanic Majesties Request" on December 8th.

New year new kids. Two rock-guys just moved into Holliston, a few houses down from drummer Joey's.

Jeff Knapp is my age and he owns a real Gibson guitar.

A brand new Les Paul Black Beauty with jumbo frets.

Brother Ken is a year younger and he has... a real *bass guitar*.

Jeff is way ahead of me on his instrument but he doesn't mind sharing some secrets.

The better guitarists down at the Framingham Music Center usually turn their backs on me if they catch me studying their fingers.

Pretty soon Jeff, Ken and I are all jamming together with Joey on drums. Creating a rapid succession of bands that include Rigor Mortis and Apple Brandy. Sometimes just the four of us, other times with added singers, or even horn players. Jeff is way into Mike Bloomfield and the Electric Flag - a rock band with a brass section.
Working with Jeff, I'm learning a lot about r&b and the blues.

We also cover "Love Eyes" and a few other songs by Phluph, a professional rock group that rehearses in Framingham. Their debut album on Verve is part of the *Bosstown Sound* being promoted by producer Alan Lorber along with MGM Records and a few other major labels. The singer/bassist of Phluph is a friend of Jeff's named John Pell. We're playing the Battle of the Bands this weekend and Pell kindly lends our band several of the big Standel amplifiers his group uses. We even borrow John's little sister, Debbie Pell, to be our lead vocalist.

I'm in bed with my headphones on. Uncle T broadcasts from midnight until 3 am on WBUR-FM. I recently discovered the FM band while messing around with a used Fisher radio tuner I bought cheap from the back (used gear) window at the Music Box.
Most of the FM bandwidth is vacant. Just the occasional opera or classical music plays here or there.

Now I can wear boots to school. And turtlenecks. I can attempt a Brian Jones/Ilya Kuryakin, 15 year-old cool. On my first day at the new school I walk in wearing Thom McCan Monkee boots, a paisley shirt and my fink vest (fake mink = fink, occasionally worn by Sonny & Cher as well as The Mosquitoes). Mother custom-made it for me.

Holliston MA 1967. My brother Sam's second birthday party. We're sitting at the Bell kitchen table and I'm wearing my fink vest.
Photo by Bill Bell

Purple Dynasty are the popular power trio here in Framingham Center, near to my new campus. Drummer Richie plays double kick drums like Ginger Baker while belting out vocals like Buddy Miles.
Dickie is the lead guitarist. He slings an old Epiphone solidbody and really knows how to make it scream. The bass player is a bit younger and his name is Steve. He's my classmate at my new school.

Steve and I become musical allies and pretty soon he invites me and my faithful drummer Joey over to his house for some jam sessions. A really big house with waxy wooden floors and hardly any furniture in it. Steve's mom looks like a TV star and his father is always away on business. We rehearse in their empty, echoing living room. I just topped-off the summer of '68 at the local Jimi Hendrix Experience show last month. The tent is only a couple miles from here. I'm all revved-up to recreate the Experience, right here in Steve's living room.

The Cave is the exclusive teen center in Framingham Center. You need a membership card or know somebody big to get inside. I've heard about this "in-crowd" venue all the way from Holliston. When Purple Dynasty isn't available, the Cave will get popular local groups like Late C.W. Moulton, Agrapinary or Indigo Blues to play on weekend nights.
Indigo Blues is led by singer/guitarist Gene Provost and his younger, bass playing brother, Ric.
The Provost brothers are from nearby Natick.

My new bass player, Steve, is a mystery man. He has long hair and looks super cool and he digs the heavy music but he also smokes cigarettes and drinks beer. Like greasers do. Anyway, Steve has lots of connections and somehow he gets me a membership at the Cave. I'm the first Holliston kid to set foot in this private cellar.
Descending the steps into the teen-filled space, the rough walls are constructed of piled-up stones and boulders, like a root cellar.

Everything is lit with black light and painted, rocks and all, in Day-Glo hues and blobby shapes. Like the conversation wall on Rowan and Martin's Laugh In.

Giant-sized wooden spools, once used to hold utility cables, are arranged around the Cave as tables. The noisy catacomb has short metal stools for the plentiful patrons to perch on. A smallish, low-to-the-ground stage, spans one wall and a little soda concession sits around the corner in an adjacent room adorned with more psychedelic posters. Unlike most teen centers, there isn't really a dance floor here. The Cave is set up for studious rock music watchers and listeners.

(5 days later)

Jeff Beck Group is playing at the Boston Tea Party tonight and I have a ticket. My father drives me into Boston, about an hour away from our house. He drops me off on Berkeley street and we make a plan to meet here again in three hours.

It's a warm October night and now I'm standing in line behind a bunch of college-age kids gathered on the corner. I've been imagining being part of this action for a long time. From listening to Uncle T and his vivid descriptions of the freaky street scenes taking over the city. I feel prepared. But standing in this queue I'm seeing, hearing and smelling things that are alien.

A big red neon YMCA sign glows down on us from the next block. We slowly snake our way up the front stoop and inside the antique doorway.

This entire city block is lined with three and four-story, brick-constructed buildings. All are at least a hundred years old. Liquor stores, rubber stamp shops, apartments. We continue climbing, double-file, up the stairs to the upper level of this, the largest building on the corner of the block.

I hand my ticket to a bearded cat and he motions me to proceed through a doorway to my left.
I enter the darkened hall. Wooden floor, no seats, no balcony. I see a half-dozen silhouettes, working up on a raised scaffolding that hugs the back wall. Busily, they alternate places behind a parade of film and slide projectors, overhead projectors and a spotlight or two. Too dark for me to see clearly, but from the acoustics, I reckon this space is similar in size to the main room of our Holliston Town Hall. Big enough to squeeze six or seven hundred kids into. A band is playing, I don't know who. Movie clips are being projected on the walls, the floor, the ceiling and all over the stage area. Felix the Cat with question marks floating over his head, a frantic chase scene from a Mack Sennett comedy.
Suddenly the room blacks-out and a pin spot illuminates a revolving, mirrored ball, hanging above our heads.
I think I saw one of these mirror balls in a ballroom scene from an old swing band movie. The lighting crew adjusts the speed of the reflecting orb and the pitch of the spotlight, creating thousands of reflections, pin-wheeling around the periphery of the hall, spinning downward. It makes us feel like the Tea Party is beginning to lift from its foundation and rise into the sky.

The band onstage is Earth Opera. One of the dozens of
area groups who recently got caught up in the Bosstown
Sound scheme. Most of the "Bosstown" bands are terrific
and they all have different musical styles. Unfortunately,
following last year's impressive invasion of the San
Francisco bands, a bunch of record company suits decided
to sign a platoon of Boston groups, en masse - and
promote all of them simultaneously - with an umbrella
"Bosstown Sound" media-blitz campaign.

The advertisements are way over the top and I begin
hearing a new term used to describe the hustle. *Hype.*
The Bosstown Sound smells fishy to a lot of the record
buying public. A bunch of talented young rock musicians
get tainted and overlooked in the process.

Earth Opera don't play the heavy music I hunger for but
they have musical genius Peter Rowan in the line-up and
their topical, introspective song "The Red Sox are
Winning" from their Elektra debut, gets played on WBCN
every day. The Tea Party light show, color slides, film-
strips, strobes, films and psychedelic liquids are being
projected across the faces and bodies of Earth Opera.

It's hard to figure out what's real and what isn't.

I'm 15 years old and I weigh 115. Easy to slither my way to
the front of this former religious temple with its ample
wooden stage. Raised about 3 feet off the ground, the
platform spans the entire end of the room. Rising up,
behind the drum kit, the back wall still bears the slogan
"Pray Ye The Lord" spelled out in bold block letters,
framed below an arched wooden moulding.

Chained from the ceiling, protruding over the front of the
stage, is a wide, multi-cell-horn speaker system. Perfect for

projecting vocals. Large wooden boxes, mid-range and
bass bins, are stacked on both ends of the stage. The hefty
loudspeakers are actually teetering over the outside edges
of the platform. They've been lashed together with heavy
ropes, hopefully well-secured, because I'm right here in
front, house right, eyeing the spot my hero will soon
inhabit. If this wall of PA speakers tips over, I'll be flat as a
cherry pancake.

The Yardbirds played on this same Boston Tea Party stage
just six months ago, back in April.
Two months after that, in June, Yardbird guitarist Jimmy
Page was in New York City to greet the new Jeff Beck
Group as they stepped onto the jetport tarmac.
Beck had been to America several times, during his own
stint with The Yardbirds. Usually to play the current hit on
TV go-go shows or travel through America on a Dick Clark
rock'n'roll caravan tour. But this June was the first time
the rest of his Group had ever played in the USA.
The Jeff Beck Group were in Manhattan to do some live
dates preceding (and hopefully inducing) the delayed
release of their Truth album on the Epic label.
Beck isn't surprised when Page tells him the New
Yardbirds have finally decided to call it quits.
Jimmy continues, sharing details about the new band he
wants to put together.

The Jeff Beck Group's first American shows include a
couple nights at the Steve Paul Scene (301 West 46th St.) a
basement club in midtown Manhattan, where the Group is

But somehow he always does, creating musical suspense and an exciting cacophony along the way.

Nicky Hopkins hammers away on the keys of his upright piano but it's hard to hear him. I'm the son of a son of a sound man, so I understand how difficult it is to get a mic'd upright piano high enough in the mix vs. electric guitars and drums, without tempting feedback.

You Shook Me morphs into Let Me Love You, both from Truth, the album every rock guitarist has been spinning non-stop ever since it came out two months ago.

Jeff Beck turns sideways and I see the Les Paul he's slinging is severely ravaged. Up at the top of the neck, it looks like the entire headstock has been replaced after being totally smashed-off somewhere along the line. From the looks of the repair, it might be a headstock from a whole different guitar. The colors and finishes of the Gibson neck and the headstock don't match-up. The rough surgery looks like it might've been performed in an auto body shop rather than on a luthier bench.

The Group rockets into the groovy LP-opener Shapes of Things, proving that they, like the Jimi Hendrix Experience, can replicate their recorded sound, right before our ears. The swirling guitar patterns and the interplay between Ron Wood's non-stop bass lines against Jeff Beck's measured, hyper-dynamic approach, is thrilling.

Jeff underplays through long sections - before releasing stunning musical uppercuts to the jaw.

For "Blues Deluxe" the Group brings down the volume
level so we can finally hear Nicky Hopkins, whose piano-
garnishments are so familiar to anyone who grew up with
The Who's Anyway Anyhow Anywhere, The Stones She's a
Rainbow, The Kinks Sunny Afternoon...
But the guy who is getting just as much, and even more
attention, is the unusual looking lead singer, Rod Stewart.

Eight years my senior, Rod Stewart is 23 years-old. Like
the rest of this band, he's wearing a tight tee shirt with
flashy trousers. Rod's are flared at the bottom over flat-
soled shoes. Stewart's hairdo and his beak are pronounced
and he sings in a much higher range than Jimi. Throwing
back his head, strutting in place, singing full throttle, up to
the rafters. His tone is passionate, gritty and he uses his
tripod-based mic stand as a prop, swinging it around and
over his head, inverting it, waving the tripod legs aloft as
he crows the choruses, marching in time, rasping into the
upside-down SM58.
Hard not to notice this cat.

I Ain't Superstitious is next and it's the one we all want to
hear.
This is the cut from Truth that WBCN is giving the most
airplay, a Howling Wolf original with voodoo lyrics.
A showcase for Jeff's rock-a-billy licks meet blues guitar
fireworks. Pumped through the far-out sound of the new
Vox Wah-Wah pedal.
Ain't Superstitious brings down the house - but Jeff
immediately tops himself with "Jeff's Boogie" a number
I've read about - but never actually heard.

Jeff's Boogie strings together a score of Beck's most fantastic, gimmicky riffs.

His Gibson musically echoes the chimes of Big Ben, songbird cheeps and a Zed car siren. Beck picks Chet Atkins-style, then he quotes from the Yardbirds' Over, Under, Sideways, Down - and then - a headlong rush into the Beverly Hillbillies TV theme-song, picked banjo style with 3-finger rolls.

The Boston crowd is elated. Jeff Beck turns out to be everything we hoped for and even more.

Bidding us adieu, The Jeff Beck Group cap off the night with Rock My Plimsoul and I leave the Boston Tea Party - my second rock concert - on cloud 9.

And that's the Truth.

Now I'm alone, except for my Aria electric guitar.

Trying to recreate sounds and riffs I watched Jimi and Jeff perform live.

I mix my attempts with bits I've already mastered and solo patterns that my neighbor Jeff taught me last summer.

I take a break from my fretboard on December 6th to pick up the new Rolling Stones album.

Every song is great.

Street Fighting Man, Jigsaw Puzzle, Stray Cat Blues, Sympathy For the Devil...

This one is called Beggars Banquet. Folky acoustic numbers alternate with bluesy, driving rockers, topped with smart, sometimes scary, sounding lyrics.

A totally new direction for the Londoners, following the whizbang carnival of Their Satanic Majesties Request and the regal, pop/blues/fuzz-tone masterpiece, Between the Buttons.

Playing my Aria guitar in the forward cabin of my father's Triton sloop, the Kialoa.

{ 3 }

The God of Hellfire and Black Sun
1969 begins. LBJ steps down and on January
20th, Richard Nixon becomes 37th president of
the USA. Three days later I turn 16.
Black Sun is the name Steve and I come up with for our
new band. Joey on drums as always, Steve on bass, me on
backing vocals and guitar. We play heavy music. Stuff from
Jimi Hendrix's three albums, Jeff Beck's Truth, some
Cream and a few songs from the groundbreaking debut
Led Zeppelin record, it just came out on January 12th.

But we also have these other two, way different songs,
"White Rabbit" and "Somebody to Love" where Steve's
girlfriend joins us to sing lead.
15 year-old Merry is icy cool. A 15 year-old knock-out with
a Germanic, blonde, Nico look.
Merry smokes Newport menthol cigarettes and wears her
long golden tresses like Peggy Lipton, the current TV star
covergirl from the Mod Squad. Merry also has a very
professional sounding rock'n'roll voice. Black Sun makes
our debut at the Cave and we go over well.
Especially when teenage beauty, Merry, steps to the mic.

Steve continues playing bass with Black Sun even after
Merry decides she'd rather be my (first) girlfriend.
On April 5th, Merry and I go into Boston together. A
wrestling venue called the Boston Arena occasionally

brings in big rock shows, like Chuck Berry or The Doors.
We have expensive five-dollar seats. Up in the stands but
directly in front of the stage, for the "Second Annual
Boston Rock Festival." First up, is a solid sounding band
with a horn section.
I think they're called Ascension.
Next up is a band I've heard a lot from, The Youngbloods.
I'm excited to see their guitar player, Electric Banana.
Led by Jesse Colin Young (vocals/bass) of Queens NY and
local guy Jerry Corbitt (vocals/keyboard) of Cambridge.
But Banana owns the stage, in a goofy Monkees kinda-
way.
The Youngbloods hit the charts in '67 with "Grizzly Bear,"
a honky-tonk dance number.
Also released that year was their anthem "Get Together."
The anthem was a little ahead of its time, so now in 1969
Get Together has been re-released and this time around its
burning up the Hot 100. Their new LP also features a
spooky tune called Darkness, Darkness, that gets constant
spins on the underground FM dial.
The Youngbloods rock the Arena for a solid forty minutes
until the last of the empty seats fill up.

One of the last year's coolest records was Fire.
I'm not referring to Jimi Hendrix Experience's Fire or
The Doors's Light My Fire.
No. The Crazy World of Arthur Brown gave us *Fire* and it
burned its way straight to number one on the British
singles chart and number two on Billboard's Hot 100.

Arthur Brown sings and dances and he *is* crazy. Vincent Crane works the Hammond B3 organ and Brown's drummer tonight is a fellow called Carl Palmer.

So, just like the Mechanical Onions, if you don't count the singer, this is basically a two man group.

Arthur Brown is a front man without peer. He hypnotizes us with strange invocations. Rail thin, his gaunt face is painted a skeletal black & silver.

Carl Palmer's drum rhythms rise to a crescendo and Brown snaps into a bizarre dance maneuver. Face to the left - right arm up. Face to the right - left arm up. His legs and torso sync-up and he begins ratcheting, stiffly around the stage like a tin-man on acid. It all makes perfect sense when the trio segues into I Put a Spell On You, the warning made famous by Screamin' Jay Hawkins, godfather of shock rock.

Arthur Brown brings us to our feet as the Crazy World dives headfirst into their international hit "Fire." Disappearing briefly behind the amplifiers, Brown re-emerges with a metallic helmet strapped to the dome of his head. Gyrating to the apron of the stage, Brown triggers the bunsen burner hidden within the bronze headpiece. Flame blasts from his skullcap. I grasp Merry's hand, wide-eyed and totally awestruck by what we're witnessing.

Fire leaps and licks out of Arthur Brown's cranium, the conflagration rises, making the God of Hellfire - prancing before us - appear to be at least thirteen feet tall.

So who wants to follow that?
The Canadian-American band, Steppenwolf.

These guys play the heaviest, hardest-hitting hits to ever
hit the AM radio dial.

Born to be Wild, the huge smash of last summer, followed
by the deliriously delicious Magic Carpet Ride. They
recently released Rock Me Baby, from their third album,
and it's already rocketed into the Top 10.

Five guys. Same instrumentation as the Jeff Beck Group
but a whole different sound and style. Jerry Edmonton
(drums), Goldy McJohn (keyboard), Michael Monarch
(lead guitar from L.A., replacing Mars Bonfire), bassist
Nick St. Nicholas and lead vocalist John Kay. The band
looks good on stage and there's plenty for me to study.
John Kay is wearing leather trousers, like his Los Angeles
neighbor, Jim Morrison.

First time I've ever seen pants made of leather in real life.
Mr. Kay wears a wide, leather belt with silver conchos,
slung beneath a tight Mexican peasant shirt. John has a
thick, dark mane and he never removes his dark
sunglasses. Except for the sunglasses, Kay seems to be
wearing Jim Morrison's Doors wardrobe.

Or perhaps Jim takes his fashion cues from John?

Equally intriguing is the bass player. Nick St. Nicholas.
Nick has been with this band off and on, ever since they
began in Canada as Sparrow, a couple years ago in '67. I
read that Nick's supposedly afraid to fly and he suffers
from a lot of weird, fatalistic superstitions.

Like me, St. Nicholas has been cursed with a golden head
of curly-curls. Unlike me, Nick likes to set-off his pretty

hairdo by wearing ladies jewelry and a dress onstage.
Tonight it's a long, very pretty, gown.
Jerry, Goldy and Michael don't wear girl stuff. Far from it,
the rest of these guys look tough - like the lead singer -
born to be wild.

John Kay spends most of his time at the center stage mic
but he grabs a guitar during the mystical Magic Carpet
Ride. Kay plays the slide guitar embellishments during the
jam, sounding just like the record. He doesn't say very
much to us, the band just keeps rolling out familiar songs:
Sookie Sookie, Don't Step on the Grass, Sam, The Pusher,
Everybody's Next One, along with their multi-million
selling hits.

Steppenwolf doesn't have a spotlight player who
monopolizes the limelight. No, these guys play like a team.
Goldy holds down overdriven Hammond B3 chords on top
of Monarch's concise riffing. Sustained organ notes
shimmer at first but begin to jangle from sweet to tart, as
counterpoint notes from the bass and guitar revise the
flavor of each chord. Drummer Edmonton provides just
the right measure of dramatic drum fills and accents.
Following the encores, the Boston Arena houselights come
up and we join the mob of fans, slowly making our way to
the exits. Back to the reality of St. Botolph Street.

That's when I hear sobbing. Merry? I spin my head to the
right, extremely surprised to see Steppenwolf's bass
player, Nick St. Nicholas, still in his gown, trotting right
for us.

He's crying. Merry's shocked too, seeing the headliner
scoot right alongside us, gushing with tears. Apparently
things didn't go well for Nick back in the Steppenwolf
dressing room. So the bass player bolted, leaving his band
behind, and now the weeping rocker is trying to slip out
the front door of the Boston Arena, along with Merry, me,
and the rest of this buzzed crowd.

Black Sun keeps trying to get famous. Except for the Cave,
we don't really play out much. The occasional church
dance or local teen center gig.
Bass player Steve talks to a booking agent and manages to
snag us a try-out in a bar in Revere.
I doubt Steve told the agent our real ages (16).
Despite its wide ocean boulevard and sandy beach, Revere
is supposed to be a pretty tough town. Merry isn't
interested in this road trip, so Joey, Steve and I head out to
play the bar gig on our own.

I've never really been inside a bar, unless it was attached
to a restaurant and my mother was leading me through it
by the hand, on our way to the rest rooms.
This place isn't out on the main Revere beach boulevard.
No, it's a couple streets back, more of an alley than a
street. Entering, I feel dread.
There's about a dozen people inside. No women. No young
people. Just a bunch of stiff-looking old men.
Hunched over the bar, staring at the Red Sox game playing
silently on a 27" Zenith.

Music is playing. I walk over to the jukebox where a Dean
Martin 45 spins. Dino is crooning a quasi-Italian love
song. I flip through the juke's musical menu.
Al Martino, Tony Bennett, Sergio Franchi... and page after
page of Frank Sinatra.
No Led Zeppelin, Jimi, Jeff Beck Group or Steppenwolf.
Not even the Rolling Stones or the Monkees. No rock, just
songs from the grown-ups who warble on Ed Sullivan
before the rock group finally comes on.

We don't see a club manager, so we begin setting-up our
amps and drums while ol' Blue Eyes sings Witchcraft,
Chicago and Come Fly with Me.
The elderly patrons have their backs to us, nobody looks
our way.

When it's finally time to play, we open with
Communication Breakdown. Several of the grandpas fall
off their stools and run out the door. By the time we kick
into Rock My Plimsoul, there's only a couple seniors left in
the joint. Probably deaf.
A door in back swings open and a serious-looking guy
wearing a tailored suit emerges. He steps up to the
bandstand and motions for us to stop.

"Okay kids. That's enough. Time to go home now."

Steve looks mad.

"Hey, no. Wait, we're Black Sun and we're just getting started. The agent said you'd pay us seventy-five dollars for the night."

The suit inches over to Steve's side of the stage.

"Listen son, you're done. Get it?"

He slides his right hand into his trouser pocket as he speaks, allowing his fitted jacket to open just enough for us to see something hanging from his shoulder.

Steve and I decide that standing up for our rights is a lousy idea after we spy the discreetly exposed revolver, holstered across the thug's chest.

Spring 1969. The Jeff Beck Group is returning to the Boston Tea Party.

I make it into the city and over to Berkeley Street on a warm night on the first week of May, proudly wearing the blue, crushed velvet pants I bought at Krackerjack's boutique on Mass Ave in Cambridge.

The store clerk, Charles, a supercool black cat with an afro wrapped inside a pirate scarf, helps me locate the incredible trousers, tucked away on the highest shelf.

These are the kind of pants guys in Ten Years After or Small Faces would want to wear.

Inside 53 Berkeley, I make my way up the wooden staircase, hand over my ticket, turn the corner and BOOM, the light show is projecting on every surface, just like I remember it from last time.

The Boston Tea Party is shaped like a square cube, lots of head room and very high, spacious white walls, perfect for the large images the resident company "Lights by the Road" are projecting.

Opening the show tonight is Seatrain from Marin County, California, but now re-settled just up the coast in Marblehead MA. They have Andy Kulberg on bass and flute. Andy was formerly with the Blues Project and their "Flute Thing" is still one of the most played tracks on WBCN. Seatrain also has an electric violinist, Richard Greene. They don't play fuzz-tone, heavy music like Black Sun, but they're still great.

Second up is The Nice. A remarkable power trio.
Lee Jackson on bass and vocals, Brian Davison on drums.
Leader, Keith Emerson, mesmerizes this audience much like Hendrix hypnotized the Carousel crowd last year.

Like Jimi, Keith's a master player who doesn't mind putting his axe through a public torture trial. But Emerson doesn't seem to share Jimi's humor or friendly vibe. No, just the opposite. This British keyboard player looks downright dangerous and he acts deranged.

The Nice play aurally exciting, challenging arrangements, based on themes from Dave Brubeck, Bob Dylan and Leonard Bernstein. Visually, Keith Emerson takes things to the extreme. He straddles his Hammond organ, climbs atop it and humps it. He rips the back-panel off his instrument, he climbs inside it, he re-wires the thing while he's inside. Re-emerging, he begins stabbing the keys of his bleating B-3 with silver daggers. Pinning down chords while adding counterpoint melodies on a second keyboard. Keith whips more hunting knives across the Tea Party stage. The blades penetrate the helplessly-whirling Leslie speaker cabs.

 The Nice whack me hard upside the head. How the hell is Jeff Beck going to follow this sound & fury? Maybe Jeff and his band are thinking the same thing...because a few minutes later I hear a ruckus in the crowd behind me. I'm smooshed up front against the stage, waiting for the headliners to appear. Turning around, I spot the rooster top of singer, Rod Stewart, followed by comrades Ron Wood and the star, Jeff Beck.

The whole band just entered the Tea Party through the front entrance and now they're slowly winding their way through the audience. As they get closer to me, nearing the

stage, I can see Rod has a bottle of Mateus Rose wine
hoisted high over his head.
Beck and Wood appear to be crying with laughter,
stumbling. All of them are singing, perhaps a football song
or maybe a sea shanty. The group clambers up onto the
boards and I have a bad feeling about this.

I only see four of them, no Nicky Hopkins this time 'round.
The drummer is different too, that's not Mick Waller.
They begin the show and about half the setlist is new stuff,
including some Elvis Presley covers.

I guess this is material from the Beck-Ola LP that's
supposed to come out next month. Tony Newman is on
drums and I bet he's good when he's sober. The JBG goes
down okay with the crowd but I'm disappointed at how
sloppy they sound compared to a few months ago.

Oh yeah, one other thing about tonight.

I'm taken aback when I realize that the Boston Tea Party's
resident stage announcer, a super hip looking smooth-
talker, a dude everyone calls the "Master Blaster" is none
other than my friend, Charlie Daniels. By day he's the clerk
who sold me these crushed velvet pants at Krackerjack's
clothing boutique.

Two weeks later, the much talked-about rock opera by
The Who is released.
"Tommy" immediately becomes my favorite record.

Still, no luck getting Black Sun a booking at Boston Arena or the Boston Tea Party.

I think it's my age. You have to be old in order to be taken seriously in rock'n'roll. At least 18 or 19.

The really big guys, I mean groups like Paul Revere and the Raiders, the Chambers Brothers, the Monkees or the Kinks...they're all ten years older than me.

Except for Dino, Desi and Billy, all the really famous groups are old.

Andy, Sam and Mach Bell. In our living room on Christmas morning.
1967

{ 4 }

Terry Reid, Tommy Bolin and Katy the Donkey.

My band isn't making much headway. In June I tell my folks I'm leaving. Hitchhiking out to the West Coast. I'll go to San Francisco. I think that's where most of the hip kids and the rock action is.

Several of my friends have attempted the trip and most had good luck. I neglect to mention that Merry will be tagging along with me. For the past few months, Merry's father has warned me to

"Stay away from my daughter."

He's a stern-looking guy. A high school math teacher. Merry's dad reminds me of one of the bad guys on Hogan's Heroes. He doesn't dig my "free" school, my longhair or my weird clothes.

So Merry tells her pop she's going into Cambridge with a girlfriend, to see a rock concert.

Instead, the two of us go to Shopper's World and hop a Peter Pan bus. Bound for New York City.

We start out on a bus because I don't want to get spotted together by anyone who knows us. Can't be caught standing at the entrance ramp to the Mass Turnpike with our thumbs hanging out.

Four hours later, we arrive at the NYC Port Authority. I
study the subway map. Looking for a stop that sounds
good for camping. Harlem? Flushing Meadow? Astoria?
I've become fairly skilled at urban camping. Even in
heavily-settled areas I can usually find a garden, park,
cemetery or some sort of off-the-beaten-path area where I
can unroll my sleeping bag and catch a few winks.
Hey, Merry...this sounds like our destination.
Rockaway Beach.
During the long subway journey to the beach, I imagine
sand castles and sea shells.
Arriving at the final stop, we drag the back packs and
bedrolls out to the curb. Fumes, buses, triple deckers.
Still in the city.
Getting dark. We trudge up Livonia Ave. Finally beginning
to see some marshy looking flats. Bullrushes and cattails.
It begins to sprinkle rain as we mush off the road, back
into the wetlands.
We find a dry enough spot to unroll one sleeping bag. I
shove the bag inside a large plastic liner, basically a big
garbage bag. Dog tired, we both manage to squirm inside.
I can't tell you much about the rest of our evening, but in
the morning - at around 4:30 am - we wake to the scream
of jet engines, directly above us.
Merry springs bolt-upright, as a second jet whizzes right
over her head. The morning light reveals an airport, dead
ahead, probably JFK.
We've been sleeping in a swamp at the foot of a jet runway.

One day this will become known as the summer of
Woodstock. VW busses with flower-power stickers are

criss-crossing the USA. Hippie drivers stop to pick up anybody groovy looking. It's pretty easy to get a ride. If you manage to get picked-up on the Interstate, let's say I-70 in Pennsylvania, there's a pretty good chance the ride might take you all the way to Ohio or maybe even Kansas. A nice long ride.

A fellow traveler we meet along the way advises us to always ask the driver,

"Would you please drop us at the last HoJo's or truck stop plaza on the Interstate before you exit the highway?"

In a highway rest stop we can survey and work the ever-changing, road-tripping crowd. We scope around and try to find someone cool who might help us with a lift.

I introduce myself politely and chat before asking about a ride. Merry does the same.

The tactic works out pretty well for us. That's how we find Caesar Geronimo.

Geronimo is wearing some sort of military outfit, dark glasses and a cap that partially hides his wild eyes, scarred scalp and stubbly haircut. We pile onto the front bench of his sedan and take-off.

Geronimo drives really fast and he talks like Clutch Cargo. Merry doesn't believe his name is for real. Caesar Geronimo hands her his ID as proof. Caesar picks up another hitchhiker in Ohio.

The new kid asks me about our destination.

"You're headed for San Francisco? I'd stay away from there. The Haight is a mess. Kids are getting hassled. You guys should check out the Hill instead."

"The Hill? Don't think I've heard about it. What part of California?"

"No, man. Not California. *Colorado*. Boulder's where it's happening man. The Hill in Boulder."

I don't respond to that. I just gaze out my window at a field passing by. I see two brown donkeys looking back at me.

The Bell house in Holliston stands on a small rise surrounded by four acres of mostly wooded land. Down the hill from the house is an old barn with an adjacent meadow.
When I turned 5, my grandmother (I call her Big Mama) gave me a baby donkey for my birthday.
We named the burro Katy and she lived in the barn.
A year later my father brought home another donkey. This one was compact too but fully grown. He even came complete with a leather harness and a green cart with big wooden-spoked wheels. Cathy and I could hitch everything together and Pedro would pull us in the cart, up and down the wooded-paths, through our neighborhood and along some nearby cart roads.

Katy and Pedro got along okay together. Pretty soon a baby donkey, Pee Wee, was born.
Now it's spring. I'm nine years old and it's the middle of the night. I wake up to a frightening sound.
Screams. From somewhere outdoors.
I hear rustling and clunking coming from inside the house.
My father, usually a very deep sleeper, is out of his bed,

grumbling, trying to locate the commotion. The screams don't sound human. It's coming from somewhere down near the barn.
Flashlight in hand, Pa Bell walks briskly down to the donkey stalls.

They're empty. Our pets usually prefer sleeping outdoors when it's warm. Finding nothing amiss in the barn, my father checks the grazing field. Under a dark but moonlit sky, another, eerie, strangulated cry. It sounds like it's coming from the far corner of the donkey pen, a dense pine grove, heavily overgrown with underbrush.
Father advances slowly into the thicket, inching along under the long-needled white pines that block out most of the moonlight...Another scream.
Coming from just ahead - but echoing in an unearthly way.

From the safety of my bed, I hear the screen door creak open, my father has returned. Now he's talking to my mother, but I can't hear what they're saying.
The front door swings shut again, slamming loudly this time. I wait a long minute. Gunshot. And another.

After the birth of Pee Wee, my father had enlarged the donkey pen. Our property features some sunny, open spots, perfect for mother's gardening.
The woods that stretch between our kitchen door and the homes of our playmates (we call them "the-up-the-street-kids") is a friendly forest, akin to Christopher Robin's Hundred Acre Woods. A well worn path wanders past

rhododendron bushes, Tarzan's Rock and dozens of sweeping birch trees.

But the mysterious quadrant of property my old man recently fenced-in for our growing donkey family is vine-covered, prickly, unexplored territory. Cathy and I stay away from the poison ivy, brambles and thorny bushes that thrive down there.

We don't like to play in that stuff - but it's exactly the kind of vegetation donkeys enjoy munching on.
That's exactly what Katy was doing that night.

Why so late? Who knows. Full moon maybe?
Anyway, Katy was back there, deep in the weeds, munching peacefully when the dirt beneath her hooves suddenly crumbled into dust and she fell.

Straight down. Into the earth.

Katy plummeted down the shaft of a forgotten well.
It could've been dug a hundred years ago. Maybe more.
But then, back in history, somebody laid heavy planks over the top of the abandoned pit in the ground.
Over the decades, the forgotten well-shaft became overgrown with vines and weeds.
When Katy wandered onto the spot, time was finally up for those rotting timbers.
The long, deep plunge broke her neck - but it didn't kill her.
My dad had to finish-off my pet with his rifle.

"Hmmm...the Hill, huh?"

"Yeah. I was out there last fall and now I'm heading back.
You two would fit right in."

Merry and I talk it over. We take the stranger's advice.
After speeding, hypnotically, through miles of flat plains,
flat pastures and flat farmland, Mr. Geronimo drops us all
off at the Colorado state line. A few rides later, I begin to
see the Rocky Mountains emerging in the distance.
With every mile we traverse, the wall of mountains comes
into clearer focus. Towering, glorious.
We pass Denver and less than an hour later, we enter
Boulder.

University Hill is crawling with kids our age. Runaways,
flower children, vagabonds. We wander into the park
where a hippie soup kitchen is set-up, cranking out meals.
You kids want a free sandwich? Some minestrone?
Next to the kitchen is the free clinic. Kids are lined-up
beside signs for Lice, Mono, VD, Crabs and Pregnancy
testing. I don't want any of those, so I just line-up for the
free sandwich.
We see signs for shelters.
One area for girls to crash and one for boys.
Merry and I are a team, so we shoulder our packs and walk
southwest on Broadway, heading toward the Flatirons.

After not too far, we get to the edge of civilization. Looking
up at the foothills of the Rocky Mountains.

Blasting up out of the Earth like a tilted row of
skyscrapers, we see the parade of towering rock
formations called "the Flatirons."

Boulder CO 1969.

The Flatirons and me at age 16.

Photo by Merry

Spreading down from the rising rocks is a wide grassy
meadow and off to the side, a sprawling green barn.
On closer examination the "barn" is really an old theater,
the Colorado Chautauqua.
I remember learning the word "chautauqua" from an Elvis
Presley movie called *The Trouble with Girls*.

Merry and I hike up the grassy field, all the way to the
tree-line that stretches beneath the Flatirons.
There, in the shadows, seemingly waiting for us, is a tiny
house.

On further investigation, it's more of a shed. No door.
Most of the back wall has fallen down. But there's a floor,
three walls still standing, and a roof. All sound.
Inside, in the middle of the abandoned hut is a car engine,
propped up in a cradle. The engine has been re-tooled, the
drive shaft is attached to a large steel wheel...

"Oh, I get it. This must've been some kind of ski area. The
grassy meadow we just climbed was a ski run and this old
hotrod mill probably powered a rope-pull, towing skiers
up to the top."
We make camp and nobody bothers us up here. If anyone
comes hiking in our direction, we'll spy them a mile off.
Like Swiss Family Robinson.

Merry and I walk back into town every couple of days, to
re-fill our water jug and buy some macaroni, rice or a pack
of hot dogs. I purchase a $2 claw hammer and repair the
back wall of our mountain chalet. All the missing boards
are still lying around on the ground. We lounge out front
and the view is astonishing. The city of Boulder and the
University of Colorado are below us. As the sun sets
behind us, the city of Denver lights up, thirty miles to the
east.
That's where all the top rock musicians are arriving for the
Denver Pop Festival this weekend. Jimi Hendrix

Experience, Frank Zappa and the Mothers of Invention, Three Dog Night, Johnny Winter, Creedence Clearwater Revival, Joe Cocker, Iron Butterfly and Big Mama Thornton will all be here. No way can we afford tickets ($6 day/$15 for the 3-day weekend). Barry Fey is the promoter and the huge concert is at Mile High Stadium.

Several days later, we score a lift from some locals who correctly identify Merry and myself as rock musicians. Now we're all heading up a twisting gravel road to a neighboring mountain-top for a free rock concert. Arriving, we see dozens of hippies and a flat-bed trailer (stage) with electricity supplied by a rattling generator. A band is already playing.
Boulder's own David and Candy Givens, are on bass and lead vocal. They called themselves Zephyr and they just got back from warming-up the Mile High Stadium crowd on two different days during the Denver Pop Festival last weekend. Candy has a sweet face, frizzy hair, a tiny body and an enormous voice. The lead guitarist, who moved here recently from Iowa, is named Tommy.

Tommy Bolin is 18 years-old, two years my senior. He's a cool looking teenager. Long brown wavy hair, bell bottom blue jeans, a leather vest, a Gibson Les Paul guitar connected to a Marshall stack. Next to his amplifier, Bolin has a mysterious little gadget strapped into a baby's highchair. Zephyr play a very heavy set of original blues and hard-rock. Blonde bassist, David Givens, has a strong, rockstar look and Tommy Bolin mostly-plays lead guitar but he solos on a flute a couple times too.

We're in luck, because they say there's another band here.
I'm shocked when British singer/guitarist Terry Reid
climbs onto the mountaintop stage with his trio.

"Bang Bang You're Terry Reid" is one of Merry and my
favorite records and Black Sun rocks a decent replica
version of Reid's "Tinker Tailor."
20 year-old Terry doesn't look as dazzling as he does on
his album covers. His sexy shag haircut has grown out,
now it's long and stringy.
Today he looks less flash and more hippy.
But that voice...yikes.
Reid has a new LP out, called Superlungs. According to
rumors, Terry and his band will join the Rolling Stones on
their upcoming American tour. The Stones first US tour in
three years.

The weeks go by, we take care of our cabin campsite and
listen non-stop to my little transistor radio. AM hits play
over and over. These Eyes, Get Back, In the Ghetto, Bad
Moon Rising, Hair, Good Morning Starshine, Aquarius/
Let the Sun Shine In and Pinball Wizard.

I haven't touched a guitar in a month.
Time to see what's rocking back East.

{ 5 }

The Led Zeppelin

Arriving back in Massachusetts on July 3rd.
Just in time to hear crushing news.
Brian Jones, multi-instrumentalist and founding leader of
the Rolling Stones, drowns in the swimming pool of his
Hartfield, Sussex home. Cotchford Farmhouse.
Jones got sacked from the Stones a few months ago
- and now this. It sure won't be the same Stones anymore,
not without Brian.
But I'm also just in time to see the movie everybody's
raving about, *Easy Rider*. The ending is shocking and the
music is amazing. Instead of the usual orchestral score you
always hear on every film soundtrack, the background
music of Easy Rider is comprised of songs from
underground *rock albums*.
Never heard anything like it before. Steve and I go back to
watch and listen to the movie several more times.

August 15-18 is coming up. A bunch of my friends will be
hitching to Hudson Valley to attend The Woodstock Music
and Art Fair. The concert has a nice line-up: Jimi Hendrix
(but without the Experience), The Who, Crosby Stills,
Nash & Young, Joe Cocker and the Grateful Dead.

Jeff Beck Group won't be at Woodstock. Neither will the
Rolling Stones or the Troggs or the Kinks. I don't have the

bread for an $18 ticket anyway...but the real reason I'm staying home, is this...

A couple days after Woodstock, on August 21st, our local Carousel tent is featuring The Led Zeppelin.

That's what the posters all say anyway.

Those guys only have one record out and I've been playing it just about every single day.

Ever since it was released back in January.

Top tickets for The Led Zeppelin are going for six dollars and I would have bought one too, if it wasn't for Orpheus.

MGM Record's Orpheus is a quintet fronted by singer/
guitarist Bruce Arnold. I think they started out in
Worcester, 30 miles west of where I live. One of their
songs, "Can't Find the Time" is a romantic prom-ballad
along the lines of the Association's "Cherish." I don't know
if the Orpheus ballad did well in your town, but here in
Framingham it's a teen sensation. A cotton-pickin' smash!
That's why all The Led Zeppelin tickets got snatched-up so
fast. The popular Orpheus will be opening the show for the
hitless headliner.

On the evening of the concert I wander through the
Carousel parking lot. I see a few freaks and rockers but
most of these kids are greasers with straight-looking dates.

Girl in the crowd: "What's The Led Zeppelin, anyway?"
Boy passing by: "Don't ask me, I think he's some singer
from England."

Hot night. Hopefully some of the tent flaps will be raised.
I scramble to the dusty berm that surrounds the back of
the tent. A few other guitar players (one of them is my
future bandmate, Brad Whitford, but I haven't met him
yet) and drummers are sitting here. We listen and study
the Orpheus set. Like most of the other Bosstown Sound
groups, these guys harmonize and play great. It's just not
the heavy music I want to specialize in. The tent is packed
and the crowd rises up, cheering, as Orpheus glides into
the intro of Can't Find the Time.

Then it happens.

The moment the final *ba da-da, da da, da da* harmony dies out, the crowd jumps to its feet and scrambles for the exits.

Not just dozens. No, hundreds of folks have zero interest in hanging around to hear some guy named "The Led Zeppelin" sing a song they've never heard of. I watch in amazement as the empty seats multiply inside the tent. Cars piled-full of Orpheus fans line up and pour out of the parking lot.

Minutes later, a rough looking man with a beard and an accent peers out of the tent. Staring at me and the other freeloaders, sitting here on the embankment.

"Aye, you blokes up there. Into the bloody tent. *Hurry it up.* Everybody inside."

I didn't get his name that night, but I bet it was road manager Richard Cole who invited us inside the tent to occupy some of the abundant empty seats.

The Led Zeppelin saunter onstage and quickly swing into Train Kept A-Rollin.' My free seat is a couple rows from the stage with a perfect view of everything.

Jimmy Page is wearing orange crushed-velvet trousers over black Beatle boots with a matching orangey-colored t shirt. Twin Marshall stacks power Page's sunburst Les Paul guitar.

Robert Plant wears black pants over flats and a silver, v-necked top with lace cuffs.

His mic is on a straight stand with a round base. Not a tripod stand like Rod Stewart uses. Robert prefers to remove the mic from the clip and grasp it while he sings, sorta like Roger Daltrey does.

Robert Plant is wearing a wristwatch too, or maybe it's a bracelet that looks like a watch.

John Paul Jones is in dark clothing tonight, a tank top with a beaded necklace.

He's got his Fender bass running through two big Acoustic amps. Center stage, seated low on his drum throne, is John Bonham.

The drummer's 5 pc Ludwig kit is set on the floor, no riser. Double floor toms, oversize kick and a big gong in the back.

I'm weirdly fixating on Jimmy Page's guitar lead.

Lead - that's what they call a guitar cable in the UK. Jimi Hendrix and Jeff Beck both had coiled ones at their recent concerts but Jimmy's using a straight cable. It's very skinny and very long. It looks like lamp wire.

I'm fascinated because I've been told that guitar cables are supposed to be well-shielded. Furthermore, high impedance cables measuring over 18 feet are supposed to be noisy. Jimmy Page's cable is too skinny to have much shielding and it looks to be at least 30' long.

How is this scientifically possible?

The Led Zeppelin power through an extended I Can't Quit You Baby before settling into Dazed and Confused.

This band doesn't stick to the recorded arrangements like Jimi did last summer. Hendrix sped-up a lot of the tempos, which shortened the live presentation of some of his album tracks, but the Experience stayed pretty true to the recorded arrangements.

Led Zeppelin goes the opposite way, taking songs at a more deliberate tempo and wandering off the established pathway whenever possible. I'm a jammer too and I'm fine with all that...until the violin bow comes out.

I dig showmanship and I love the *idea* of playing an electric guitar with a bow.
On the recorded version of Dazed and Confused it sounds like Page monkeys around with the horsehairs for maybe a minute or less. Tonight's interlude has already lasted a whole lot longer than that.
As you all know, I'm a cellist, so I know that it's impossible to coax real rock music out of a bowed electric guitar.
Weird sci-fi noises, yes - but rock'n'roll, no.
It's the bridge's fault.
Orchestral strings, cellos, basses, violas and violins, all have steeply arched bridges. Each string is raised to a different height above the body of the instrument. This allows the bow to easily access each string individually. Bowed passages are sharp and distinct.
Electric guitar bridges are not arched, they're flat. Each string sits at nearly the same plane. Except for the first string and the sixth string, none of the inside strings are singly accessible to a bow.

Valuable minutes where Jimmy could be schooling me with his arsenal of rockabilly licks and blues riffs are being wasted...
I lose hope, as I spy each of Page's three bandmates tip toeing away from the little Carousel stage.
Babe...I'm gonna leave you.

After a few more minutes of uninterrupted, back & forth sawing, The Led Zeppelin loses altitude and grinds to a halt.

Maybe in Page's imagination his violin bow has become some sort of multiplying, glowing saber. Well, there's no magic light show here at the Carousel. Just a tepid wash of red and blue, par can lighting. Jimmy must be getting paid by the hour because he's still standing there, head drooped down, sawing away. Back and forth, over and over again, across all six strings in unison. Unpleasant flashbacks of endless cello lessons are flooding over me.

I gotta get out of this place.

Ejecting from my free seat, I retreat out the same tent flap I entered.

I pass fellow concertgoers and I can see from their moony, glazed looks that Mr. Page is providing a droning soundtrack for the grooviest acid trip of the summer.

I hike around the perimeter of the tent, trying to clear my ears.

The unnecessary sound of the bowed Les Paul drones on and on. There's nowhere for Page to go musically.

He can either slap the bow down on all six strings together - or he can fiddle the bow across all six.

How Many More Times, Jimmy?

About twenty minutes later, the wonderful whap of Bonham's snare drum finally breaks the curse.

The Led Zeppelin reunite onstage, trying to revive the song and bring some energy back into the tent.

The coast seems to be clear, so I scamper back inside and return to my still-empty seat, right in front.

The show picks up considerably from there.

These guys are good.

Teenager Robert Plant just turned 20 yesterday.

John Bonham's a few months older, he's also 20.

John Paul Jones is 23. At 25, Jimmy Page is the eldest.

You Shook Me is next.

Almost as good as Jeff Beck Group's live version of the same Muddy Waters song. Then a new one I never heard before, called What Is and What Should Never Be.

I'm thrilled to hear Your Time is Gonna Come. The lads really work together on this one and it does sound heavy, just like the recording.

John Bonham favors us with a showy, very physical, drum solo. Love it. And finally, How Many More Times.

Black Sun does a killer version of How Many More Times, but Led Zeppelin's version starts off even better than ours. It rolls and rocks through the different sections, past Oh Rosie, past The Hunter, and finally reaching the ticking prelude to Plant's soaring, wailing, epic scream.

"Cause I got you... in the sights... of my ..."

Oh come *on... What* are they doing *now*?

No Robert Plant scream?

Jimmy Page steps forward - instead of the singer - to jangle-out the opening riff to Chuck Berry's "Schooldays" and boom, Zeppelin bounds off, down a rabbit hole.

They segue from Chuck Berry to a bit of Jerry Lee Lewis and who-knows-what-else before *finally* returning to the long awaited scream/climax of How Many More Times.

Don't get me wrong, I love "Up in the morning, off to school" and "Whole lotta shakin' goin' on" - but who's bright idea was it to insert a rock'n'roll history lesson - right in the middle of my favorite part of How Many More Times?

It just doesn't square. Not with this 16 year-old rock student. The group finishes with Communication Breakdown, played straight, and the lights come up.

The Led Zeppelin concert gives me a ton to think about.
My expectations were incredibly high for this concert.
I love the record, but live, Led Zeppelin don't knock my socks off, not the way Jimi Hendrix Experience and the Jeff Beck Group did.
Maybe it's me.
My ears and eyes might be changing now that I'm 17, with some professional rock shows under my belt.
The Experience are riveting, from start to finish.
The Beck Group's high-energy Boston debut held us spellbound.
Led Zeppelin, tonight anyway, are maddeningly uneven.
Jimmy Page seems to sabotage the momentum with oddly-timed jams. To my ears, they knock it outta the tent when it pleases them - but they also seem content to noodle aimlessly (and at the perfectly wrong times) before finally getting back into the pocket.

Or maybe Jimmy Page was just pissed-off tonight.
Seeing the Carousel empty-out just before his group made their Framingham debut.

I admit it was Page's slow motion, violin bow half-time show that really set me off.
But I should give The Led Zeppelin a break, they invited me to watch their concert for free after all.

On Oct. 22nd, the second Led Zeppelin album is supposed to be released.
I'll be the first to buy it and my studies will continue.

Frank Connelly's 2-pole Carousel tent. Framingham MA
This is where I saw Jimi and Led Zeppelin.

{ 6 }

Altamont and Love It or Leave It

Altamont and Love It or Leave It

In the aftermath of the summer of '69, the rock concert business mushrooms overnight. The huge turnouts for the Atlanta International Pop Festival, Toronto Rock and Roll Revival, Texas International Pop Festival, the Denver Pop Festival and the Woodstock Music and Art Fair have clued the corporate world into the huge youth audience for "underground" rock.

The kind of music being played on album rock FM stations like WBCN in Boston.

I gotta admit, while watching these struggling rock bands at the local Carousel tent or at Boston Tea Party gatherings, I often wonder to myself,

"How much longer will it take, before the kids back in Holliston and across America get hip to Jimi Hendrix? The Led Zeppelin? Keith Emerson?"

I'm noticing that rock music, especially the lyrics, have changed tremendously since I got my first Zim Gar electric. Early Kinks and Yardbirds records were made for dancing and the singers mostly talked about good or bad relationships, love and other emotional stuff. The British Invasion groups played riffs and sang songs based heavily on the works of rockers like Chuck Berry and Bo Diddley or Howlin Wolf, Jimmy Reed, Muddy Waters and the other Chicago and Mississippi Delta blues artists. Meanwhile, at the very same time, a folk music boom was going on. Pete Seeger, Joan Baez, the Guthries, Buffy Sainte-Marie, Tim Rose, Peter, Paul and Mary and Bob Dylan to name a few. Not so easy dancing to folk songs, but these acoustic minstrels aren't just bemoaning lost love like the blues and early rock artists. The socially conscious folkies sing about civil rights, unionizing, stopping wars and other big issues that are blowin' in the wind.

So, inevitably, the political messages of the folk movement get sucked-up into the rock'n'roll scene. Suddenly we have groups of folkies-gone-electric, like the Byrds, Barry McGuire and Buffalo Springfield, setting political lyrics to a rock dance beat.

By '69, headliners like Steppenwolf, Country Joe and the Fish, Crosby, Stills, Nash & Young, Creedence Clearwater Revival and Jefferson Airplane are all writing and singing about social issues and even political revolution.

The political-rock trend goes straight to the top. The Beatles begin peppering their repertoire with ditties about taxes, the British class system, Prime Ministers and warm guns. The Rolling Stones and the Kinks follow suit.

Back in the USA, Ann Arbor's MC5 raise things up another notch. Kick Out the Jams is recorded in October 1968 and released the following January. The outspoken band, whose startling debut will climb to #30 on the Billboard album chart, is managed by John Sinclair, founder of the militant, leftist, White Panther Party.

Of course, my buddies and I are all keenly aware that when our 18th birthdays roll around, we'll all be making a required visit to the Selective Service office in Framingham to register for the draft.
The war is on. Uncle Sam needs more boys to go out and defend America (girls don't get drafted).
Not many of my friends have volunteered for the jungle assignment, so random numbers picked from a hat will decide who gets called next.
Being forced into military service dangles over our necks. The draft has politicized the entire teenage male population of America. Ever since I turned 15 I've been toting around the latest issue of the counterculture Ramparts Magazine and sporting a Ban the Bomb button on my fink vest.

1969 ends with the Rolling Stones. December 5th sees the release of Let It Bleed. The album is great but bittersweet for me, as this will be the last recorded peep from my favorite Stone, the uniquely talented Brian Jones.
The day following the record release, Mick and the Stones headline the Altamont Free Concert in California.
300,000 kids show up, hoping to catch some good vibes at "Woodstock West."

My bass player, Steve, shows up at band rehearsal with a thick stack of bumper stickers he just liberated.

"America: Love It or Leave It" the decals proclaim, in vibrant red, white and blue.

I've seen cars plastered with the lame slogan ever since President Nixon's veep, Spiro Agnew, began talking about America's "Silent Majority."

A majority of citizens who (according to Spiro) support the war, the draft and regular haircuts for boys.

Spiro Agnew is disturbed by young people protesting the draft in the streets or at music festivals. Like lots of kids in the USA, my bassist Steve and I have been attending peace marches and moratoriums. We're beefing up our setlist with edgier material like Eddie Cochran's Summertime Blues (by way of Blue Cheer), Morning Dew and a heavy version of Country Joe's brilliant "Feel Like I'm Fixing To Die Rag."

We decide to ratchet up our anti-establishment image. With scissors, we carefully trim the word "America" from all the bumper stickers.

Okay, that's more like it. Forget Black Sun - our band is now officially named "Love It or Leave It."

Over the next days and weeks we refinish all our speaker cabinets, adding red & white stripes to some, others will get a blue field with five-pointed stars. We remove the grille-cloths from all the speaker panels and replace them with swatches of Old Glory. While the paint dries, Steve and I both strip the finish from our guitars and repaint them in the same Betsy Ross motif. Our drummer, Joey, must've missed *Easy Rider*. He doesn't want to change the color of his drum set, he just shakes his head at us.

My band. Love It or Leave It.

And we already have our own custom bumper stickers.
Welcome to 1970.
My subversive new group manages to land a few high
school dance bookings. Merry has drifted as faraway as
possible from my half-baked political experiment. So we've
found a guy named Rob to sing lead vocals.
Rob doesn't have much of a voice or look, but he does have
one those clunky Shure 55 mics from the 50's that looks
like a space heater.
We open with a ripping version of MC5's Ramblin' Rose,
followed by Kick Out the Jams, leading straight into Helter
Skelter. The high school kids stand back. Way back.
Are they gonna Love it? Or Leave it? I don't think they're
getting my revolutionary message.

After laying an egg at the Sherborn Congregational church
hall and stinking up the Holliston Town Hall, my quasi-
political experiment, Love It or Leave It, calls it quits.
It's February and today I run into an old acquaintance,
Jack Bialka.
I grew up in East Holliston and Jack grew up a few miles
away, on the western edge of Holliston.
Jack is a year or two older than me.
The first time I met him was back in '66.
Back then, George Masters was in my elementary school
class and George was briefly a member of The Effective -
or maybe it was the Mechanical Onions...
A few months later, George invites me over to his house to
mess around on our guitars together. My little white
ZimGar can't hold a candle to George's multi-pickup

Teisco Del Ray. His axe has a row of rocker switches and a striped, silver & black pick guard.

Maybe George's guitar has better action than mine, or maybe I'm just slow but whatever it is, Masters can play the barre chords and inversions that I'm still struggling with. It gets worse when George's neighbor, Jack Bialka, shows up...carrying a cherry red *Gibson* SG Special guitar. Jack and George start strumming the chords to "Cherish" and begin to sing, *in harmony*. They made a monkey out of me, still wrestling with my first position chords.

That was four years ago.

Now, Jack has just dropped-out of Boston's Berklee School of Music, after nearly completing his first year there. In the Berklee program, Jack's primary instrument is the jazz saxophone, but what Jack really needs to do is sing and play rock'n'roll.

Following a few meetings, we put together a whole new idea. Jack tells me about his friend Rick,

"He jumps around the room and plays riffs on a flute."

Remembering how deftly Jack handles guitar, I suggest that I switch to the bass.

I already have my eye on a cheap one. A white teardrop model over at Music'n'Things.

Jack has a deep, Elvis-type voice and I can sing a little, so even if we sound rough at first, I still have my secret weapon - Joey on the drums.

We name the new band after my birthplace,

Yellow Springs, Ohio.

Our debut show is at Dennison Hall in Framingham, a nice venue with a big stage and a balcony. I've got all my gear piled in the back of my old man's station wagon, he gives me a lift to the concert.

To complement my white teardrop bass guitar, I've decided to wear all-white tonight. White bell bottoms under a white Nehru shirt that I bought at Truc. It has a built-in white scarf stitched to the collar.

I even dyed my shoes white.

We get to the hall and a lot of kids are outside waiting for the show. After unloading my gear, I slam the tailgate of the wagon shut - *OUCH*.

Mashed inside the tailgate - my right fore-finger.

Slammed in. Real good.

The door is totally latched and my digit is stuck in there. Damn...no choice, I yank the tailgate open and blood comes gushing out of my squished finger.

Squirting all over my white shoes, white bell bottoms, white scarf. Alice Cooper would faint if he saw this gruesome scene.

We're supposed to be opening for the popular Newton group "Landlord" in just a few minutes. I manage to slow the stream, tightly wrapping my finger in one of my socks before hitting the stage. But once I begin rocking, the finger resumes gushing.

All over my white bass guitar, dripping across the stage.

{ 7 }

Faces and Tulagi
The public schools are still enforcing strict dress codes. No boots, no turtlenecks. Correct hair-length is monitored daily. I've been out of the state-controlled school system for over a year and my wardrobe and hair are enjoying their newfound freedom.
Long blonde and curly, kinda like Roger Daltrey or Robert Plant's.
I don't wear clothes from the boys department at Sears or Zayres like a lot of the kids in my town. My non-conforming rock'n'roll wardrobe is pieced together with items from Harvard Square boutiques like Truc and Krackerjack's, mixed in with my Flagg Bros, calf-high, laced moccasins, my well-battered Thom McAn Monkee Boots and my signature fink vest.

Around Holliston most of the kids call me faggot.
I just mind my own business - but I draw weirdos like a magnet every time I venture off my parents' property. Walking up Washington street, motorists will lean out of their windows, leer at my butt and make lip-smacking noises.

"Hey chickie. C'mon cutie. Why ya walking so fast?"

Rolling along behind me in their cars, horny guys hang out their windows, they slobber, shout and honk their horns while they look me over, up and down.
Once these idiot males get closer...they continue to drool and offer their stud services. Eventually, somebody in the car usually realizes that I'm not the hottest chick on the planet.
Hey. That babe is...a guy!
When the salivating goons realize that they've been loudly professing their lust for a bro, they get really pissed-off.
At me.
Suddenly they don't want to feel-up my ass anymore.
Now they want to kick my ass, chop off my hair and blah, blah, blah.
I don't respond to their confused threats. I just keep walking - but it makes me angry.

Today I'm heading home from Tito's Country Store and I can hear the familiar sound of a slowing car, rolling right behind me. I keep my head down...just keep on trucking, moving down the sidewalk.

"Hey. Where do you live?" Asks a low voice.
"What're you doing in this town?" A second voice inquires.
I keep moving, silently.
"What's with the heels? Are you queer?
Trying to prove something?"
"Why the hell don't you get a hair cut?
Are you ashamed of your sex?
Is that your problem?"

These knuckleheads, whoever they are, are trying to bait me into a fight.

Don't look up. Just keep walking...

With a screech of tire rubber, the driver suddenly accelerates. The car swerves back onto Washington street and blasts past me. I see the idiots for the first time.

Two Holliston police officers in a patrol car.

This is the first time the police have ever spoken to me.

It makes me angry.

During the summer of the Woodstock festival, our little Boston Tea Party moves out of 53 Berkeley St. into a larger space at 15 Lansdowne St. The new place is an old parking garage behind Fenway Park. The space is air conditioned and has a concrete floor. The audience area is bigger, holding several hundred more patrons than before, but the ceiling height is much lower. Not enough space to project a big psychedelic light show.

The Boston Tea Party continues to be an all-ages operation. No alcohol is served.

Admission rarely exceeds $4.

I've already visited the new location a few times to see the Velvet Underground, Sha Na Na and Fleetwood Mac.

On March 27th, Cathy, Merry and I are all here, anxious to see the debut of Faces, a brand new British ensemble featuring Rod Stewart and Ron Wood. Tonight's headliner is Lee Michaels and opening the show is the band Merry and I know from Boulder.

Zephyr. With lead guitarist, Tommy Bolin.

78

Tommy still has his mysterious "Bolin Box" strapped to an infant's high-chair right beside his amplifier stack.
I recognize the sounds the box makes. Jimmy Page used a similar effect on the two Led Zeppelin records. The device can repeat musical phrases for varying lengths of time and at varying intensities, the brand name is Echoplex.
Following a heavy Zephyr set, it's time for Rod Stewart and company to make their Boston premiere.
Drummer Kenny Jones, singer/bassist Ronnie Lane and organist Ian McLagan are all from The Small Faces.
Ron Wood has traded his electric bass for a lead guitar.
My third time seeing Mr. Stewart and once again he impresses. This band doesn't have a virtuoso soloist, no Jeff Beck, but working as a team, Faces offer a rollicking, engaging set. We're thrilled with the brand new British band and the sounds they make.
Faces will prove to have a deeper effect on us than I realize.

After a flurry of bookings at the Cave, Dennison Hall and Holliston Town Hall, my latest teenage band "Yellow Springs, Ohio" is withering.
Merry doesn't come around much anymore.
I don't smoke weed and she's a little pothead.
One night I run into her and out of the blue, I announce "I'm heading back to the Hill, wanna come along?"
Merry surprises me and replies "Yeah."
She just turned 17, we're both still considered children.
I don't think I'll get in trouble for crossing state lines with a minor. I'm a minor too.

We head west in June '70 and somewhere in Ohio, a school bus covered with fun-flower decals stops to pick us up on the Interstate. Well, it doesn't really stop, it comes to a slow roll, the yellow doors fold-open and we both leap, clambering up the moving steps.

Plenty of long-haired kids are already onboard and the bus smells bad. The driver, who has a styrofoam cooler by his side, hands us each a cold drink and points to a nearby bench seat.

He steps on the gas. Topping out at about 50 mph and things begin to smell a little better as we gain speed.

I take inventory.

Half a dozen guys, maybe ten girls, a few dogs.

One of the riders passes Merry and me, he swings behind the wheel, relieving the driver who races to the back of the bus. There's a plywood wall separating us from the very last bit of the long interior cabin. A wobbly wall, with a barely-hinged door.

Oh, I get it, that must be the bathroom in the back.

A few minutes later, the captain emerges with his hand covering his face, he dashes up the aisle and takes over the wheel again. Everyone is either toking on the roach being passed around or nursing a beer.

A red-haired flower child wobbles up to the front and whispers something to the driver.

"Nah, I'm sorry" he replies, pointing to the row of windows behind him.

The redhead looks a bit dismayed. A few minutes later, after an extremely hairy guy helps her lower her window as

far as possible, I watch the girl scoop-up her puppy, kiss it
on the nose, grab it by the scruff and shove it out the
window of the rolling bus.
The little mutt is suspended in the breeze, yipping as the
traffic zips by below. A geyser of pee suddenly shoots out
of floating Fido. Motorists honk their objections.
Windshield wipers of cars down below begin whapping as
the beeps rains down.

Speaking of beeps, I've finished my drink and now it's time
to visit the washroom. I totter to the back of the bouncing
bus, meeting a few of the other riders as I navigate the
long aisle. Pulling open the door to the lavatory I'm
horrified. Even with all the windows back here propped
full-open, a hot, thick stench begins to dissolve my
eyebrows.
A five gallon bucket sits before me. Untethered. Just
plopped on the floor. Full to the brim with community pee,
topped off with a few floaters.
Rude stew sloshes over the brim, the floor is soaked, my
eyes sting. For a moment I consider leaping out the
window and joining Fido, who is still hanging 20.

After spending a penny and with my peepers watering, I
kick open the door to return to my seat.
Strangely, as I re-enter the cabin I notice everyone has
their backs turned to me.
Everyone is pushing their face out the nearest window,
even the driver. He's slowing down the bus.

"Your turn!" yells hairy.

It takes a moment for me to realize what's going on.
Stopping this bus would mean instant death for all of us.
The contents of the vile bucket would overtake our lungs
and melt our vital organs in seconds. Gotta keep moving.
What about the back door? I remember, as a kid, thinking
about trying to escape from school by evacuating out the
back end of my school bus.
But, no.
What remains of the rear escape hatch has been bolted
and welded shut on this Blue Bird.

Well, at least the bucket has a handle...I grab hold and lift.
Hippie tinkle splashes down my leg. Five gallons of beeps
is heavy as heck but I have no choice, I run the gauntlet.
Hefting the pail of stink with one hand and clamping my
schnoz shut with the other. Our captain knows the drill, he
has one hand on the steering wheel while his head is
extended (way-out) his driver's-side window. He operates
the folding-door control-handle with his right foot. The
bus slows down to around 15 mph as I descend the
stairway and lean out of the moving vehicle.
I heave the hideous, chunky-soup out the bus door and it
spills across the passing pavement of I-70.
Actually, most of it flies back and splatters against the
entire side of our flower-festooned bus.
The captain hits the gas, trying to outrun our own stench.

Arriving in Boulder, we find our old Flatirons shack
waiting for us.
Looking just as we left it last year. Incredible.

Merry hears about a free concert down the Hill on the
University campus. Not many kids show up but the local
band sounds excellent. They're fronted by a singing B3
organist and they call themselves Sugarloaf. The roadie
told me they 're really called Chocolate Hair but Liberty
Records made them change the name.
One of the new songs they play is familiar to us, "Green-
Eyed Lady" the single was released a few weeks ago and
it's already getting played on the Denver AM radio we
listen to.

Tulagi is a nightclub on the Hill at 1129 13th St.
The venue serves pitchers of Coors 3.2 beer to students
from nearby Colorado University while hosting popular
touring artists and rock bands. A few years ago, Tulagi was
the launch pad for the Boulder surf-rock band, The
Astronauts.
They were RCA Record's answer to Capitol's Beach Boys.
I saw The Astronauts play on the Hullaballoo TV show a
few times and they appeared in four excellent beach party
movies too.

Tonight the headliner is blues artist, John Hammond Jr.
I know Hammond and his music from listening to WBCN
and a Rolling Stone article that featured a photo of John
wearing some extremely cool leather boots. I'm hanging
around, watching the slightly-older-than-me crowd swarm
through the front door. Wish I had the cover charge.
Wouldn't matter though, I'm only 17, too young to be
admitted into a beer bar. Remembering the Led Zeppelin
show from a few months ago, I make my way around back.

Who knows? Maybe someone will leave a window cracked and I'll get to hear some dynamite blues for free.

I don't see any windows, but I do see a thin curl of smoke wafting up from behind an aluminum exhaust shaft. Looking down I see boots. Cool leather boots. I move a bit closer and - shit, that's gotta be him.

John Hammond Jr. Smoking a butt before his concert. Hammond looks up.

"Hey man. Coming to the show tonight?"

I explain that I'm on the road and short on funds.

Hammond smiles and asks about my journey.

I tell him a little about the trip west with Merry but I leave out the part about the overflowing bucket of urine.

"You play?" he asks.

"uh, yeah," I update John on some of my career highlights with the Mechanical Onions, The Effective, Love It or Leave It...

"Okay, listen. Don't say a thing, just follow me."

Simple as that, Hammond stamps out his smoke with one of his very cool leather boots, hoists his Gibson acoustic 6-string into playing position and strides to the stage door.

I do as I'm told. I follow.

Two zigs and a zag later, I'm standing in the wings.

John motions to an empty seat, right next to the stage.

Boom, I'm here. In a *bar*.

The Tulagi crowd bursts into applause as John steps into the spotlight.

A minute later a cold pitcher of 3.2 beer is delivered to my table.

Hammond shoots me a grin and swings into Walking
Blues.

This second trip to Boulder doesn't enhance my
relationship with Merry. We end up finding our own ways
back east, separately.
She flies. I hitchhike alone and most of my rides are
decent.
Let's get one thing straight.
All this cross country hitchhiking stuff is not really my bag.
I'm a nervous, shy kid. I mean, back home around
Holliston, I never hitchhike.
This uncanny road fever crept into me while I listened to
my older classmates bragging. Guys a year or two my
senior, telling tales of how they hitched out to Golden Gate
Park last summer and on up to Mendocino a month later.
My real dream would be to criss-cross the country with my
own touring rock band.
But for now, I'm just grabbing at whatever fragment of my
dream I can reach.

The worst part of hitchhiking is the vulnerable place it
puts me where the law is concerned. My limited
relationship with police officers has been terrible so far.
I'm here in New York, breaking the law by hitching on a
ramp that leads to the Interstate. Still 250 miles away from
Holliston, praying someone will stop for me.
A patrol car buzzed past me a few minutes ago.
An officer with a bull-horn warned that I "better not be
here" the next time he passes through.

Sweating, on my final stretch, begging for someone to stop. Every car whips past me.

I see flashing lights approaching.

Damn.

The unit pulls up to the curb about a hundred yards away.

There's another hitcher down there, about to get detained.

I watch as the police step out of their cruiser.

Should I dive over this guard rail and roll down the embankment?

Make a run for it?

I'm trembling, feeling sick. That's when out of nowhere, the most beautiful car in the world - a rusty 1967 Chevy Nova - jams to a quick stop, right in front of me.

I dive onto the front seat and we're off, merging onto I-90 and heading homeward.

My rescuer's name is Luther Rabb and he's got his car radio cranked while he sings along. Melodies, harmonies, rockers, Motown shouters, love songs...

Man, this guy sounds good on everything.

Miles up the road, Rabb tells me he's heading for a gig in Hyannis, out on Cape Cod.

His touring rock band has a show booked tonight at the Velvet Hammer nightclub.

Seattle-born Luther tells me about a Los Angeles mansion where his band lives and how they've been opening shows for his childhood friend, Jimi Hendrix.

The "Cry of Love" tour started this April at the Forum in L.A. with Buddy Miles Express and Luther's group. They warmed-up for Hendrix in Houston, Baltimore, Ventura

and Rabb tells me he just rocked the Swing Ballroom with
Jimi last week in San Bernardino.

Wow. Okay, now I remember.

I've seen this dude and his band playing on TV.

PBS did an hour special on them, they record for Columbia
and go by the name Ballin' Jack.

Luther Rabb gives me a ride all the way to the Natick exit
of the Massachusetts Turnpike.

I point out the location of the Carousel tent as we drive by.

I'll run into Luther again, in a few months.

Boulder CO 1970. With a frisbee I found. And my diary.
Photo by Merry

{ 8 }

Firebird and Joe Flash

Returning home to Holliston, I start saving up.

On Sunday afternoons my father drops me off at the Music Box where I vacuum floors for $5 an hour. First I clean the upstairs bookkeeping office where grandfather Nelson works, then the Sound Room where my father demonstrates the newest audio breakthroughs. I vacuum the spacious greeting card department - it's been part of the store ever since WWII.

Next, I clean the record department, the rest rooms and finally the Service Lab on the downstairs level.

I Windex the front and rear windows, mop the entry ways, sweep the two staircases, empty ashtrays and if there's time leftover, I make little signs for the parade of used audio gear that constantly rotates through the trade-in window out back on Church street.

I finally manage to accrue $150.

The most cash I've ever seen.

Framingham Music Center has moved across the street into a larger space, now calling itself Devine's. That's where I find a slightly-used, 1965 Gibson non-reverse Firebird, 2 pickup, solid body electric guitar, in Pelham Blue. $150 but no case.

It's hard finding a case that fits a Firebird.

I end up with an old Sears Silvertone guitar case and just cut a hole in the top of it, so the Gibson headstock can hang out a little bit and get some air.

In August, Eric Clapton releases his first solo record. It's a major departure from his star turns with John Mayall, the Yardbirds, Cream, Blind Faith and Derek and the Dominoes. Clapton is less of the focus on this record and more of a team player, grooving behind Bonnie and Delaney Bramlett (he met the duo when they were openers for his Blind Faith shows). It's not a heavy-rock record but something about it intrigues me.

Eric sings lead on the recording but Bonnie shares the harmonies and there are group-vocals as well.

I manage to convince Merry to come over and we start jamming on a couple of these new Clapton numbers, After Midnight and Let it Rain.

Another song on the Clapton record, Bottle of Red Wine, inspires us to pen our own "Sweet Wine."

While we were both out in Colorado, Rod Stewart released his second solo record. Merry amazes me with her spirited renditions of Rod's Country Comfort (written by Elton John and Bernie Taupin) and the title tune, Gasoline Alley.

I know from watching Ron Wood at the Tea Party how this song is played. Wood uses an open-E tuning. I take to the open-tuning like a diving duck.

Likewise, Merry is extremely comfortable singing in Stewart's range and she even adopts a measure of his grit into her delivery.

With these new songs under our belt, I phone my bass-playing neighbor Ken. Drummer Joey isn't around so I call Rick, the flute player from Yellow Springs Ohio. Rick owns a drum kit too, and he sounds okay on it.
Pretty soon we're all jamming together with a new direction.

Both my mother and Big Mama (my grandmother) celebrate birthdays on September 18th. I'm in the kitchen eating cake and ice cream when shocking, nearly impossible-to-comprehend news spills out of the KLH Model Twenty-One table radio.
Notting Hill, London: Jimi Hendrix, found dead at age 27.

On October 5th, Led Zeppelin release their third album on Atlantic Records.
I'll have to wait til tomorrow to listen because right now we're back at the "new" Boston Tea Party on Lansdowne Street.
Faces are back and they've moved up to the headline spot.
Warming-up tonight's crowd is Ballin' Jack.
Starring my ride from a few months ago, Luther Rabb.
I'm proud to see my friend standing center stage, on lead vocals and bass guitar.
Speaking of Rabb, he's about to become a member of Santana, and after that, War.

Faces have yet to release a second album, but singer Rod has filled the gap with his two solo albums, both are getting decent play on WBCN. The band impresses us with their progress. They've become extremely comfortable on stage, drawing everyone into their pub-rock, soccer and dobro guitar universe.

My only minor complaint is Around the Plynth.

An extended jam that is based, I presume, on the Jeff Beck Group's far superior, Plynth.

Ron Wood was a perfect bass player for Jeff Beck.

As a bottle-neck guitar player he's...improving.

Around the Plynth just goes on for too long. It's a song about basin water swirling 'round the plug-hole, and when Wood runs out of fresh slide guitar riffs - about half-way through the number - it all goes down the drain for me.

Returning to Holliston, Merry and I continue to craft a new setlist.

You're My Girl is a new, unrecorded, heavy/funk thing we just heard Faces perform live.

From memory I try my best to re-construct the number and we have fun with the results. Three Button Hand Me Down is another Rod Stewart song that fits Merry's voice amazingly well. An old bandmate swings by for a listen, I'm stunned when my talented neighbor, Jeff, offers to back me up on *second* guitar. Jeff can out-play me any day but I guess he hears potential in the direction this thing's heading in.

Jeff brings along a bassist named Peter and now I have Joey back on the drums.

Two months later, in early 1971, I spy a poorly drawn poster, scrawled in crayon, advertising a show coming to the Lakeview Ballroom. Just up the street in Mendon.

Of course I know the headliners, The Joneses.'

The popular Worcester group is fronted by the D'Angelo brothers. Joe and younger sibling Jimmy. They both have perfect shag haircuts, play Gibson guitars, often in harmony, and they both share the vocals, often in harmony.

The Joneses' are the only group with Marshall amps to ever play Holliston Town Hall.

I stare at the odd poster... I've never even heard of the opening band.

Aerosmith.

What kind of name is that?

Based on the penmanship, I figure it's a little kid band.

On Monday. I pay my 2 bucks to get in.

I'm about to get schooled by the opening band.

The guy on the drums is funky and he packs a hard punch.

The rhythm guitarist is steady and cool.

The lead guitarist looks like a British Rock Star.

The bassman is pouring a deep foundation and when I see the singer leap into action - I can hardly believe my ears and eyes.

I'm almost 18 years old and I've seen a whole bunch of rock stars in concert but this local band measures-up to, and occasionally exceeds them all.

Nobody here at Lakeview even knows these guys names. It's cosmic.

All we can do is stare in astonishment. Glancing at each other, thinking the same thing,

"Whoever those guys are, they're gonna be huge!"

From the first song it's just so glaringly obvious.

Aerosmith are headed for the top.

We hear "Somebody" and "Mama Kin" for the first time
that night. They also play the Stones "Honky Tonk
Women" and "Bad And Ruin" from the just released Faces
second LP. Aerosmith open with "Jive" which is basically
"Mother Popcorn" minus the vocals. The rubber-faced
frontman just jigs across the stage, banging a cow bell.
Showstoppers are Fleetwood Mac's "Rattlesnake Shake"
and the Rufus Thomas novelty, "Walkin' The Dog"
featuring a wooden flute solo from the odd looking singer.
During the break, my curious sister Cathy sneaks
backstage to meet the band.
She attempts to hire them for a dance at our Town Hall.
The Aerosmith frontman whips a tiny date book out of his
back pocket and quotes her a price.
"We can do it for $200.
And we want a box of malted milk balls for our dressing
room."
 I leave the Lakeview Ballroom overwhelmed. The brand
new local group called Aerosmith stuns the teenage crowd.
They sure do a number on me.

A group of my friends have been attending the town
selectmen meetings, lobbying for their own Holliston Teen
Center. They're asking for a heated, sheltered spot where
all the local kids can get together to hangout and listen to
rock music.
The effort pays off when the local Catholic Youth
Organization gives the kids use of basement space in a
building they own, right in the heart of downtown
Holliston.
The new Center will open in February.

They name the place Ararat.

The band Merry and I have been hatching for the past six months will finally debut at this new venue.

Our frequent line-up changes come to a brief halt when Jack, my singing/saxophone-playing/guitarist friend, agrees to handle bass guitar and backing vocals.

During rehearsals, Cathy and her girlfriends sometimes get carried away during the frantic choruses of After Midnight or Brown Sugar. They begin Stewart-strutting and shouting Wooo! in unison. The same routine works well for some of the Faces songs we cover, and since Cathy and her friends work for free, we hire 'em all to be our "Screamin' Ya-Ya Girls."

On Feb 19th the new band debuts at the Ararat opening. The underground teen center is decorated with kaleidoscopic murals and tin foil. The ceiling height is low, not enough headroom for a raised stage or a psychedelic light show. But, the basement space fills-up quickly.

Merry is always an attraction. She draws boys like flies and the local girls seem to be fascinated by her too.

Unexpected bad news. My secret weapon, drummer Joe Hamwey, *resigns*.

Right before the big gig.

I'm stunned. Joey has been with me for years, ever since the lean days of the Mechanical Onions.

I'll admit that most of my bands have flopped, but tonight, for the first time in a longtime, I've finally put together something with potential.

Holliston MA 1971. JOE FLASH debuts at the Ararat teen center.
Merry on vocals
and me with my
Gibson Firebird.

Joey stuck with me through all the rotten times, even my
"Love It or Leave It" fiasco...but tonight, just as we turn
the corner towards something with possible commercial
appeal, he calls it quits.

A good humored drummer, named Mark, who plays in the
Holliston group Integrated Sound (aka Flower Power),
steps-in to save the day.

The local press reviews Ararat's opening night and there's
a big picture of Merry on the front page. Oh yeah, I named
the new band Joe Flash.

Our set goes down great, Merry nails the lead vocals on our Rod Stewart, Stones and Dave Mason songs. When she takes a break, Jack and I rocket into a Sly Stone/Isley Brothers/James Brown mash-up with Mark keeping time behind us on the drums.

I take over the singing for the high-energy, call-and-response numbers.

The night is a big success, for the new teen center and for my new group.

Holliston 1971. JOE FLASH at Ararat. Me, Jack, Merry and my sister, Cathy Bell.

Besides being a nice guy and a good rock musician, our
bass player, Jack, knows his way around a wood shop.
He grew up around power tools like I did.
We spend lots of hours down in my dad's shop in the cellar
of the Holliston house. Building speaker boxes. With some
locally sourced black Tolex, silver grille cloth from Radio
Shack, nickel-plated hardware and Jensen speakers from
the Music Box, we create reasonably pro-looking cabinets
that could almost fool Leo Fender.
We're using the Craftsman table saw to rip through 4'x 8'
sheets of plywood.
Jack looks up, pointing with a confused-smile. He asks
"What's that?"

An icy night, in the Winter of early 1961.
We've finished dinner and now we're sitting around the
circular kitchen table, laughing with my grandparents,
Big Mama and Bun. They're visiting us from their home in
Burlington Vermont.
A loud yelp comes from the other end of the house.
My grandfather jumps to his feet, he races out of the
kitchen.
Bun runs through the dining room, past the staircase and
throws open the door to the living room.
"Call the police!" Bun yells to us over his shoulder.
Mother darts to the kitchen phone.
Grandmother tries to remain calm, she turns to my six
year-old sister, Cathy, and then to me.
Little brother Andy continues eating his Oreo because he's
only two.
Rescuers take a long time getting up to our house.

They can't back the ambulance up the icy hill. The weather is really bad. While mother and Big Mama tend to the children, I gather my courage and creep towards the living room.

Peering inside nervously, I see blood.

Splattered all across the floor and straight up the wall. The bloody trail continues all the way across the ceiling, drips back down the opposite wall and continues back across the floor again.

It's a gruesome, circular pattern, and it's been sprayed around the large room several times.

Crumpled on the floor, in the middle of the gory, Spirograph-like design, is my father.

Bun is hunched down beside his son-in-law, applying all his weight to the stump end of my father's left arm.

Besides selling top-notch audio gear, my father runs a brisk side-business, designing and installing custom cabinetry to house his customer's Ampex tape decks, Marantz tuners and Thorens turntables.

An experienced builder, my workaholic father is also in the midst of completing a sizable addition to our house. He's turning a narrow sun room into a spacious living/music listening room.

The house was originally built in 1799, as Holliston's first schoolhouse.

My parents, both fans of Colonial history and architecture, often bring the family to tour Old Sturbridge Village, a recreation of an early 19th Century New England neighborhood.

Holliston 1964. Mother in her new Corvair. That's the Bell house in the back. Photo by my father, Bill Bell

Cathy will admire the horses and stables while I visit the clockmaker or the candle-maker. Meanwhile, my father busies himself, measuring moulding details and studying door and window frames.

On this icy night, my dad had his Craftsman table saw set up right in the middle of the under-construction living room. The interior is still very rough, with plywood sub-flooring and unfinished sheetrock walls.

After dinner, he excuses himself to the living room, where he's finishing work on a custom job for a Music Box customer.

Cutting openings in a face-panel for an audio cabinet.

The initial cut involves lowering the face-panel down onto the bench saw - right on top of the spinning 12" carbon-tipped circular blade.

Somehow, my father's forearm ends-up stretched across the sheet of birch plywood as the blade came tearing through. Ripping through the lumber and continuing to saw off my old man's ulna and radius bones. All the nearby muscles and nerves are severed, as well as the three main arteries to his left arm.

It takes a full hour but they finally manage to carry him out. Strapped to a stretcher. It's a slow job, maneuvering the stretcher down the slippery hill to the lower part of the driveway where the ambulance and most of the town's sleet-covered squad cars have gathered, radios humming and lights flashing.

Also on the stretcher, right beside him, is my dad's forearm and left hand.

Even though all the bones and veins are severed, the dismembered arm is still attached to him by a bit of arm skin that escaped the saw blade.

Later on, my grandfather tells me what he saw.
When Bun entered the living room, my father was passed-out on the floor from loss of blood.
Motionless. Except for the stump of his arm.
The stump was still swinging around like crazy, painting the walls and ceilings with fresh squirts of blood with every beat of his heart. Pa had the presence of mind to let out a very loud cry, just before he fainted and collapsed. Yelling - not from horror or pain - but from the knowledge that he was bleeding out. Once he conked-out, alone in that room, he wouldn't survive very long. Thank goodness Bun was visiting. He's a strong ex-Navy man and he knew exactly how to handle the emergency.

The surgeons at Framingham Union Hospital do a magical job re-attaching the arteries and nerves.

"It's like sewing together strands of spaghetti," one of the doctors tells me.

Bill and Paddy Bell. My parents met on the first day of school at Antioch College in Yellow Springs OH.

Bill Bell wore a cast for a long time after that, waiting for the muscles and bones to mend. He would never regain feeling in his left pinky or ring finger - which led to funny moments when we'd see him rest his left hand too close to a stove burner, causing the numb fingers to begin smoldering.

My father never said anything to me about the accident, never a complaint about pain or loss of feeling. I think he was embarrassed by the whole thing.

Woodworking is a passion of his and he doesn't want to admit that one of his power tools got the better of him.

The only lasting trace of the incident is right here,
dangling above the bench saw.
A tourniquet.

It's April 9th and I've been listening to the great new Alice
Cooper LP, titled Love It to Death, released last month.
Jack is driving us to Hopedale in his Rambler station
wagon, a push-button automatic.
Arriving at the Town Hall - it's a warm night for this time
of year - and I listen to all the kids talking outside the
building.
"That's David, the manager of Aerosmith" says a brunette.
She's points to a guy seated behind a card table, near the
door of the Hopedale Town Hall.
Aerosmith's manager is a teenager named Dave.
He's got a little cash box and he's counting a pile of one
dollar bills.
My sister has learned the names of a few of these
Aerosmith people. The singer is Steven and the lead
guitarist is named Joe.
According to the teen-buzz, it seems that Joe lives right
here in this dinky town. We pay the two dollars admission
and join the growing throng inside the hall. The Aerosmith
concert is great but there's a stranger playing onstage with
the band. A blonde-haired guy, not much bigger than me,
he has a Gibson Les Paul sunburst guitar.

"I know him, he went to Berklee with me" nods Jack.
"That's Brad Whitford."

{ 9 }

Michael Nesmith and the Floral Steakhouse

Jack phones me the next day.

"Hey, I got us a gig."

"A gig? Where? When?"

"Floral Steakhouse. Sunday. It's in Wrentham."

We manage to cram Merry, drummer Mark, sister Cathy plus an extra Screamin' Ya-Ya Girl and all our gear into the bass player's brown Rambler.

Jack wheels us down to Wrentham, on a Sunday afternoon.

Wrentham MA 1971. JOE FLASH entertains at the Floral
Steakhouse. Photo by Jon Read

Strange gig. They want us to set-up inside the main dining room of this stuffy old restaurant. All the tables and rugs have been pushed back, exposing the wide wooden floor. Joe Flash is supposed to play from 2 pm until 5 pm. My friend from school, a younger kid named Jon Read, shows up to take some photos.

Wrentham MA 1971. Lead singer Merry.

Photo by Jon Read

Once Joe Flash begins playing, the joint starts filling-up
with kids, mostly girls, looking to dance. We motor
through our repertoire of Faces, Traffic, Nazz, Stones,
Small Faces and Badfinger songs.
Merry and Jack have all the harmonies down.
Girls and guys become semi-hypnotized whenever Merry
takes center stage.

Wrentham MA 1971. JOE FLASH. Merry and Jack.

Photo by Jon Read.

After she's done with them, Jack and I take over, with our
"soul-revue" portion of the set.
This is the part where I work the mic, shouting bits and
pieces of every Sam & Dave number I can remember.
We run through James Brown's repertoire too.

Wrentham MA 1971. JOE FLASH. I take a turn at the mic.

Photo by Jon Read

A pumping, jumping, elongated version of Sly Stone's "Dance to the Music" comes next and by now the dance floor is hopping.
Girls wearing hot pants frisk about, bell-bottom boys do the stomp, everybody bounces all over the place. The manager congratulates us and hires Joe Flash to return next Sunday, the Sunday after that - and the following Sunday too...

It's still April and my band is suddenly busy, playing weekend nights at Ararat, the Cave and the other teen centers followed by our regular Sunday afternoon gig at the Floral Steakhouse. All these commitments are more than the Ya-Ya Girls bargained for.

One by one they retire from show business, leaving only
Cathy, to ya-ya alone.
In other rock news, the Rolling Stones release a new album
this month, called Sticky Fingers. Another good one.

The photos Jon Read took at the restaurant come out
pretty well.
"Have you guys thought about going into the recording
studio?" he asks me.
"Well, yeah, of course, Jon. That's all I ever think about.
Writing songs. Recording. Going on tour."
Jon recently earned his Class 3 radio license.
Even though he's high school age, Jon's been allowed to
intern at WTBS-FM, the radio station on the campus of
Mass Institute of Technology in Cambridge.
"They have a good recording set-up at the station. A decent
size room with nice mics and a mixing board."

Sweet Wine, the song Merry and I wrote together several
months ago, is now a highlight of the Joe Flash show.
I penned a bottle-neck guitar rave-up called "Saltine Pete"
that's a crowd pleaser. I nicked the best riffs from "Around
the Plynth" Ronnie Wood's slide-guitar showcase with
Faces. But my version is briefer than Ronnie's with a more
straight-ahead melody and easy, join-in choruses.
We load up the Rambler and head into Cambridge where
Jon Read, who might be 17, engineers my first recording
session.
This studio usually gets used for live, in-studio interviews
or live musical broadcasts, so there's no multi-tracking.

We aren't playing live over the air, so we can stop the tape
as needed and do multiple takes on each number.
But we can't go back and adjust the individual track levels.
Every note we play goes straight to the master, 2-track,
quarter-inch tape.
We end up with an okay-sounding, three song demo reel.

One of the (former) Screaming Ya-Ya Girls is jumping up
& down about some Irish kid she just met. The guy works
for a flea-bag tent show called Circus Bartok. They're set-
up in a field near the old high school. Cathy, Merry and I
head over to catch the afternoon performance.
It's a meager spectacle. No lions, no elephants, no human
cannon balls.
I think the best act is a girl who rides a see-saw with a big
dog sitting on the other end.
I watch the Irish kid as he works. He took our tickets out
front and during the performance I see him carrying props
for the juggler and now he's roaming the stands, trying to
sell flavored ice-shavings to the small crowd of spectators.
Later, I'm introduced to the Irishman and after he sizes-
me up, he suggests I join the show. They're about to pull
up stakes and head for the next town.
I grew up watching Circus Boy and Toby Tyler, so the idea
of leaving Holliston with the circus sounds like a fantasy
come true.
If not for Joe Flash, I'd be packing my rucksack for sure.

Drummer Mark has obligations and drops out of the band
in June.

Jack reminds me that his friend Rick, the guy who played flute in our short lived Yellow Springs Ohio, also possesses a drum kit. With a bit of cajoling and some serious rehearsing, Rick comes aboard and rekindles his drum chops.

Just in time for Joe Flash to win first place at a Battle of the Bands held at the S.A.M. hall in Framingham. We're still the house band at the Floral Steakhouse every Sunday, and now with the Jon Read-produced demo tape making the rounds, even more prestigious gigs are coming our way. Joe Flash goes over well at a huge Cambridge Boathouse frat party.

Then we get a call from George Papadopolous.

Mr. Papadopolous recently moved his Unicorn Coffeehouse to a roomier location near the Berklee School of Music.

The Unicorn, originally located at 815 Boylston Street, is where the Paul Butterfield Blues Band, Jefferson Airplane, Spirit and J. Geils played to full capacity houses - of maybe 75 people - a couple years ago.

George Papadopolous also operated the Psychedelic Supermarket while it lasted. Like the Boston Tea Party, the Supermarket had no seats and no age restrictions. Located at the end of an alley at 590 Commonwealth Ave. and envisioned as a counter-culture supermarket with head shops and hippie-clothing stores sharing space with a live music showroom (capacity 400).

Joe Flash gets a call to come into town and audition for George Papdopolous on stage at the new Unicorn.

This is my first time setting-up the gear inside a "name" venue, where groups like Gross National Productions, and other bands with songs on WBCN, perform.

The Joe Flash audition seems to go okay, but the future of the Unicorn is in question. The Boston Tea Party closed up shop a few months ago. Rock ticket buyers have multiplied in number following Woodstock and the top bands are suddenly charging way more than the parking garage clubs and tents can afford.

Meanwhile, back on the super affordable band scene, Aerosmith is playing a free outdoor gig right down the road from my grandfather Nelson's house in Dover MA. It's July 17th and we all jump into our bass player's Rambler. Jack navigates the circular roadways, laid out concentrically, that make getting into-and-out-of Dover a challenge. We arrive at a breezy art camp where a bunch of paint-smeared kids are running amok. The concert set-up reminds me of the mountaintop jam where Merry and I watched Terry Reid and Tommy Bolin perform.

Same flatbed trailer. Same admission fee too.

The opening band is called Sacrifice and they're playing hits identified with the Woodstock festival. The rhythm section boasts a Hammond B-3 and several percussionists. I recognize the sound system, it's the one Aerosmith carries with them and even outdoors it sounds loud and clear. Several Bogen 100 watt power amps are rack-mounted inside a roll-around cart. Driving four large speaker columns, two on each side of the stage, probably made by Temple. Sacrifice wrap-up their energetic set with

"Soul Sacrifice," the drum extravaganza made famous by
Santana.

Aerosmith begin their show, extremely entertaining as
always - but for some reason, I'm confused.
The guitar players, Joe and new hire Brad, have melded
into a startling force. As a fellow lead guitarist, I study
every move they make...but that funny-looking singer - my
attention keeps going to the singer. Every time I see this
group it leaves me questioning my own musical path...
Joe Flash is gaining fans and finding work but still...
something isn't right and I can't figure it out.

A couple weeks later, Who's Next is released and our latest
drummer quits Joe Flash that very same day.
Rick is in such a hurry to eject from the group, he leaves
his entire drum kit behind.
The mood of this band is impacted greatly by the mood of
Merry and myself.
Our tattered romance is constantly on the rocks.
Brightening the mood, our favorite Monkee,
Michael Nesmith, is opening for Dan Hicks and his Hot
Licks tonight. We arrive at Paul's Mall just in time to learn
the headline band is delayed. Dan Hicks can't make the
show. Promoter Fred Taylor makes it very clear,
"You kids can go inside if you want. But all you'll get
tonight is Mike Nesmith."
That's fine with us.
No problem scoring a ringside table either, there's barely a
soul in the place.

Michael Nesmith moseys out onstage with his acoustic guitar, smiles at the slim house and sits just a few feet from us. Performing his hit compositions "Joanne" "Listen to the Band" and "Different Drum."

The concert turns out to be only a start, because following a brief, post-performance chat, Michael invites Jack, Merry and me to join him for an after-show snack at the Bulkie Delicatessen, just a few doors down Boylston St. As we stroll down the sidewalk, Wool Hat pulls out a pipe and lights up. Merry joins him for a few puffs.

We all squeeze into a plastic and formica booth with the TV star.

Four years ago - in '67 - Nesmith and his band sold more records internationally than the Rolling Stones and the Beatles, *combined.*

While he munches his grinder, we pepper Michael with questions about his TV series and details regarding the Monkees/Jimi Hendrix Experience tour dates. He tells us about a "club house" NBC constructed on the Monkees TV soundstage. A hideout where the four actors could hang around, smoke, listen to records and stay out of view of the network suits. A system of colored lights alerted each of them when their scenes came up.

"Jimi had a huge impact on me. Did you notice how I ditched the Vox and began using a Marshall 100 watt stack on the show?" Yes, we did.

We also ask about that lightning quick, Spanish-style lead guitar break, that runs throughout the Monkees "Valeri." Nesmith tells us that he played the part himself, but an octave lower.

112

"They recorded me at 7 1/2 ips and then sped the machine up to 15 ips during mixdown. The trick doubled the speed of my picking but also raised my pitch by an octave."

According to local gossip, Merry makes a sneaky trip back into Boston the following day to move into Michael Nesmith's hotel room at the Sheraton for the balance of his stay. Not sure if the story's true - but I'm pretty sure it is.

We find a young drummer called Tarzan.
An excitable boy, he tends to speed up every song we play.
On November 8th the latest Led Zeppelin record comes out. Their fourth effort is an un-named LP... but it's nothing to be ashamed of... it has some strong songs.
Rock and Roll, Black Dog and a lengthy number dubbed Stairway to Heaven.
Okay, but a different, brand-new record is the one I find myself listening to even more. Killer.
Also released this month, Killer is from the Alice Cooper band.
Be My Lover and Under My Wheels are templates pointing in the direction I think rock should be heading. I'm fascinated by Alice and his flagrant, anti-authority, hard-rock approach.

On my 18th birthday I go into Framingham to register with the Selective Service.
Now I can get drafted and shipped off to fight the reds.
One glimmer of progress - the military draft recently switched from a random drawing to a lottery system.
Every birthday now has a lottery number attached to it.

If your lottery number is in the Top 40 you better pack some bug spray because you're headed for the jungle. My lottery number is bubbling under, in the low 200's, so I can stay here in New England for the time being.

Rounding out my birthday festivities, the drummer quits.

Tarzan swings out the window and Brooks, a fuzzy-haired guy from Wellesley, joins Joe Flash. Brooks is a spectacular drummer and I wish we found him earlier.

My guitar playing is in a rut. I've become disillusioned with my band. I need to shake things up but I'm not sure how. I'm searching high and low for a kick-ass, front person. A guy who does what Alice Cooper, Crazy Arthur Brown and John Kay do.
A super confident, sane, natural performer. Someone I can rock behind, work alongside and hopefully write some songs with and even draw inspiration from.
Where is my phantom lead singer hiding?

{ 10 }

The Big Bird Cage
In our spare time, Brooks and I mess with songs
from Alice's Killer LP.
Then I get a call from Dave, an okay local singer who often
works with Brooks.
"Listen man, you wanna do three gigs with me? I don't
wanna mess things up with you and Joe Flash, but I have
three solid dates booked. One of them is at the Women's
Penitentiary."
Dave isn't much of a frontman but he just got my
attention.
I saw *The Hot Box, Big Doll House* and *The Big Bird Cage*
when they got held-over at the Natick Drive-In.
"They Caged Their Bodies but Not Their Desires"
*"Ravaged...Savaged...Licked by the Fiery Tongues of The
Hot Box."*
I definitely gotta rock the All Girl Prison.

Dave sings, Brooks plays drums and I'm the guitar man.
I found a bass player while visiting my old school in
Framingham. I graduated last spring but I still go over
there to visit with classmate Jon Read and check to see if
any new musical talent or interesting girls have enrolled.
Vogt is only 15 but he's a really good bassist.
He's got a huge amplifier to boot.

Our setlist features the new Alice Cooper tracks from
Killer, a few T. Rex songs off Electric Warrior. I rekindle
some of my MC5 favorites and a few originals.
We manage to patch together an act in time for the first
gig, in the ballroom of the Newton Marriott Hotel.
I think we were a little strong for that crowd.
Next up, is a high school dance and we do a bit better.
Okay, now it's time for show number three.
Off to prison we go.

Framingham State Prison is the longest running female
correctional institution in the country. From the outside it
doesn't look like the Hot Box or the Big Doll House, it
looks more like a public high school.
All our gear is carefully inspected by uniformed guards.
The band members are searched and questioned at various
checkpoints lining an echoey corridor. As we move deeper
into the facility, iron doors clang shut behind us. Like the
beginning of Get Smart.
We're in. We set-up our instruments on a raised stage at
the end of an empty mess hall.
Vogt starts riffing Jailhouse Rock and I tell him to cool it.
Alarm bells ring and I can hear the prison doors swinging
open in the main cell block. A minute later the hall fills up
with a couple hundred young women.

We plunge into our exciting set. The prisoners stare at the
stage with vague interest. Not the man-hungry, lusting-
with-desire harem I've been dreaming about. These
prisoners don't look beat-up or strung-out either.

116

On the contrary, a lot of the inmates are smartly coiffed, most are wearing lipstick, fingernail polish and appear to be quite healthy. Brooks begins his drum solo while singer Dave explains to me that this prison believes in rehabilitation through work. Lots of these girls are interested in hair and make up, so the institution teaches those skills and even runs it's own in-house salon. The yardbirds practice their skills on each other, perfecting the latest cuts and cosmetic trends until everyone looks like a covergirl.
Desperate for men? I don't think so.

A lot of these cons look like they've moved up the ladder from men. Guys are nothin' but trouble. Men are probably the reason a bunch of these dolls ended up in here.
While jamming on Jeepster, I take a closer look at this gallery. Girls are pushing hard against each other, fingers combing through each other's locks.
Women in chains take care of their sisters.
Modern Girls. They're happy with each other.
Someone should write a song about it.

When bands like Led Zeppelin, Faces or any of the Woodstock groups come to town, they all end up at the Boston Garden now.
I was lucky seeing most of these guys on their way up, playing local venues a couple years ago for $4 or less.
I'm disinclined to pay a lot more to see them playing inside a huge, reverberating sports arena, seated among thousands.

Now that the Psychedelic Supermarket and the Crosstown Bus are history, I try to catch upcoming bands in nightclubs like Paul's Mall or the smallish Fenway Theater. A 2700-seat movie house called the Orpheum played its final double-feature film show in January 1971.
The venue is now called the Aquarius Theatre and I've been seeing some good shows there.

On May 18th, the Aquarius has the Jeff Beck Group (touring the Orange album) with opener Todd Rundgren. Todd's masterful Something/Anything LP came out a couple months ago and it's full of brilliant songs.
But instead of playing a normal rock set with his band, Rundgren has this elaborate, show-within-a-show concept, involving yet another group, called Hello People, who perform a couple tunes before calling Todd onstage to join them.
A few songs later, Todd's regular band enters, while the Hello People all sing in the background.
This onstage coming-and-going, clearly pisses off the inflexible Jeff Beck road crew.
It doesn't help that the Hello People have their faces painted like french mimes. Todd is in the midst of performing "I Saw the Light" when all his amps go dead. The stage goes black. My sister, Cathy, is here too. Mainly to see Todd Rundgren.

Cathy: "I was standing in the wings during Todd's set and I got upset when I saw Jeff's roadies pull the plug on him. Steven and Joe from Aerosmith were back there too. Those two are always hanging around. Trying to soak-up some

118

rockstar magic I guess. Todd came running off the stage in tears. There was a lot of yelling and commotion. Beck's crew are onstage, dragging Rundgren's amps out of the way. The mimes huddle around poor Todd. That's when I notice the sneaky Aerosmith guys, backing away from a wide-open Jeff Beck road case. Then they turn around and go galloping out the back door, straight down the alley. One of Beck's crew members chased after them but he came back inside a minute later.

"Those two yanks. They nicked Jeff's bloody foot pedal!"

Being young, nubile and fearless, my sister is very crafty at meeting her favorite musicians everywhere she goes. One time Cathy smuggled a bottle of Martini & Rossi vermouth into the Music Hall (4,800 seat) on Tremont Street.

"It's for Rod" she told me.

"Good luck with that, Cathy. The Tea Party days are over. There must be five thousand kids in here. Look at all the security people up front."

About an hour into the concert, just as Mac begins his piano intro for Maybe I'm Amazed, I spy my sister, as she is (somehow) catapulted above the heads of the front row crowd. Quick as a cat, Cathy dashes into the spotlight, presenting Rod with the booze.

Stewart accepts the gift, he smiles at Cathy and even bends down a bit, to let her rifle her fingers through his rooster-top - before bodyguards escort her away.

A few months later, Cathy announces,

"I have to speak with Ray Davies."

A bunch of us are down here in Hartford CT at Dillon Stadium.

The Beach Boys with Carl and Dennis Wilson headline today along with openers the Kinks. Also on the bill are The Doors, currently a trio, since the death of their lead singer last summer.

The Doors began making the latest LP, Other Voices, while Jim was living in Paris. Guitarist Robbie Krieger and organist Ray Manzarek sang all the lead vocals. It was pretty obvious that Morrison was drifting away. This new Doors album follows the chartbusting L.A. Woman.

The first single without Jim Morrison is called Tightrope Ride. Ray sings lead on this one, sounding very much like Jim. Tightrope Ride gets a lot of play up here in New England but tops-off at #71 on the Billboard Hot 100.

Today's outdoor show is set-up on a steep, raised platform. Towers of scaffolding frame the stage, supporting generous amounts of lighting and sound. During the Doors set, I see dozens of kids trying to scale the stage front, before falling into the waiting arms of security goons who punt the kids back out onto the field.

I hope Cathy wore her crash helmet.

The Kinks present a strong set, incorporating a few of their bedrock British Invasion classics, numbers from Village Green Preservation Society, their rock opera, Arthur and a newer song that a lot of the teenie-boppers in today's crowd came to hear, last year's smash "Lola."

During the Beach Boys set, my sister finally reappears, emerging from the backstage gate. Mission accomplished.

"How the hell did you pull that off?" I demand.

"Well, I was going to run across the stage and go look for Ray, but when I got near the front, things looked pretty dangerous. Big guys warned me to back off.

"Don't even try it, kiddo."

"Yeah, I get it Cathy. I was standing back here the whole time, watching the whole thing. I saw dozens of kids getting tossed from the stage.'

Cathy continues, "When the drunk guys in front of me started yelling and climbing up the scaffolding, I dropped down to the ground. There was a rip in the canvas covering the stage front. I crawled through it. Nobody saw me. Everyone was looking up at The Doors, nobody thought to look down at the ground. I saw lots of cables in the dirt under the stage, so I had to be careful. It was dark under there. I inched past the steel support pipes while avoiding wires until I popped out the other side."

"You crawled through the dirt all the way to the backstage?"

"Yup. And Ray Davies was sitting right there. Sipping a cup of tea."

"You gotta be kidding, Cathy."

"No. I went right up to Ray and asked, what's Waterloo Sunset really about?"

"What'd Ray say?"

"He rolled his eyes at me and whispered, It's about a lot of things actually."

{ 11 }

Piggies and T. Rex
Good news: It's May 1972 and a new Rolling Stones record, Exile on Main Street, has just been released.

Weird news: There's been a drastic sea change in my town. The townies have suddenly stopped calling me a faggot. The jerks who used to chase me, harass me and call me names are trying to catch-up with the times.

Overnight, Holliston High drops the strict dress code requirements.

Conformists who tormented me with scissors and taunts, repressed loudmouths who treated me like a sub-species, are now shopping for their very own hippie-style bell bottoms.

The jocks want to be groovy like Neil Young.

The High School adds an outdoor quadrant for student lounging and a sunny spot for the kids who like to smoke cigarettes. Peace and love has arrived in Holliston.

Even the teachers are growing their beards and hair and sideburns. It happened in an instant. After totally missing out on the 60's, the state-run schools are attempting a cultural leap, out of the 50's and straight into the 70's. Everyone wants to conform to the hot "new" 1969 Woodstock-look. It's all the rage in '72.

Guys who made my life miserable smile at me now.

Some even claim to be fans of my music.

It makes me angry.

Croz plays guitar with Sound Rebellion, a local rock outfit
with tri-corner hats and uniforms. They do a routine
inspired by Paul Revere and the Raiders. His group made
it all the way to the Battle of the Bands State Finals, held at
the Carousel tent.

Croz drives an MGB. I've been lusting for one of these sexy
British Leyland sports cars. Triumphs and MGs. They're
all over the place and I want a convertible MGB, just like
the one Croz tools around in.

A used 1966 model goes for around a grand. That's a
thousand more than I have, so I take a job at Wood
Engineering, a metal fabrication shop right down the hill
from our donkey barn.

Wood makes things like the metal boxes CB radios get
mounted into. Each piece of metal moves from station to
station, being sanded, bent, drilled or etched in an acid
bath. I get moved around the factory, from machine to
machine, like a robot. I'll spend an entire shift running
hundreds of steel sheets through the sander or tapping
holes in hundreds of steel sheets with a drill press or
inserting rivets into more steel with a foot operated press.
Sometimes we double-up on jobs with another metal
fabrication plant a couple towns over in Hopedale, called
Draper Corporation.

That's where another MGB owner, Joe Perry, works.

Joe Flash finally falls apart, so I fall in with a whole new
gang. Claire is an artist. She and her artist friend Linda
spend every afternoon in Claire's barn studio, painting and
listening to Seals and Croft. The Hendricks brothers, Bob

and Michael, move to neighboring Medway from their home state Florida. Both are surfers and rock musicians. Pia works at Music'n'Things, she and her sister Kersti live in downtown Holliston. 16 year-old AnneMarie has a part time job as a dental assistant just around the corner from Music'n'Things. AnneMarie is a short, cute, smiling, curvy, blonde. She's the first girl I take for a ride in my new sports car, a 1965 MGB ragtop in British Racing Green.

The James Montgomery Blues Band and The Sidewinders are playing an outdoor show at Wellesley College. The Music Box provides the sound system. Grandfather was one of the first sound men in America. In 1929 he quit Dartmouth College the same day the first commercial loudspeaker hit the market. Nelson bought a truckload of 'em and he was the first to bring amplified-sound to Fenway Park, Boston Garden and the surrounding fairs and horse racing tracks. Nelson's sound systems were used for public address, to amplify speech or play pre-recorded music, they weren't rock'n'roll sound systems.

I get hired for the afternoon, helping Ernie put together sound reinforcement for the college rock concert. Ernie and I roll a couple Klipschorns down onto the outdoor amphitheater stage. The bass horns of these Klipsch, folded-horn systems don't really work correctly unless they're placed in the corner of a room. Using several 4'x 8' sheets of plywood and a stack of 2"x 4"s we construct two "corners" to place the loudspeakers in. I set up some EV microphones and wire everything to a stack of 100 watt Bogen amps.

The Sidewinders are a pro sounding Anglo-influenced pop-rock band fronted by handsome Andy Paley. The lead guitarist sounds good too, Wellesley's own Billy Squier.

The headliner, James Montgomery, is a 23 year-old bluesman from Detroit. James recently relocated to Boston and his band is super tight. They're about to sign to the Allman Brother's label, Capricorn Records.
Old Ernie watches silently, arms folded, as the rhythm section cooks and the guitarists trade licks.
"I just don't know how it's gonna fit in."
"What's the matter, Ernie?"
"Well...the lady on the phone told me the main guy is supposed to be a harp player... but I can't understand how a harp is going to fit in with all that other noisy stuff. I didn't see a harp when they were unpacking the other instruments."
Montgomery finishes singing the refrain, pulls a little Marine Band harmonica up to his mouth and begins riffing. Ripping into a tasty James Cotton-style blues lick. I guess this is why I got sent out on this job, to translate for Ernie. He's still scouring the horizon, wondering if some harp-playing angel might descend from the clouds.
"Uh...Ernie, I think she was talking about a mouth harp, y'know, like a harmonica."

June '72 and Alice Cooper is back with his biggest hit yet, School's Out. Alice's lyrics are direct and fresh. No fairies or Tolkien imagery or re-worked Willie Dixon boasts. Alice sings about cars, telephones, high school, mom & dad, sex and dead babies.

My folks have sailed to Maine for the summer, so I invite
some of my musical buddies to jam in the living room. The
Hendricks brothers, Bob on harmonica and vocals, Mike
on congas and vocals, Vogt on bass. Mark, who played
with Joe Flash, returns to play drums. I really like all these
guys but our musical goals don't align. They don't share
my fascination with T. Rex, Blue Cheer, Alice, MC5...
One artist we can all agree on is Jeff Beck, so we mess
around with Situation and Goin' Down.
We write some stuff and the setlist grows.
We begin to take some gigs. Ararat, Wellesley Youth
Center, Holliston Battle of the Bands (3rd place) and the
Andy Lattanzi Festival. Michael names the band "Piggies."
I'm not a big fan of the tag but this jam is just a lark for
me, something to tide me over until I can find a ballsy lead
singer to build my next real group around.

T. Rex is in Boston at the Aquarius on September 12.
I'm really amped for this concert, I've been following Marc
Bolan's career closely for the past two years.
Pia and I have pretty good seats and we arrive just as the
openers take the stage. An unknown California band with
a goofy name. The Doobie Brothers. I've seen their album,
its on Warners, produced by Ted Templeman, but I never
gave it a listen.
The Doobies open up with a harmony-laden tune called
Listen to the Music, and hey - they're not so bad.
By the time the Doobies finish their set with "Jesus Is Just
Alright" everyone is getting into it, these guys are more fun
than most of the other Bay Area hippie groups.

After the Doobies equipment is rolled off stage there isn't much left. A conga, a small drum kit and a couple amps. The houselights dim and a single spotlight follows Marc Bolan as he dashes out from the wings. Reaching the microphone stand at center stage, Marc does a high jump, guitar held high, legs folded beneath him.
And then...oh no...Marc Bolan falls. Right on his ass.

The little glamster sits in the spotlight, frozen for a moment, trying to collect himself. Darn it, what a crappy way to begin the show. The rest of T.Rex take their places and begin playing Telegram Sam. Bolan's butt isn't the only thing that gets hurt in the fall, his Gibson SG is knocked way out of tune. Brown notes cascade from his Gibson, making Telegram Sam a sour listening experience. I can't wait for the first song to end - so Marc can grab another axe - or tune his SG. But no, they forge right ahead into Hot Love. The de-tuned strings are wrecking everything. Apparently T. Rex is traveling with only one guitar on this American tour because no back-up ever appears and Marc never pauses to re-tune.

A couple days later, I'm driving through downtown Holliston in my MG, bringing AnneMarie back to her parents' house.
It's almost 11 pm when a Holliston cruiser spots my passing car and pulls out. Trailing me.
The lone officer at the wheel tailgates my little green sports car up Route 16. I slowly pass the five & dime store and Goodwill Park. There are no other cars on the road. Just us. I think the patrolman is trying to make me nervous.

About a mile later, I hang a right onto Underwood Street and the police car is still stuck to my rear bumper. Deep in the woods now, I'm passing the water tank when the squad car suddenly sounds it's siren and flashes blue. I've never been stopped before and what happens next is so disheartening... I've spent a lifetime trying to block it out.

I do as I'm told and give the policeman my driving license and registration. He's craning his neck around the inside my MG, sniffing around, shining his flashlight in our eyes. AnneMarie is afraid that something really bad is about to happen. She begins to cry. Maybe I didn't show the proper respect to the peace keeper and I admit that I was very nervous too. If we'd been high or drunk I guess the policeman would have felt vindicated - but we don't have time for that stuff - and it makes the officer really upset.

After finding no evidence of liquor, drugs, narcotic paraphernalia or anything else illegal in my automobile, I'm dragged out of my car, searched and thrown to the pavement while AnneMarie screams her pretty head off. I try to get up. Punches are thrown. None by me.

A few hours later, I'm released from the handcuffs and locked inside a cold, brightly lit jail cell at the Holliston police headquarters. Nothing but a bare steel bench and a steel toilet bowl with no lid. I have a swollen eye, my clothes are torn and my lips are bleeding.
I've been charged with assault and battery on a police officer.

Bill Bell comes down to the station the next morning to
bail me out of jail.
I don't like this tale. It still makes me angry. When it
comes time for my district court hearing, the judge in
Framingham attempts to get a new color TV set from the
Music Box in exchange for dropping charges. My father
balks at the obvious bribe. He leaves the judge's chamber
extremely upset with the court. The bogus charge against
me is finally dropped but I'll never forget being ambushed
and beaten by a frustrated Holliston policeman.

In November a really talented young drummer pops out of
the woodwork, inspiring Jack, Merry and me into trying
another go at Joe Flash. With the addition of Steve on the
skins our band gains a fresh sound. Public schools are
trying to catch up with what's happening and the bookings
come pouring in. Besides church halls and dances, Joe
Flash is a top draw at local teen centers in Medfield,
Wellesley, South Natick, Framingham, Dover, Holliston
and Bellingham. We even score some college dates.
But compared to Led Zeppelin, Steppenwolf and the
Troggs, I feel like I've barely moved an inch in my quest to
rock the nation. Touring America, making records, hearing
my songs played on WBCN. That's my goal.
I'm 19, I've played guitar in a dozen groups and performed
at well over a hundred shows - but I'm still nowhere.
It's confusing.

In December the most inspiring thing I've heard in ages is
released: Slade.

Chas Chandler, former bassist with The Animals, discovered and became co-manager of the Jimi Hendrix Experience. Chas produced my favorite Experience records. Now Chandler is managing this ballsy UK quartet called Slade. The new album is called "Slayed?" and the lead singer is Noddy Holder.

"Slade both looked and sounded different from most club bands on the scene at that time. They were a welcome change from the immobile, introvert rock musicians who hunched over their instruments trying to impress fans with spell-binding virtuosity that often amounted to little more that a thirty-minute jam session. Slade were a direct confrontation to all this. They sounded crisp and tight. They kept their numbers short and they had no illusions of grandeur about their musical ability. They were a good time. They were spearheading the march back toward extrovert behavior. Excitement and glamour were on their way back and Slade knew it."
Chris Charlesworth, Melody Maker 1972

Speaking of new bands...
Cathy amazes me again when she drives her Datsun 1200 to Manhattan, all alone, on New Year's Eve 1973. She hopes to track down a group called the New York Dolls. These guys are barely on my radar but Cathy heard about them and has to meet them. 17 year-old Cathy finds Broadway up near the Bronx and stays on it all the way down to the Broadway Central Hotel at Mercer and 3rd Street.

Ten rooms in the back of this dilapidated hotel are known as the Mercer Arts Center, Manhattan headquarters for film makers, rock musicians and other artists.

The Center opened in 1971, incorporating a rehearsal space, a bar, a theatrical room, a cabaret room, an experimental video room and the Oscar Wilde Room - the room where the New York Dolls hold court.
On her return to Holliston, Cathy regales me with detailed stories of the outrageous, glittery quintet - and the sordid, after-midnight goings-on in all the different rooms at the Center.

Five days later our favorite local band puts out their first album. It's called Aerosmith and the cover art and liner notes look kinda flimsy, considering it's a Columbia Records release, but the LP sounds fantastic.
Also in January, I turn 20 and the re-united Joe Flash breaks up for good. In February, Alice Cooper releases Billion Dollar Babies. Along with Alice Cooper, I've got "Slayed?," "Brain Capers" by Mott the Hoople, and the Aerosmith debut on constant rotation.

My musical career takes a wrong turn when I lose my concentration at Wood Engineering. I'm about an hour into my shift, kicking a giant foot press that drives metal rivets - after I've carefully positioned them - into sheets of steel. Its only March but there's a warm breeze today and the doors of the loading dock are wide open.
I glance out to the parking lot.
Whap.

The press slams down before I lift my left index finger out of the way. Pointer immediately splits-open and for the first time, I can see what my finger-bone looks like. The force of the blow pulverizes my nervous system. I don't feel pain, blood doesn't spurt out.

Halfway to the hospital everything comes undone, now I'm bleeding and throbbing. Damn. I'm left-handed but like most guitarists, I strum my guitar right-handed. I do all my chording and riffing with my left hand. My first finger is an important one...

Now it's April.

I'm sitting around trying to heal. Checking out the new album Led Zeppelin just put out last week. They call this one Houses of the Holy.

Bad News usually comes with some Good News. I don't realize it yet but a new state law just went into effect on April Fool's Day. It will impact me and every other rocker in Massachusetts and way beyond. The new bill allows 18 year olds to drink in bars and buy booze in liquor stores. Beginning today, April 1, 1973.

I'm no politician and I wasn't around for the debate but I think this new legislation came about, in large part, due to the military draft of 18-year-old boys and lingering feelings about the war. "If they're old enough to fight the war - they should be old enough to buy a drink."

It's June and my pointer has healed together pretty well. Missing a bit of the tip, but enough leftover to bend a note or barre a chord. We get Piggies back together for an appearance at the 2nd Annual Andrew Lattanzi Festival.

Held on the green in downtown, just steps away from the
hall where The Effective got Wiped Out by a backline of
hairy hula dancers.
By now, dozens of local guys can play rings around me on
the electric guitar. Amazing players like Johnny Press from
Gross National Productions, Barry Minor of Chester
White, George McCann and the Lean Street Sliders, David
Amato from Dave and the Essex... But I have a show biz
streak inside me. I like putting on a big show even if I
don't have the best chops.
We're about to go on and once again, my lead singer
forgets to show up - so I guess its up to me.

The guys in Piggies are cool and they play well but they
aren't flashy and they don't share my mania for the heavier
sounds. Our setlist includes stuff from Spirit, Derek and
the Dominoes, Sly Stone, Jeff Beck and Dave Mason.
No choice, I take over the lead vocals, doing the best I can
on the Firebird with my wonky finger.

I've learned a few tricks that can liven up a crowd.
Traffic on Route 16 slows down as more people hop from
their cars to join the party. Mark and Mike get into a good
groove on the drums and congas while I venture out onto
the grass, walking through the crowd. Still riffing, singing,
I start shaking with some girls and pretty soon the whole
crowd is up and dancing.

I can't recall how I ever met Pam Green - a nice kid from Medway - but a few minutes after our show ends she pushes up to me, announcing
"I have someone here for you to meet." Pam steps aside - and for the first time - I see Bobby Edwards.

Bobby is a good looking kid. A few inches taller than me, straight blonde hair falls past his shoulders, firm handshake, friendly smile, he's two years younger that me, just 17. Bobby Edwards is a drummer and he lives a couple miles away in Medway. He's already put together a group. They just need a lead singer.

"Welcome to the club," I think to myself.
Everyone is looking for that same kickass lead singer.
I've been trying to find him for years.

"So can you come down to our rehearsal space tomorrow?"

"Well, I don't know... my finger's kinda messed up.
I haven't played my guitar in weeks - except for today."

"No man. Forget about the guitar.
You're gonna be our lead singer."

{ 12 }

Kill the Singer. Biggy Ratt '72

I arrive at the address Bobby gave me. A nice suburban house in a newer development. The guitarist lives here. I can feel a heavy kick drum beat booming out back. Now I hear really strong, meaty guitar riffing.

I approach the open bulkhead doors to the basement as a bass guitar locks into place.

Descending the cellar stairs I see Bobby Edwards on drums, his friend Big Bill on the Gibson SG guitar. The guy on Fender bass is Barnett Kim Childress.

I listen and watch as they run through a powerful number called Cities on Flame with Rock and Roll (Blue Oyster Cult). The guitarist has great control, he doesn't cheat on any of the notes, his riffs are dirty sounding but precise. Drummer Bobby has obviously grown-up playing alongside this guy, they're tight as ticks. Out of the corner of my eyeball I see a very attractive blonde chick, sitting on the sidelines, chain smoking, watching the bass player. Must be Barnett's girl.

I'm wearing black jeans, a fake lizard-skin belt, heeled boots and a white peasant shirt like the one I saw in a Jim Morrison photo. I know that Bobby is 17 years old. I think these other guys might be a year or two younger than me. Big Bill is a tall teenager with scruffy black hair. His blue jeans are adorned with dozens of patches. The bassman, Barnett, has a more delicate appearance.

Long-haired with a mustache and dark eyes. Barn seems friendly but for some reason he has the single word *"suck"* stenciled on the pick guard of his bass guitar. It's written an inch high, in Blackmoor font.

I introduce myself to everyone and the guys talk about some of the songs they're trying to replicate. Rat Bat Blue (Deep Purple), Rock and Roll Queen (Mott) and Louisiana Blues (Savoy Brown). These heavy teens have a good look and they're mining a vein of weighty-rock similar to the one I've been chasing.

BIGGY RATT 1972 Standing: Bobby & Barnett.
Seated: me and Big Bill. Photo by AnneMarie Martins

Til now, Bill and Barnett have been doing their best to fill
the vocal parts on these tunes while simultaneously
holding down the riffs and solos. I know the feeling.
Lightning bolts exploded in my brain after Edwards spoke
to me the other day. Me? A lead singer? But what about
my classical training on strings? My Firebird and the back-
up Fender Mustang guitar I just bought for $75? My Sunn
amplifier head and all those guitar speakers I built with
Jack? Everything I do and own is guitar-related.

I remove the mic from its perch on an Atlas boom stand. I
flick-open the aluminum tripod stand with a trigger
clutch-release that I dug out of the very back of the Music
Box warehouse. I believe it's the same model tripod stand
Rod Stewart hoisted when I saw his debut at the Boston
Tea Party in 1968. Big Bill launches into Route 66. I bear
down on the Shure SM58, growling out the lyrics - or a
reasonable facsimile - of this Perry Como standard,
covered by the Stones, the Dead and Aerosmith among
others. Digging the new feeling, concentrating purely on
the job of singing and leading the charge without having to
worry about tuning or the key of the next instrumental
break. Guitarist Big Bill sounds better too, now that he's
freed from mic duties. He can fully concentrate on carving-
out riffs.

Ain't Got You, You Really Got Me, You're My Girl and
Walkin' the Dog follow. My feet strut around the basement
as I vocalize. Lifting my mic into the air, telescoping the
stand and shoving the mic beneath Bobby's snare drum
just as he unleashes a double-stroke roll. Snapping the

windscreen back to my face in time for the pay-off refrain. Bobby and Big Bill are digging my stunts, my apparent confidence and, I guess, even my vocal skills. Not so sure about bassman Barn or his girlfriend. They seem to be unmoved. Me? I'm too stunned to know what to think. So the score is 2 yes/ 2 not-so-sures, and 1 stunned.

Bobby Edwards is a smart, strong kid. His drumming skills are off the chart. Moreover, Bobby is the guy who finally solves the riddle that's puzzled me for the last 7 years. I've been scratching away at my guitar while foraging around for a lead singer I can march into battle behind. I've been imagining exactly how this phantom singer should dress, speak and conduct business. I knew all along, in detail, just what I was looking for. So did Bobby Edwards. While he watched me rock with the Piggies, he figured the whole riddle out. Bobby found me working in the wrong department of the rock'n'roll supermarket. His vision and faith in my ability to become a frontman is all I need to make the jump.

Biggy Rat and Itchy Brother are the villains on TV's King Leonardo cartoon show. Bobby and I think Biggy Ratt will make a good band name for our new ensemble. Biggy Ratt is received enthusiastically on the local dancehall circuit and at the high schools. Nobody says boo about my transformation from guitarist to frontman. The path forward suddenly opens-up for me. Pam Green and her brother Wally rave about Biggy Ratt to anyone who'll listen and a guy from Holliston named Frank signs-on as our first roadie. AnneMarie's younger brother, Mike, who I call Mick, will soon come aboard as Bobby's drum tech.

BIGGY RATT '72. One of my first appearances as a lead singer. I built the amp rack in front of the stage. It's a pretty good copy of the PA system Aerosmith used in 1971.

We run into an ambush at the Medfield Youth Center. I've played this hall dozens of times over the years with Joe Flash and Black Sun. It's usually a nothing gig, just a gaggle of girls, made-up in mini skirts, dancing around while the local boys try to act cool. Biggy Ratt is about half-way through our set of James Gang and Humble Pie numbers when I see a gang of really large guys pour into the teen center. I think the building used to be a two-room schoolhouse, most of the interior walls have been removed to create a large, open space with a dance floor. We're up on a high stage, at the end of the hall, a couple feet off the ground. The army of giant-sized dudes approaches the bandstand, cutting a swath as they advance. The regular-sized teens scurry off to the sides of the room.

We're in the middle of our Biggy Ratt version of The Ocean, a cut from Led Zeppelin's latest record. The gang draws closer. One guy, I'll call him Kong, obviously the leader of this mob, crashes up against the stage, eyeballing each of us, his gaze finally rests upon Barnett's bass. Kong points at the little word *suck* that is painted on the Fender. He decides to take it as a personal insult - an insult directed at him and his minions.

Kong points a beefy finger at my face and grunts "No. You suck" as two of his goons plant their butts on the edge of the stage over by Barnett.

Fingers pointed at me, the goons shout along with Kong, "You suck. You suck, You suck."

We keep rocking, but these loudmouth guys are nearly drowning-out the music with their catcalls. This is my stage and my job is to defend it - but it would be nice if I had some help. Are there any chaperones here? A security guard? Anyone who can lure the noisy trespassers off the stage and de-escalate this uncomfortable situation?
No. And now they're starting to swat at us and paw at our legs and even the guitars. The dancers are frozen, watching the situation heat up, waiting for the ass-beating that is apparently about to go down.

So, it's up to me. The lead singer. I grab a mic stand - not the lightweight aluminum Rod Stewart stand I usually toss around. No, I grab an old-school Atlas stand with a round, heavy, cast iron base. I stare down at Kong who is still leading the "You suck" chants. Swinging the mic base out over the stage, I hold it high and steady. Suspending the steel base directly over Kong's cranium.
"Back off " I command.

Kong doesn't seem to notice the iron weight dangling over his dome. What happens next, happens really fast and in a blur. I only remember a couple of Kong's buddies giving him a shove and the feeling of his hairy hands on my legs and that's when I let the full weight of the iron base come crashing down on the invaders skull.
I'm not sure but I think I heard it crack open.

Blood. Screams. Kong's whole platoon are down on the floor, trying to revive the big ape. Bobby and Big Bill yank me behind the amp line. Two hundred teenage dancers are all craning their necks, crying, hollering at the stage. Minutes later the Medfield police department floods into the hall. The dancers are quickly herded outside. Kong is removed on a stretcher and I can hear an ambulance leaving the scene. Biggy Ratt sits all alone in the suddenly empty venue. Frank and Mick hustle our gear out the loading door. We can hear a growing commotion ringing the entire building. Flashing lights and sirens encircle the property. Looks like I'll be spending another night in jail. Maybe a lot longer than just a night...I sure hope I didn't kill the big guy.

The mob outside begins yelling "It was the singer!"

"Kill the singer."

Long minutes later, the entire police force file back inside the teen center. I guess they figure I won't be leaving without a fight. The Chief stares the four of us down. "Okay. Listen up you guys. Stay out of this town. From now on. Got that?" We all nod.

"The kids outside want to kill your singer. We'll try and hold them back. When I give you the signal, run to your vehicles - and *drive like hell.*"

The way the Chief is looking at us I don't think he knows which of us is the singer and I don't think he gives a hoot. He just wants us gone. We gather at the back door, about 100 feet from where the cars are parked. The policemen, batons drawn, form two lines flanking the exit door. The Chief waits for the right moment, finally he shouts *"now."* We scramble out the door and bullet straight down a loud, angry human corridor. Dozens of kids are pushing

forward, right behind the officers, cursing and whipping
rocks at me.

I dive into the shotgun seat of Bobby's car and he tears off
the lot, full speed ahead, five or six cars are in hot pursuit.
Bobby the backseat-Romeo knows all the dead ends and
quiet lanes in this neck of the woods. Bang, we squeal a U-
turn and briefly lose the trail of angry teens. Bam, up a
side road and here's Micky waiting for us with his motor
running. I vault into Mick's car and Bobby cruises back
toward Rt. 109. A minute later our innocent drummer's
Impala is being trailed by the entire parade of angry kids,
honking and yelling. Meanwhile, Mick and I tool out of
Medfield, undetected.

The police never follow up on the case. I will always
wonder if the big galoot I creamed at the teen center was
the town bully, a suspected thief or the local brawler.
Someone the Chief figured was well-deserving of a severe
head bashing.

{ 13 }

Duke & the Drivers, Aerosmith and the **Sunset Strip** A few days later I get a call from Mickey's Restaurant in Ashland. When we arrive I don't see much food being served, looks more like a bar to me. They hire Biggy Ratt for the night and once the sun sets we can't believe how fast the parking lot fills up. All kids. 18 & 19 year-olds. They pack into the club and we play four shows, featuring our versions of T. Rex, Spiders from Mars and Joe Walsh hits 'til the 1 am closing time. Biggy Ratt scores and we're hired back for next week, Thurs- Sun, four nights, 16 sets.

BIGGY RATT at the Foss Reservoir. Photo: AnneMarie Martins

In a matter of weeks, the entire Teen Center circuit I've toured these past eight years will shut down.

Ararat, Wellesley Teen Center, the Cave, South Natick Teen Center - they all go dark. Rock bars like Mickey's spring-up in every town and the older teens have a new home. The younger ones too, if they can pass for 18 or scrounge up a fake ID. The same thing is happening all over New England and New York as the dip in the drinking age becomes law. Bands like mine are jumping from the high school dance circuit straight into this teen rock bar scene, literally overnight.

On April 13, 1973, David Bowie and Mick Ronson drop the trail blazing Alladin Sane LP and in July "Mott," from Ian Hunter's Mott the Hoople arrives. Also new in July is the debut album from the New York Dolls. Rhinestones, glitter, boas, satin, platform shoes...rock goes glam.
I'm almost 5' 7" and I weigh around 120, I can squeeze into just about anything.
Cathy keeps yelling at me to stay out of her closet but it's hard to resist borrowing some of her high-heeled boots, scarves and shiny blouses for the shows we've got booked at Dean Junior College and Mickey's teen bar.

Charlie Farren is singing up in the loft at Timothy's Too when Bobby, Big Bill and I enter the Route 9 nightclub. We're scoping out the place for a possible booking.
The placement of the stage is odd, but the room is packed. Tonight's the first time I've heard Farren sing but I'm well aware of his band, Live Lobster. I always see their name plastered all over the club listings.

Then we get this odd booking. It's a high school dance in Wellesley but they want my band to start playing way past midnight. They've decided to book an all-nighter at the high school on the same night as the prom. An attempt to keep the kids off the roads, out of the bars and out of mischief.

Biggy Ratt is hired as the support act for a new - supposedly upcoming - band I've never heard of.

The other group is supposed to begin at midnight, then sometime around 2 am Biggy Ratt will rock til the sun comes up.

On the evening of the all-nighter we watch as the other band sets up their gear. A Hammond B3 organ, a decent drum set, several amps and a contraption that one of the roadies calls "electric bongos." There's a few hundred kids in the gymnasium when the concert begins. The headliners walk on, they look a few years older than us, they cruise into their set. Not glam, not heavy stuff like Biggy Ratt... No, these guys are more funky and bluesy and all six of them sing. Well, at least five of them.

Lots of big catchy choruses.

The electric bongo player steps to the mic.

"Good morning children. We are Duke and the Drivers. It's sincerely a pleasure, having this opportunity to play for you tonight. At this particular time, I must apologize for the tardiness of our dear, beloved band leader. The Duke. As you can plainly see, the Duke is missing tonight..."

The rhythm guitar player leans forward to add,

"Rest assured the Duke is safe and resting comfortably. He phoned us to say he's laid up at the Days Inn in Peabody. Recovering from a severe case of sheet burn."

"What the heck?" I think to myself. "How unprofessional. We're opening up for these guys and the star of the band isn't even here?"

I think it took me almost a year to realize that the "Duke" was nothing but a fiction created by this loony but solidly entertaining bunch.

Aerosmith are coming to town. Well, not my town exactly, the next town over. Since their first album came out in January the quintet has kept busy doing road dates. I guess it's all on them because the record company doesn't seem to be doing much. Rolling Stone didn't review the record. They won't even acknowledge the band. Only one Boston DJ, BCN's afternoon host Maxanne, will play it. A medium-sized Aerosmith billboard has been hoisted not far from the neon Citgo sign in Kenmore Square. The Aerosmith sign faces up Comm. Ave towards BU, but that's about it for advertising. Locally, the only hope for Aerosmith is coming from WVBF, a medium-sized FM station next door to the Framingham garbage incinerator. Thanks to constant requests from young callers, deejays Charlie Kendall, Buddy Ballou and Bash Freeman are the first in the nation to regularly spin Dream On, a track from the Aerosmith LP.

The big gig is out on Route 9 at the Monticello Dinner Theater. The venue where *Laugh-In* sock-it-to-me-girl Judy Carne starred in "Cabaret" for several weeks last summer. Cathy and her friends were reporting back to me every time they saw Judy and her boyfriend, Joe Perry, sitting together at the Copper Kettle, Bickfords or one of the other all night eateries on the Route 9 strip, following Carne's nightly curtain calls.

I guess Joe might have met Judy while he was working across the street, rehearsing with Aerosmith upstairs at The Meadows. An old supper club, once owned by band leader/pop singer Vaughn Monroe (Let it Snow, Cool Water, Riders in the Sky). Monroe's weekly, national *Camel Caravan* radio show was beamed from The Meadows starting back around 1946.

Biggy Ratt should be opening the Aerosmith homecoming show, but no, the warm-up is provided by Reddy Teddy, a group from Winchester, just north of Boston. They're currently being courted by Mercury Records. August 11th is the show date and I'm much too jealous to attend. Some of my bandmates and friends go - everyone returns gushing about both bands.

BIGGY RATT 1973 At Dean Junior College with new gear.
Bobby Edwards and his famous Ludwig drum set.

Bigger gigs and larger crowds mean that it's time for Biggy Ratt to upgrade to heavier gear.

We all save up, work part-time jobs or sell everything we own in order to pull this off. Barnett moves up to the Ampeg SVT, a 300 watt amp head with a pair of 8x10 cabs. I purchase a Klipsch La Scala theater speaker system, for cost, from the Music Box.

Big Bill graduates to the brand new, hard-to-find, 100 watt amp stack made by the Orange Music Electronic Company of Kent, England. Bobby orders a matte black, over-sized, eight piece Ludwig drum set from Jack Adams of Jack's Drum Shop fame. The upgrades not only look a lot more professional, they also improve our sound significantly.

Bobby and I have bonded. I've taken over the spare bunk in Bobby's room, where his older brother Elliot used to sleep. The Edwards family rolls out the red carpet and treat me like family. A long lost son.

Musically, Bobby and I see eye to eye on just about everything, he's a major fan of Steppenwolf drummer

Jerry Edmonton and session man Steve Gadd. Bobby is
clever about business too. He understands the importance
of promotion, being out there, hanging posters in pizza
shop windows, continually campaigning and making new
connections. Bobby isn't scared of hard work, travel,
crowds, growing the band and reaching higher.
I'm not certain if Big Bill and Barnett are on quite the
same wavelength. That's when I start seeing two white
vans, with the name Doc Savage painted on their sides.
Parked out in front of a yellow and white Victorian house
right in the center of Holliston.

I turn 21 in 1974 and shock everyone that Spring by
announcing that I'm leaving for Hollywood. I'm not sure
how this all came about, it happened so fast.
For a reason I can't quite fathom, I'm once again yearning
to hit the open road and head West.
My bandmates and the Biggy Ratt road crew are taken by
surprise. Bobby is really upset with me. Hitchhiking has
gone out of vogue now. The Boston Phoenix runs a weekly
classified ad for the Green Tortoise hippy bus that goes
back and forth between Boston and San Francisco every
week or two. There are similar, amateur, cheap bus lines to
choose from. I book a spot on something called the Grey
Elephant, bound for San Francisco.
I'll hitch the rest of the way down to Los Angeles.

Good morning. I'm in Brighton, a Boston neighborhood,
with a backpack and a few dollars stuffed in the heel of my
boot. Last week I sold my Gibson Firebird to the guy who's
playing lead guitar in Merry's new band. I see the old
school bus parked on a hill, a bunch of boys and girls are
milling around. Minutes later a bearded guy (he looks like
Mr. Natural from Zap Comix) comes out of a nearby
coffeeshop and begins collecting the (cash only) fares.
He charges $70 to ride across country. Then he beckons
everyone inside his bus, where he waves his hands and
recites a very short passage that sounds like a sermon.

Turns out Mr. Natural is Father Natural and this former
school bus is currently registered with the Commonwealth
as a house of worship - in order to avoid paying taxes on
the operation.

Now he orders all the men to disembark the bus.
We're instructed to get in back and push. The electric
starter is shot, so he needs to get the bus rolling before
dropping the clutch. We manage to limp out of
Massachusetts but every time we stop for oil, gas or a rest
stop, all the boys need to get out and push - until the
engine kicks in again. This routine happens over and over,
until Wyatt, a Peter Fonda look-alike wearing aviator
shades, declares a mutiny.

Wyatt takes over the wheel in Ohio - using minimal force -
and guides the bus straight to the first truck repair place
he sees. Another standoff happens when Wyatt has to
force Mr. Natural into paying for the parts and labor.
Replacing the starter eats a whole travel day and gobbles-
up a major chunk of the bus fares.

Problem solved, Wyatt relinquishes the wheel to Mr.
Natural and we continue to roll through the Mid-West.
The passenger area of the school bus has no seats and is
bisected, bow to stern, by a plywood platform suspended a
foot below window level. The plywood is covered with
mattresses. Bags and cargo are stowed beneath the
platform and the passengers all flop around on the
mattresses with the nearby windows wide open, trying to
survive the baking heat. I count a few hippies, some
students, an artist or two.
Sirens wail, blue lights flash.
Oh, boy. Looks like somebodies in big trouble... wait.

Why are *we* slowing down? I see state police patrol cars
gathering behind and in front of our bus as we come to a
stop. More squad cars arrive. We wait patiently.
Officers enter the bus slowly with guns drawn.
Me and the other kids are all ordered outside. We
scramble to the edge of I-70 as passing tourists slow down
to stare at us. The officers take their time searching every
inch of the vehicle. A police photographer snaps pictures
while others gather together near the school bus's rear
exit. We watch as Mr. Natural is thoroughly interrogated
by two officers. Another hour goes by and troopers wait
beside their radios. They finally get the all clear, hop back
inside their air-conditioned units and buzz off.

I'm sun-burned and thirsty, what the heck just happened?
Turns out we were reported by a passing motorist,
concerned about the insignia painted on the back door of
the school bus.
"It's just a big grey elephant with tusks and a trunk.
I should know, I painted it." insists our driver.
Apparently Mr. Natural's elephant art looks similar to the
multi-headed, snake logo used by the Symbionese
Liberation Army (SLA), a group who've been all over the
headlines since February 4th, the day they kidnapped
Patty Hearst in Berkeley California.
Patty is the 19 year-old granddaughter and heiress of
William Randolph Hearst, creator of the largest media
company in the world.
I guess the police thought we were holding Patty Hearst
prisoner in our school bus.

Watching America scroll past my window, thinking to myself. The chick beside me is wearing a see through, macrame dress, she smells of incense. I was never a hippy. I was quick to get an electric guitar and grow my hair long - but only to copy Brian Jones and the Stones, not the Lemon Pipers. I don't vibe with the pot smoking, Seals & Crofts listening, laid back life.

I want to dress like a peacock and be bigger than life. I don't want to soothe and lull people to sleep with my music. I want to move them, confront them, kick them in the pants. I have no desire to retreat to a quiet commune in the countryside. I'm aiming for round-the-clock action, glamour, big city lights...

A few days later I finally make it to the Sunset Strip where a sensational scene is simmering. I guess my fascination with Southern California began with Disneyland.

Every kid wanted to go there and in 1964 my father drove the Bell family across country to visit Walt's park in Anaheim.

Relatives in the San Diego area introduced me to things they called skateboards, built in the garage from halved roller skates and round-nosed, plywood planks. The boards my cousins make are carpeted too.

Around that same time, I began seeing these stupefying Revell model kits. Older, teenage brothers of my second-grade friends are building these unbelievably-cool, plastic, Ed "Big Daddy" Roth creations... monsters - obviously from SoCal - driving around in hot rods with towering stick shifts. Some of the actual, full-size cars these astounding models are based-on, start showing up -

usually for a split second - in movies shot in Malibu, like
Beach Blanket Bingo and *Village of the Giants*.
TV began running the California beach party,
dancin'n'surfin' movies from American International
Pictures. The real Frankie & Annette ones, and the
imitations too. A daytime rock'n'soul program called
"Where the Action Is" premieres in June 1965 with Paul
Revere and the Raiders ponying along Sunset Boulevard to
a theme song that promises:

"Whoa! dance, dance, dance, let your backbone slip
Let's go to the place on the Sunset Strip!"

So, I'm finally here, on the Sunset Strip.
Sitting out in front of the Power Burger. A rock club called
Filthy McNasty's (8852 Sunset Blvd) is a few doors down
and there's a kustom-painted hot rod parked right out
front. Gazing up at a gigantic billboard, I see a new group
called Bad Company. Their debut is about to come out on
Led Zeppelin's Swan Song label.
Across the street is the Rainbow Room (9015 Sunset Blvd.)
and next door, The Roxy (9009 Sunset Blvd.) just recently
opened. The marquee says Rocky Horror Picture Show.
Someone told me it's not a picture show. It's a musical
with rock songs, acted-out, live onstage, every night.

I hike down to the next boulevard and find the Troubadour
(9081 Santa Monica Blvd), a haven for mellower tastes,
with singer/songwriters like Jackson Browne and J. D.
Souther. A few blocks further is the Tropicana Motel (8585
Santa Monica Blvd) where former resident Jim Morrison

paid $10 a night for his regular room. Alice Cooper is staying here now. Then it's Barney's Beanery (8447 Santa Monica Blvd) and finally another newly opened venue, called the Starwood (8151 Santa Monica Blvd). I remember the address, it used to be called PJ's, back when Trini Lopez, Johnny Rivers and the Standells worked - and occasionally recorded - here as house bands.

Hiking back up Crescent Heights to the Strip, I find Schwab's Drugstore (8024 Sunset Boulevard).
The lyrics to Over the Rainbow, a song from my favorite film, *The Wizard of Oz*, were supposedly written here late at night by Harold Arlen while he sat in a car parked out front, bathed in the glow coming from the drugstore windows. A block east I encounter the wildest sidewalk scene ever, in front of Rodney Bingenheimer's English Disco (7561 Sunset Boulevard).
Lots of really young kids, dolled-up and hoping to catch the eye of Robert Plant, Brian Connolly, Michael Des Barres, David Bowie or Suzi Quatro. I have no money to go inside. But I don't really need to be inside these clubs. Like a lot of the other kids, I'm just floating around the Strip for free, watching and listening to all the flamboyant young characters. I'm soaking it all in... the fashion, the attitude, the decadent vibe that's going round.

After Rodney's closes, I head west on the Strip, below Laurel Canyon and the Chateau Marmont (8221 Sunset Blvd.) I see another new place called the Comedy Store (7561 Sunset Boulevard). The buildings themselves aren't new. I mean, The Comedy Store used to be the rock room

"It's Boss" and before that, they called it "Ciro's LeDisc," which was home base for the Byrds. Even earlier, the same building was a movie star hangout called Ciro's. I spend the early morning hours nursing a cream soda in one of the booths at the 24-hour diner, Ben Franks (8585 Sunset Blvd) until tomorrow comes. Then I brush my teeth and wash-up in the lobby restroom of the Continental Hyatt House (8401 Sunset Boulevard.) This is the place where Led Zeppelin throws TV sets off the upper floor balconies. Hopefully they'll throw Jimmy Page's violin bow out the window too.

I scoop up a lot of pointers hanging around, observing and occasionally conversing with the diverse players in this edgy West Coast, show biz community. It's so different from the conservative New England villages where I grew up playing Young Rascals covers in church halls. Where rock'n'roll is still considered a fad - not a business or a way of life.

I'm 21 years old, a nobody, but starting tonight, I'm envisioning myself as a contender.

Hey, that could be me partying with Rodney, rocking with David Johansen, or Mick Ronson, or Andy Scott or all these other stars gliding past the doormen and into the clubs on the Strip.

I'm getting pretty full of myself, but I'm gonna need all the inner-bravado I can muster to pull this off. Listen man, I'm as self conscious as the next guy, but somehow I'm learning to suspend my own disbelief and project myself into the boots of a star. A fearless frontman.

A certified rock'n'roll singer.

{ 14 }

THUNDERTRAIN 1974
A week later, I'm leaning against Turners Liquors, making a quick phone call to my family back in Holliston. My brother Andy gets on the line, telling me Ric Provost, the bass player from Doc Savage, is putting together something new. He's looking for me.

Ric Provost and his guitarist brother Gene, fed up with Doc Savage, begin hammering together a new rock group in the Spring of 1974. Natick's Provost Brothers have made good music with their earlier groups Farm and Chester White. I saw them at Ararat in early 1973 and they had a Moby Grape, Buffalo Springfield-type sound.
Ric Provost is looking to create a breathtaking, sexy, scary, colossal, rock club attraction.
The 9th Wonder of the Modern World.
(King Kong is the 8th).

His first attempt at constructing the ultimate rock band was dubbed Doc Savage. They should have been great. The frontman is a hunky, Jan Michael Vincent look-alike with big eyes and a shag hairdo. Lead guitarist Jimi is a skinny black cat who plays his Stratocaster like...Jimi. Lictor is the drummer and he's got a sprawling double-kick set-up. Doc Savage has all bases covered - the looks, the chops, a band house, two vans.

The Provost brothers are fun-loving guys but they know
how to channel their lunatic energy into positives for their
musical enterprise. That's not the case with the rest of the
irresponsible, dysfunctional Doc Savage bandmates.
The group sparkles for a brief, exciting moment before
crashing & burning. Ric goes back to the drawing board,
looking for solid, mature guys, committed to the long haul.
He nabs drummer Bobby Edwards from the dissolved
Biggy Ratt.

I return to Holliston, head buzzing from the Sunset Strip.
Balanced on platform shoes... glittering... all glammed up,
acting like...
Well, I guess I act like I know what I'm talking about, dead
certain that the dazzling L.A. rock energy is ready to sweep
across the whole nation. It's just up to me to lead the
charge. After a brief meeting with Ric, it's obvious that he
has the fire, the talent and the nerve to get his vision off
the ground.
Ric is tall, dark, intense and a year my senior. You could
power the entire Indy 500 with his enthusiasm. Ric stops
at nothing.

During their brief career, Doc Savage ventured down to
Norfolk VA to play clubs on Virginia Beach. That
accomplishment is hugely significant to me. Leaving town
in a van with your band, headed for some faraway gig...on
Virginia Beach...wherever that is...that's my idea of
heaven. I've been gigging around in circles, stuck in
Middlesex County for eons.

I'm also impressed that he's corralled two duos, the Provost Brothers team and the Mach & Bobby team. Being a lone wolf is cool, but being part of a dynamic duo moves things up the road apiece. Bobby and I share a sixth sense. I know what he's doing next on the drums and I'm right beside him, magnifying his efforts, as a team-player frontman should. Bobby shadows me musically, he accents my stage movements and my offhand remarks with deft, occasionally hilarious, drum accents.

Ric and his rhythm guitar playing/singing brother Gene, are locked-in musically as well as physically. Together, they create a rumbling, sonic rampart and when the music begins to redline, the Provosts fall into a vigorous, brotherly choreography. It feels natural and totally unplanned.

ZZ Top is a power trio from Texas and they have an album (their second), Tres Hombres, that's getting some radio play up here. So the hombres visit Boston and put on a free outdoor exhibition. The Provost brothers and I head into town for the event. ZZ Top is set-up in the Hatch Shell on the Charles River Esplanade. The weather is great and thousands show up for the July 15th concert. From where we're sitting it's impossible to make out the brand name of the string of gigantic, sandy-colored amplifiers lining the rear of the bandshell. ZZ Top strides onstage and totally kick our collective asses. I'm having a great time but watching this fantastic show makes me even hungrier to get our own group off the ground.

The Thundertrain line-up is cemented on August 4th 1974, the day lead guitarist, Steven Silva, arrives from New Bedford in his white 1966 Mustang - with a Gibson SG and a Marshall stack wedged in back. Ric has us in downtown Boston, jamming in a cellar hole, deep below Jack's Drum Shop at 1096 Boylston St.

We blaze through a bunch of Silverhead, Lou Reed and Alice Cooper covers. Our sound is loud, energetic and pretty much what I've been hoping for - but Silva's bottle-neck slide guitar solo on Silver Train leaves my head-spinning.

I grew up immersed in the Peter Green, Dave Davies, Keith Richards School of British heavy blues/rock. His shag-cut

hair might be straight off the Kings Road but this Steven Silva cat plays his SG in a distinctly American style.
His template being the recent Rick Derringer album All American Boy. "Rock and Roll, Hoochie Koo," the lead-off track, is a current radio favorite all over America. Prior to cutting the solo record, Derringer toured and recorded with Steven's other high-energy inspiration, John Dawson Winter III aka Johnny Winter.
Steven's passion for Winter & Derringer throws us for a loop. From Silva's look, we were expecting he'd maybe be a Mick Ronson or Ariel Bender-style player.
Or at least one of the big three, Clapton/Page/ Beck.

Steven makes a strong first impression.
I immediately sense he's the elusive puzzle piece I've been searching for. Big Bill is a super guitar player, but somehow he's the wrong fit for what I have in mind.
Ronson/Bowie, Richards/Jagger, Plant/Page, Wood/ Stewart - visibly, those guys just fit together for some reason. I have no idea who might fit with me -
until Steven Silva walks into my life.

We all adjourn to the pizza place next door. Even though we're all Massachusetts boys, Steven's hometown of New Bedford is foreign to us. The coastal, fishing town is known as Whaling City, probably best known as the locale of Melville's Moby Dick. Our new lead guitarist grew up in that Portuguese-American community, sixty miles from our Middlesex County. Steven peppers his speech with funny sounding Portuguese words and phrases he must've heard growing up, over at his grandmother's house.

Unlike the rest of us, Steven is an only child. His dad teaches physical education in the local public school. Besides rock'n'roll, Gene and Ric Provost share another common bond with Steven Silva. All three of them are the products of parochial schooling.

Bobby and I rarely set foot inside any house of worship, unless we're hired by some religious group to play a dance in the adjoining hall. But underneath the glittery rags and platform shoes, our three bandmates have all been schooled the hard way - by Catholic nuns.

After pizza we cruise past Boston Common, to Beacon Hill where my Holliston, artist friend, Linda has an apartment. Linda recently re-invented herself as Miss Lyn.

Lyn almost falls over when Steven Silva strolls in.

He's my height but he's got dark, bedroom eyes and a dark, shiny shag haircut. Miss Lyn immediately flips for the cute new lead guitar player and believe me, she won't be his last victim. The TV is glowing and all eyes are on the White House in these final few days and hours before President Nixon resigns.

While Tricky Dick sweats, we throw around band names.

"Hot Chrome? Showbiz Kids?"

Junior member Bobby suggests Thunder Train.

"Thunder Train?" hisses Miss Lyn, wrinkling up her nose at the idea.

"No, replies Steven. *Thundertrain*. It has to be a single word. Thundertrain."

"But what does it mean?" sniffs Miss Lyn.

"Thundertrain has nothing to do with storms or cabooses," explains Edwards. "Thundertrain is a new word - it defines the five of us - and the music we make."

After some debate, Bobby's motion with Steven's amendment are agreed upon.

Ric and I suggest that billing Thundertrain as "Direct from New York City" sounds better than the truth. Everyone seems to be all-in with the line-up and the band name - but I'm not sure Steven is 100% onboard with all the glitter, boas and make-up the rest of us have in mind.

You couldn't find an empty seat after 8 o'clock at Crosti's Grove. Live entertainment was provided by Helen, the owner's wife and featured singer. Forty years ago it was just another barn in Ashland, down by the railroad tracks. In truth, the barn housed a speakeasy, a hideaway serving alcoholic beverages during prohibition.

Once the 18th Amendment was repealed in '33, Italian-born Crosti re-modeled the barn into a fancy restaurant, putting his daughter, Ida, in charge because she could speak English. One of the family left to take over the nearby and burgeoning, Framingham Liquors retail business in 1948, but Crosti's Grove continued to expand. A bowling alley was added and automatic pin-setting machines were installed during the 50's.

The sprawling Crosti property eventually becomes The Cricket Lounge. In the early 70's, an enterprising bar manager named Fran Horne transforms the bowling alleys into a dance hall with a wide, shallow stage across the back wall. The lay-out resembles the interior of

Lakeview Ballroom, up the road in Mendon, with its wide dance floor and gaudy, sequined stage backdrop. When the drinking age falls to 18, Fran brings in headliners, the New York Dolls, the Raspberries (Oct. 73 w/ Reddy Teddy) and Aerosmith to his Ashland rock spot.

A year later Fran decides to split the too-big space in half. He carpets the "good half" for better acoustics, installs a new, multi-tiered stage, adds larger bars and begins booking popular cover bands like Calamity Jane, ITMB (Incredible Two Man Band), Sledgehamma, Fate, Celebration and Live Lobster. They play weeklong engagements, performing four shows a night every Wed-Sun.

Thundertrain ends up in the "bad half" of the Cricket Lounge. During yesterday's excellent rehearsal in Boston, an antique dealer adjacent to Jack's Drum Shop thinks the big one just rumbled through the Back Bay. Objects' d'art fall from her shelves and smash all over the floor. The neighbor's damage results in the first of many Thundertrain eviction notices. Ric has already scoped-out our next rehearsal nest, seeing what Fran unwittingly created by chopping his Cricket showroom into two pieces. Here we are "Direct from New York City" setting-up the Ampegs, Ludwigs & Marshall stacks on the hardwood floor of the darkened Cricket backroom. The original, sequined stage where David Johansen, Joe Perry and Eric Carmen strutted their stuff, not-that-long-ago, is right over there to my left. The raised platform, sadly abandoned, is currently littered with power tools, stacks of lumber, a table saw and cobwebs. Wiring hangs down from the ceiling, there's no ventilation, no windows, the acoustics stink. Every few hours a freight train, rolling on tracks directly behind us, shakes the foundation of Thundertrain's new Home Sweet Home.

THUNDERTRAIN 1974 Mach, Bobby, Steven, Cool Gene and Ric
on the railroad tracks behind the Cricket Lounge in Ashland.
Photo by Michael Pirrella

Speedy Ric has already invited the manager of Natick area favorites, Sledgehamma, to stop by and check out a Thundertrain rehearsal. We're in the midst of the chorus of Slade's "Gudbuy T' Jane" when a tall, serious looking man carrying a briefcase strides in.

Close-cropped curly hair, aviator shades, playboy tan, gold chains in his chest hair, Al Jacques takes a seat on an extra speaker cabinet. He listens to us rehearse and watches intently through dark glasses.

Five boys. Tall bass player. Sexy-looking lead guitarist. Energetic lead singer...hmmm.

Mr. Jacques currently manages a dance club on nearby Route 9 called The Meadows. Prior to that he worked as underling to the powerful New England promoter, Frank Connelly. Al Jacques ran errands for a rock band Frank managed, Aerosmith. Our set comes to a crashing finale and Al speaks.

"You guys don't sound too bad. Those last two... original songs?" We nod.

"I want you boys to come out to the house. Tomorrow."

So, now we're sitting on the couch in the Jacques' living room in downtown Natick. A humble, double-deck, two family home in a tight-knit neighborhood. Adele serves us coffee and tea while her husband holds court, Al's wife smiles at us but she never opens her mouth.

"That's where we broke Dream On," boasts our host, pointing to the telephone mounted on his kitchen wall. According to Mr. Jacques, the first Aerosmith single, released last year in June, languished in the lower half of the Billboard Top 100.

"That's when Father Frank told me,

Al. Get that damn single into the Top 10!"

"So I sent Adele to Stop & Shop to buy Hoodsie Cups and bags of popsicles. She filled-up our freezer. I talked to the kids upstairs and they talked to all their friends. Pretty soon I had a parade of neighborhood kids, trading phone calls to WVBF for treats. The line grew and the kids kept calling the radio station and requesting *Dream On*. All day, every day. Adele kept handing out Hoodsies until Aerosmith hit #1 on 'VBF."

It becomes apparent to us that Al Jacques thinks Thundertrain might possess the potential to become his very own Aerosmith, but this time around he isn't gonna get left behind. Al wants us to meet his colleague, Frank Borsa, of Collegiate Associates. Borsa booked a lot of the local Aerosmith high school concerts during their rapid ascent in 1971 and '72. A day later, Borsa and Jacques show up at our daily Thundertrain rehearsal. Soon we're all back in Jacques' living room, looking at a management deal. Seems kinda premature to be signing anything, I mean, we've never even performed publicly.

Talks sour when Borsa hands around the production deal. I see the name of record producer Alan Lorber on the contract and I freeze. Alan is the guy behind the famously botched "Bosstown Sound" campaign that drowned a flotilla of upcoming local bands in a sea of music biz hype. We balk. Nevertheless, Al and Frank agree to represent us on a simple handshake. Frank Borsa gets busy, booking Thundertrain all over New England.

When we're not over at the Cricket, rehearsing, we've taken over the Provost's house in Natick as our headquarters. Mom,(Mrs. P.) is employed as a nurse. As long as we don't bring any groupies upstairs, she's extremely hospitable. Ric and Gene lost their father to illness a few years ago. They have two sisters and a younger brother named Phil. I call him Dueg and he's a rock musician too, a drummer. It's August 18th and Dueg is all amped-up, returning home from the "greatest rock show I ever saw."

Duke and the Drivers sign to ABC Records soon after Biggy Ratt plays with them at Wellesley High. The debut Drivers LP, "Cruisin'" is cut during 1973 at Electric Lady Studios in NYC. They even have Eddie Kramer producing. "What You've Got (Sure Looks Good To Me)," the first single, is doing great on popular WRKO-AM so Frank Connelly invites the Drivers to open Aerosmith's first huge outdoor show. Today, out on Route 9 at the Westboro Speedway. The ticket price ($6) is steep but Dueg returns from the concert totally inspired. Aerosmith are pushing their second record, released last March. This one's called Get Your Wings. Opening today's Aerosmith show is Mad Angel, starring Jimmy D'Angelo, formerly of The Joneses. Today's Speedway crowd is estimated at a staggering 15,000.

Ask us where the first Thundertrain show happened and we'll all give you a different answer. The launch is not a smooth one. We have a tremendous pile of gear but no way to transport it properly. Ric drives a sporty Cougar convertible, his brother has an even smaller Camaro. Steven's Mustang doesn't hold much either. Luckily, AnneMarie's '61 Impala is a barge and Bobby's rust bucket is even roomier, a real banana boat.

So the band and a few of our loyal friends with similar clunkers each take a few amps, guitar cases and parts of Bobby's colossal drum kit. A parade of shitboxes rolls across New England to whatever booking Ric or agent Borsa manages to scrounge up.

Once we begin playing, our volume is immediately off the charts.

THUNDERTRAIN Photo by Lynn Ciulla

We won't receive many call-backs and sometimes we don't even make it through the first set before the axe falls. Even worse, just as we begin gaining a tiny bit of traction, our lead guitarist Steven, who is already an integral part of our sound and the Thundertrain image, suddenly falls ill. He gets carted away to the hospital. Steven is diagnosed with mono, jaundice and who-knows-what-else. In a curious twist of fate, my friendly sister Cathy, comes down with the exact same symptoms as Steven, on the exact same day.

Yellow-eyed and weak, Steven will spend the next month on his back, trying to recuperate. The timing is exceptionally crappy, he falls ill on the eve of our first big-money booking, a five-night engagement in Newport RI at the Electric Elephant. As an unknown, just-starting-out band, it would be career suicide to cancel on such short notice. With only a couple hours left before showtime, we resort to phoning Biggy Ratt guitarist, Big Bill, begging him to race down here and fill in for Steven.

Now I'm really feeling pressure. Ric and I scouted this club last week. The place was jammed full of rich-looking kids, all dancing to this lipstick smeared, decked-out cover band from Long Island called Twisted Sister. Dee Snyder and company sing Rebel Rebel, Rock and Roll Queen and a bunch of other songs we try to copy. I was already nervous about following such an established, tight act into this big room. I try to look calm on the outside but the anxiety is way too much. I need to impress this crowd and the club owner with my fantastic new band - just as my guitar riffing-sidekick conks out by the wayside.

I'm on the floor in the upstairs dressing room, chugging a bottle of Maalox when Big Bill arrives, breathless. Bill might be even more tense than me. He hasn't played with Bobby in almost a year. He's never heard a note of Thundertrain. Bill barely knows any of our Slade and Silverhead repertoire. Somehow we manage to fake it, limping through the week of shows - but just barely.

Ric keeps grinding away, keeping our spirits afloat and moving Thundertrain forward. I watch as his older brother, Gene, crafts a few glowing paragraphs about our band. Gene sends his composition, along with our group photograph, to the local free handout Night Life Magazine. The next issue comes out and I'm amazed to see our picture and Provost's article reprinted, word-for-word.

Thundertrain

Another fine product from New York City, Thundertrain acts as though they invented hard rock. This powerhouse is definitely one of the flashiest, high energy acts to hit this area in a long time.

Thundertrain was originally scheduled for a short tour of New England but the boys decided they "like the area and we just haven't had enough time to rock the population." And for the ladies! Mark Bell, Steven Silva, Ric Provost, Bob Edwards and Gene Provost all claim that they "do not mind being considered sex objects," (the boys look as fine as they play). If you are out to get crazy and you hear that train a-comin', don't do something you will later regret when your friends tell you of the wild time you missed. Catch Thundertrain!!!

Jon Read, the youngster I met while at school in Framingham, and who later recorded Joe Flash at the MIT college radio station, is old enough to drive now. He shows up at a Thundertrain gig.

Up til today he's been busy doing club dates, mixing sound for Merry and Jack's latest band, Foxfire. I guess something changed on that front - so we offer him the job of running sound for Thundertrain. Jon Read is a major score for us. He gets to work, tightening up our sound system and figuring out how to bridle our noise into something more listenable. Our crew takes shape, with sound man Jon joined by Mick Martins who works the lights and takes care of Bobby's Ludwigs.

Transporting the band, the crew and the growing mountain of equipment we've assembled has become a problem. Al Jacques comes to the rescue. Al's other band, Sledgehamma, has a sneaky deal going with Joe, the owner of the local rental place on Union Street.

Joe rents everything. Popcorn machines, chain saws, U Haul trucks and stacks of folding tables and chairs. Clients will call Joe whenever they need banquet seating for say, a million people. Joe delivers, sets everything up and a day or two later, following the event, he hauls away all the 8' foot tables and folding chairs.

Well...actually, Joe doesn't move any of the stuff himself, that's where Sledgehamma - and now Thundertrain - come in. In exchange for our youthful manpower, setting-up and retrieving billions of chairs & tables, Joe allows us free use of the U-Haul trucks on his lot. Good ol' Joe even shows the roadies how to quickly disable the truck odometers. Thundertrain's U-Haul use is never recorded or reported to the home office. We still have to pay for our gas, which has risen sharply in the past year, now at 53 cents a gallon.

Ralph Mormon is singing at K-K-K Katy's this week. It's the hottest rock nightclub in Boston.

Ralph's band, BUX (formerly Daddy Warbux), is another Frank Connelly-managed group and Thundertrain's Gene Provost is related (through his girlfriend's family) to their drummer Tommy Bonarrigo. Gene raves about BUX, their incredible singer Ralph and their flamboyant guitarist, Punky Meadows. Provost also raves about the club itself. "We gotta get Thundertrain in there."

Frank Borsa makes some calls and manages to land Thundertrain a Sunday showcase.

Thankfully, Steven Silva recovers from his month-long illness just in time for the gig. K-K-K Katy's is part of the Kenmore Club complex, at 533 Commonwealth Ave, operated by the notorious Henry Vara. The multi-level complex houses three night clubs (with ever-changing names) that dominate Boston's dance/rock music scene. Narcissus, Lucifer, Lipstick and Celebration are a few of the monikers the Vara clubs operate under.

K-K-K Katy's is the basement space.

A large dark room with three bars and an ample stage. The New York Dolls and Aerosmith both played seven-night engagements here. The Boston Police have tied club owner Henry Vara to various illicit activities all over the city - but that doesn't slow us down for a second.

My girlfriend, AnneMarie, is enrolled right up the street at Boston University. In the theatrical department. Down in the dressing room at K-K-K Katy's, AnneMarie applies stage make-up to our eyelids and faces.

Glitter, mascara, even some face paint.

When she's finished, we resemble the New York Dolls but when we hit the stage, something different happens. Rhythm guitarist Gene can pass for a Slade member and silver-booted Ric's bass lines meld seamlessly with his brother's riffing. Blonde drummer Bobby Edwards provides more than enough propulsive energy.

But what about those two guys showing-off out front? They're all mixed up. The singer is dressed a little bit like David Johansen and he does a decent Noddy Holder holler - but wait - he just veered-off into nasty, Jim Dandy/cock-rock territory. The androgynous guitar player looks like a glam-boy until he begins firing-off Beaumont Texas-style Johnny Winter boogie-rock licks. Glitter rock? No. I don't think so...

What the heck *is* this Thundertrain anyway?

Courtesy of the Howie Burnham Archive

{ 15 }

The Stadium. 1975
We flunk the K-K-K Katy's audition. I'm worried.
The Thundertrain roll-out has been a dud at best.
Hardly anyone gets us. No call backs. Several tense
situations where we nearly get our asses kicked by irate
audience members. One venue throws us out before we
finish the first song. This Friday we're at another school
dance and most of the audience ends up pointing fingers
and hooting at us. Bobby claims there's a new group out of
New York called KISS who wear just as much make-up as
us but Steven isn't digging the make-up crap anymore.

So tonight, Saturday, we roll up Route 1 through Foxboro.
Rolling past Schaeffer Stadium, it opened three years ago
to house the ever-struggling Patriots football team. A team
that can't win. The Patriots are even worse than the
forever-cursed Boston Red Sox.
Two miles further up the highway we pull up to a shabby
motel. The rusted sign says Stadium Motor Lounge.
Steven Silva says something under his breath in
Portuguese and it doesn't sound good. Frank couldn't find
us any paying work tonight, so he booked us into this
pitiful pit. Playing for the door. Our drummer's brother,
Elliot Edwards, came along. We hope he can collect a
dollar admission if anyone shows up.

We enter a dark, cheaply paneled, stale-smelling, raggedly carpeted room. Beat-up tables are arranged around a gummy, parquet dance floor. The stage is big enough for a polka trio. Maybe. Jon and Micky jigsaw our gear, as best they can, onto the corner platform.
We hear chuckles coming from the bar.
Three middle-aged-men are poking fun at the pissed-off gal serving them drinks.
The drunkest of the three is Harvey. The proprietor.

"Is there a dressing room?" Harvey bursts out laughing.
"Dressing room? They keep the cleaning supplies over in that closet... you can have that if you want."
We pull-on our shiny stage rags but Steven nixes the warpaint. We decide to follow his lead.
Jon cranks up the intro tape "Blues Theme" from the Roger Corman biker flick *The Wild Angels*. Thundertrain hits the tiny stage as the tape's Harley Davidson exhaust pipe outro, revs'n'roars off into the distance. Bobby counts us into "Hello New York" a Michael Des Barres/Silverhead cover. I scan the empty room as I sing.
Wait a sec, two girls just walked through the door.
A Slade song is next and a few more kids trickle in.
The first two girls are already up on the dance floor.
We pivot into "Sweet Jane" where Silva/Provost do their best Wagner/Hunter impersonation while I wail a lyrically pot-holed version of Lou Reed's masterpiece. Steven leads us into his original tune "Backseat Boogie" and I answer back with one of my own, dubbed "Single Action Pump."

Wrentham MA 1975 - THUNDERTRAIN at the Stadium Motor
Inn. Photo by Lynn Ciulla

Sharing the Stadium stage with us is a bomb. About four
feet in length. One of Dueg's friends liberated the missile
from the nearby Natick Army Labs during a midnight raid.
The Thundertrain bomb features a nosecone and fins and
we stenciled it with our band-name of course.

178

I'm not sure whether or not the thing is loaded with TNT
but that doesn't stop me from hoisting the weapon up to
my crotch and threatening the kids on dance floor.
My antics seem to be getting those first two girls all
worked-up.
I see other kids lining up at the pay phone, dialing and
yelling. We bash through our pile of Spiders from Mars, T.
Rex and Alice Cooper covers. We see the room filling up.
Fast.
Steven has another new one called "Tribute to Johnny"
and I follow it with "Cindy is a Sleeper" a thing I wrote.
Now the dance floor is packed, people are pushing
forward, yelling and applauding. The crowd continues to
expand, all the way to our grand finale, another Michael
Des Barres tune that begins quietly with just my voice and
one guitar:

"You're mama raised you to be quite a nice boy,
But then they found you playing with a most unlikely
toy...."

That's the cue. Jon detonates the explosive flash box
hidden behind me as I shout the title lyric:
"Bright Light" Sparks fly as Thundertrain bursts into full-
blown action all around me.
The overflow crowd is blinded - taken by surprise when
the generous pile of magician's flash powder ignites into a
fireball of flame and smoke. While the haze rises,
Thundertrain shifts gears into double-time and I rocket off
the stage astride the bomb. The audience, choking and
squinting through clouds of smoke, deliriously cheer-on

the mounting insanity. This is it. We've cracked it. As we leave the stage, I'm feeling the same Sunset Strip energy I felt in L.A. last Spring. This crowd doesn't want us to stop. Ric and Bobby charge back to the stage and unleash a sweaty stomp-beat that morphs into the Rolling Stone's Silver Train, a groover expertly covered by Johnny Winter - but owned tonight by Thundertrain.

THUNDERTRAIN '75. Mach & Steven at the Stadium.
Photo by Mary Johnson

Lynn Ciulla is an attractive, Lois Lane-looking, brunette
with big eyes. She works as a secretary at a booking agency
handling adult comics and hypnotist acts.

They also represent the kind of show bands that carry horn
sections and wear ties. In her personal life, Lynn prefers a
rowdier brand of rock music. She's standing right out
front. Thundertrain has been held-over at the Stadium and
the place is jumping. Mary and Kathye, the two under-age
girls who discovered us first, are back with more of their
friends. After listening and watching our act, Lynn
introduces herself to the band.

"You guys are amazing. I think David Woo would be very
interested."

Aerosmith's other huge outdoor show last summer was
Freedom Jam. Produced by David Woo and Don Constant
at the Stepping Stone Ranch in Rhode Island on 7/6/74.
Sha Na Na headlines the 12-hour festival along with
Aerosmith, Mahavishnu Orchestra and Brownsville
Station. Lynn photographs the event for David Woo and
she's apparently pretty tight with him.

A week later Thundertrain is headlining at the Echo
Ballroom in Walpole. Just a town over from the Stadium.
Most of our new converts have followed us here, Mary and
Kathye are seated right up front. Mid-set we see Lynn
Ciulla enter the dancehall with a short, business-like, very
well dressed fellow.

Must be David Woo.

Moments later Al Jacques and Frank Borsa barge into the
Echo Ballroom. Looking worried and anxious.

THUNDERTRAIN
1975 ....
Photos by Lynn Ciulla

Backstage on our break, Ms. Ciulla introduces us to the
expertly coiffed Mr. Woo. Her hunch is right, David
immediately begins talking about signing Thundertrain to
a management deal.

He's in the midst of his spiel, going on about New York
recording studios, tour buses and an upcoming slot on a
concert he's producing, when the dressing room door flies
open.

Frank and Al push their way into the small room before
David Woo can finish his presentation. A tantalizing
presentation, studded with name-drops and promises of
the riches that wait ahead for Thundertrain.

Frank Borsa is red in the face.

"Hold on just a minute. I'm the manager of this band."

Mr. Woo spins around, smiling.

"Really? You have a contract with these gentlemen?"

Borsa backs off for a moment, fuming. Al Jacques is silent.

Woo continues. "I like the Thundertrain sound but I see
room for improvement in your stage clothing and
production. I'll take care of all that."

Frank Borsa explodes. "Money? You can spend money?
Well... I can throw around the money too!"

Digging deep into his pants pocket, Franks pulls out cash.

He throws it down on the table. Dramatically.

We all lower our eyes to the tabletop.

Two lonely one-dollar bills.

Crumpled and embarrassed.

Stifling his laughter, David Woo continues to woo us.

Borsa bolts from the dressing room with steam blasting
out both ears. Al and Lynn remain inside, mouths clamped
shut. Whichever way this ends up, they want in.

A few weeks later David Woo presents his first Thundertrain concert.

Reprinted from the New Bedford Sunday Standard-Times 3/2/1975.

7 Arrested at North End Theater

A Friday evening rock concert at the Capitol Theater was an artistic success according to its promoter, David Woo, but it also created a host of police problems, according to the New Bedford police.

Problems of crowd control, vandalism and rowdiness outside the North End theater and smoking and drinking inside, were spin-offs amid a crowd of 900 music lovers who flocked to hear the James Montgomery Band and the group Thundertrain in concert.

New Bedford police reports, still incomplete, relate that one person was arrested inside the theater during the concert. At least six others were arrested in the general area of the theater on disorderly conduct or interfering with police officer complaints during and after the concert.

Police reported initial problems among a portion of some 200 patrons who were in line at the theater doors around 7:30 pm on Friday, one half-hour before the concert was scheduled to begin.

Inside the theater, police on duty reported the crowd was drinking and smoking both cigarettes and marijuana.

The concert promoter, David Woo of Three J Productions, said that the smoke in the theater was probably caused by a fog machine used by Thundertrain in their act. "It is a dry ice machine that produces a mist."

Reports also indicate a group of youths broke into the dressing room and removed clothing of the performers.

The clothing was later found hanging on a fence outside the theater.

It was even worse than that.
Wanting to make a big impression at our first professional concert, crew member Jon builds two additional, mega-flash boxes and rents the biggest fog machine the local theatrical supply warehouse has in stock.
As the fog machine belches a Skull Island-worthy bank of haze, Thundertrain proudly takes the stage. Our grand entrance is lost on the beclouded crowd, gasping-for-oxygen. Nobody can see us until the third song ends and the mist finally rises.

The middle part of our set goes okay but then we get to Bright Light. Jon trips the detonator on his synchronized, turbo flash bombs and the explosions immediately top-up the auditorium with even denser smoke. Thunder-smog flows up the aisles, permeates the lobby and billows out across Acushnet Avenue.
Blotting-out the flashing lights of the theater marquee, a passerby sees smoke and pulls a nearby fire alarm.

Thinking the Capitol Theater has gone up in flame with 900 teenagers inside, the New Bedford Fire Chief launches a massive response. Seconds later sirens are wailing. Ensconced in our dressing room, toasting our triumphant concert debut, Thundertrain is confused when firemen wearing full battle gear push their way past us, searching for the fire.

Bluesman James Montgomery and his bandmates, who've just inked a major record deal, won't go near the stage, "We're not going on until it's safe out there."
A large portion of the audience has evacuated out to the sidewalk, while industrial blower-fans are set-up onstage, gusting Thundertrain's contrail out the door.

Thundertrain continues to feature our unpredictable flash box finale, until one fateful night at Dover/Sherborn Regional High School. Good ol' Frank Borsa books the gig. As far as managing Thundertrain is concerned, Mr. Woo goes up in smoke right after our fiery Capitol Theater debut. So, here we are in this local high school gymnasium. It's spring 1975 and a lot of the kids seem to be digging Thundertrain.

As the climax of the evening nears, I jump from Bobby's drum riser onto one of Ric's Ampeg cabs. Reaching higher, I grasp the metal framework supporting a glass backstop behind the basketball hoop that hangs above our stage of portable risers. Cool Gene begins playing the solo chords leading into Silverhead's Bright Light. I'm thinking about the moment Jon sets-off the flash powder. I guess I'll leap over the backdrop, maybe even slip through the hoop, before landing center stage at the exact moment Steven rips into the double-time riff.
I figure out this stagecraft stuff as I go along.

Jon hits the switch but everything goes terribly wrong.

In an attempt to create an even brighter flash, Jon's latest bangbox is constructed of much heavier lumber, lag-bolted together. BRIGHT LIGHT I shout.

The lever is thrown - and the heavy box splinters into a thousand pieces. Shards of wood and metal rocket-out into the crowd of students. Part of a lag bolt stabs me in the knee, leaving me bloodied and dangling over the stage in pain. I see kids rolling on the floor. I hear a girl crying.

I drop from the backboard and hit the stage. Hard.

An eerie quiet fills the gymnasium.

Thundertrain limps back to the locker room.

The crew works fast, loading out our gear, trying to hide evidence of the explosion. My heart stops when an adult, a chaperone, comes backstage with grim news.

Lots of kids suffered minor scuffs and scapes but one youngster, only 13, got hit bad. Right in the face.

It's serious and she's on the way to the hospital.

Cool Gene tells us to dry off and get dressed quick.

An hour later we're still sweating as we pace nervously in a hospital waiting room.

"She got cut pretty deep. The debris entered just above her right eye."

That's a surgeon talking and my gut is churning.

"Half an inch lower and it would've been a lot more serious. She's awake now. She says she wants to see you."

The doctor leads Thundertrain into the recovery room.

A young lady with curly, mahogany-colored hair and a large head bandage manages a smile as we enter.

Her mother and father, seated nearby, turn away from us in stony silence.

For once, I can't find my voice.

Ric greets the victim but Cool Gene quickly takes over, offering the child and her family a very kind and truthfully sincere apology.

Incredibly, the kid seems excited to meet us.

She asks for our autographs and thanks each of us for playing at her school dance.

Weeks and months pass, the volatile story is never reported to the newspapers. Not a peep from the victim's parents, the school system or authorities.

We even got paid.

Jon buries the remains of Thundertrain's bright light pyrotechnics after the too-close call.

During 1975 we write more songs and get our act together, playing more high schools and clubs. The Stadium Lounge in Wrentham is home base to Thundertrain on any left-over weekend nights.

We're mid-set when I see AnneMarie enter the Stadium with Reddy Teddy's guitarist/writer Matthew MacKenzie and lead singer John Morse.

I guess John is AnneMarie's latest part-time boyfriend. I've been spending most of my offstage hours with Lynn and her two Siamese cats, so it doesn't phase me too much. Anyway, Reddy Teddy is talking about cutting an entire album at Northern Studios in Maynard MA with Willie Loco Alexander and WBCN's Maxanne Sartori producing.

{ 16 }

Northern Studio, Monson Mania and Howard Stern

On February 24th Led Zeppelin releases a new record. This time it gets a title, Physical Graffiti. Every time I see the album's cover photo it reminds me of Eddie Kent, a clever fashion designer, currently employed as a fabric retailer in Framingham. He works in a drab brick building that contains a shining wonderland of textiles & sewing supplies.

The place to get fabric for the pattern you found in Woman's Day magazine. Or the metallic material required for a space suit you need.

Sewing a parachute?

A sloth suit? No problem. Sportswear in Framingham has the best selection of this stuff. Better than you'll find in the garment district - or even Chinatown.

After experiencing a few Thundertrain happenings down at the Stadium, Eddie Kent invites me to take a quick tour of his workplace. I point out some flashy looking bolts of cloth and Eddie goes to work, creating some memorable Thundertrain stage clothes for me - particularly my trousers - I neglect to wear a shirt most nights.

Eddie Kent possesses the mug of a Warhol superstar. Wait. I forgot. You guys have all seen Eddie plenty of times. (Fast forward - seven years). In July 1982, the Rolling Stones shoot their most famous video,

"Waiting For a Friend," outdoors on the stoop of the
"Physical Graffitti" apartments at 96–98
St. Mark's Place in Manhattan. That's the building where
Eddie is renting an apartment. Director Michael Lindsay-
Hogg (*The Rolling Stones Rock and Roll Circus*) pays
Eddie $40 for the use of his front steps. The director ends
up putting the Thundertrain clothing designer in the
finished Rolling Stones video.

Exactly halfway through the heavily rotated MTV clip, just
as Mick and Keith depart the stoop, Lindsay-Hogg's
camera pans over to a blonde, forlorn, somewhat-alien
looking lad, all alone, gazing out his apartment window.
The camera rests on the sombre face for a long moment.
That's Eddie Kent.

Mach with his Eddie Kent designed trousers.

Thundertrain rolls into Bill Riseman's Northern Studios on July 28th, ready to cut our first demo. Bobby, our youngest member, is a KISS fan and he wants a deep bottom-end with a fat kick-drum sound.

The rest of us assume the "magic of the studio" will reveal our hidden genius.

But, with no previous studio experience, no producer and a $300 budget, it's a tall order.

We're disappointed when the final mix of Steven's song "I'm So Excited" (based, I reckon, on the Edgar Winter Group/Dan Hartman, 1973 Top 40 hit "Free Ride") and my "Cindy is a Sleeper" (ditto Silverhead's Candy's Gone Bad crossed with three chords from the mid-section of Zep's How Many More Times) don't end up sounding as heavy as Deep Purple's Machine Head.

We don't feel good about submitting this tape to the major labels. I try to find a way to turn the disappointment around. Billing ourselves as "Recording Artists Thundertrain" might be a smart move. I know that Reddy Teddy, after their hoped-for Mercury deal fell through, released a couple songs on their manager's own Flexible Records label. They're getting press and airplay from it too. On the last page of Billboard magazine I see a tiny classified ad for a record pressing plant down in Louisiana.

DIY record releases are unknown territory in my neck of the woods, but I manage to convince the guys to invest $200 and get five hundred 45 rpm singles pressed.

I design a United National Records logo, using press-on
lettering from the drugstore, trying to make it look almost
major. We manage to sell a lot of the singles at gigs.
Following Cool Gene's example, I'm starting to do a lot of
Thundertrain promotion. Issuing press releases, personal
notes, photos... and now records. Rock Scene Magazine
publishes one of Lynn's Thundertrain photos with a blurb
mentioning "I'm So Excited" and our address in Natick.
Phonograph Record Magazine and Playboy review the
single. Dollars stream in - we press more.

Toys in the Attic, released last April, is playing everywhere
this summer. Sweet Emotion, Walk This Way...
I gotta hand it to Aerosmith. Their debut was rock solid,
the sophomore release was as good and maybe even better,

and this new one is another step up. I guess that's the way it's supposed to go, right? - *but really - who does that?*
In Mach World, Jimi never tops his debut album and, so far, Led Zeppelin hasn't topped their first one either.
Truth, the Jeff Beck Group's untouchable debut record, is hands-down his best.
What Aerosmith is achieving is pretty damn rare.

In May we play, probably for the first time, a totally forgettable Boston dive called the Rathskeller.
All the really rocking action happens across the street at the Kenmore Clubs. Thundertrain's setlist is becoming more original by the week, cover songs are a nuisance. We don't take them seriously, just another requirement to get our foot in the door of the better paying rooms.
We've dropped the "Direct from NYC" act. No more Bright Light or Hello New York. We're original rockers looking for a Boston outpost. Tonight we end up playing for the door at this empty Rathskeller. A few confused looking Red Sox fans wander down the big staircase, probably hoping to hear some Aerosmith.
This dismal dump is definitely not a fit for Thundertrain.

John Felice, another singer/songwriter/guitarist from Natick, has a band he calls The Kids and they've managed to rent a fort-like structure in the center of town called the Natick Armory for June 21st. They add Thundertrain to the bill and together we lure a couple hundred local kids inside the acoustically-challenged venue.

Felice played with Jonathan Richman in an early line-up of the Modern Lovers. Felice is an arrogant dude, sporting a Brian Jones bowl-cut, sneering and brimming with attitude - which I appreciate. Stylistically, The Kids jangle while Thundertrain burns rubber. The Kids sing about the Boston Common, the MBTA and girls in the city. We sing about cheating girlfriends, rejection and raising hell. Thundertrain is glammed-up, I'm wearing pink velvet drawstring pants while Ric sports fur & leather. The Kids dress down, performing in jeans and t-shirts, looking more like some of the onlookers in the crowd.

THUNDERTRAIN 1975 - Bobby, Mach, Steven, Ric and Cool Gene.   Photo by AnneMarie Martins

On August 15th a second, 50,000 watt, commercial rock powerhouse debuts on the Boston airwaves. WCOZ-FM promises fewer commercial breaks and a tighter playlist focusing on the rock songs younger listeners want to hear, Led Zeppelin, KISS, Aerosmith.

Ric Provost stumbles upon a tiny local radio station I've never even heard of.

Who knows, maybe they'll be the first in the nation to roll the dice and play the Thundertrain "I'm So Excited" single. Ric tells me about his visit to WNTN-AM, broadcasting out of a humble house on the edge of Newton's, Auburndale village.

"I was coming back from the city, just cruising, and I see this weird little radio station. I figured what the heck. I grab a 45 outta my gig bag and ring the doorbell."

A young, extremely nervous guy opens the door. Ric wastes no time - he gets straight to the point.

"I shove our record in the bashful kid's hand and give him the rap. We're a Natick band, we have a new hard-rock sound. Hey, why not give "I'm So Excited" a spin?"

The radio guy stalls, he smiles but he hems and haws.

"The tall kid stares at the record, like he wants to hear it... and then he finally introduces himself, he says his name is Howard.

He's just been hired at 'NTN. Brand new and it's his first professional radio job. Howard tells me that maybe he could have played us, back when he had his own show at the BU college radio station, but he graduated last spring.

As far as I know, the odd looking new hire at WNTN - Howard Stern is his name - passed up his chance to be first-ever to play a Mach Bell record on the radio.

I move in with Lynn Ciulla and her Siamese cats. She rents the upstairs floor of an old farmhouse on the edge of Framingham. A stone's throw away from the empty field where the Carousel Tent once fluttered. We're on the corner of Old Connecticut Path and Speen St. I don't think my regular girl, AnneMarie, has time to notice. By day, Annie studies at Boston University. At night she works as a spotlight operator at Route 9's Chateau de Ville. A glitzy affair with a lobby fountain and huge crystal chandeliers. The Chateau is the largest of a chain of five dinner theaters in MA and RI that book Ed Sullivan-style headliners: Jerry Lewis, Sandler and Young, Al Martino and Charo. Jerry Roberts is the producer and AnneMarie is one of a trio of young women the stagehands refer to as "Jerry's Angels."

High school gigs can be treacherous.
Playing "dances" has been a staple of the rock business since my Mechanical Onion days. I can recall when the combos (not mine) wore blazers and ties. Replicating Top 40 hits, as best they could, while the students danced the twist or the jerk or whatever. Nowadays, the schools are usually looking to bring in more of a concert-type event. Especially in this neck of the woods, where Aerosmith left such an indelible mark during their recent lift-off, rocking local gyms and field houses like they'd never been rocked before.

But for a lot of school administrations, these "dances" are regarded as nothing but a distraction from education. A big headache.

This weekend Thundertrain is booked at Belmont High, near Cambridge, and Monson High, somewhere out west.

For the Belmont gig we bring along our own warm-up act. They're called Slash. Jeff Thomas lives around the corner from Mrs. P's house in Natick. A major devotee of Jimi Hendrix, bassist Jeff sings and writes. Drummer Dueg Provost and Jeff had a power trio called "She-Fox" which has now evolved into "Slash."

Thundertrain arrives at the Belmont show and I'm immediately concerned. Slash are already playing on the floor of the hall with all our Thundertrain gear set-to-go, right behind them on the floor. No raised platform or risers of any kind. No stage = No good.

Thundertrain has barely begun when I see a mob of ten-foot-tall jocks pour into the dance, en masse. Pushing the shrimps aside, they approach the band. Their hulking frames form a barrier between us and what was, up til now, our audience. One ugly monster, wearing a letter jacket, pokes his finger at me, braying with laughter. Another goon, with a bristly five o'clock shadow, bends down, craning his neck in amusement, inches from Steven's face.

I've been here before...the Medfield Teen Center...the night I smashed a heckler's skull with my mic stand.

There is absolutely no security here. Chaperones, if there are any, are camped-out in a lobby somewhere, far from our racket, sipping tea and gossiping about summer camps and colleges.

The atmosphere back inside the gym worsens as onlookers begin chanting, hoping for a big fight.

Ric Provost with THUNDERTRAIN. Photo by Lynn Ciulla

Bobby pauses for a moment and Ric gets a maniacal gleam in his eye. Truth is, even on his best day, Ric is forever a mere whisker away from total madness.

Boundlessly energetic, our bass player is a tightly wound individual.

Ric starts doing a disturbing-looking "slowly I turn" routine that throws-off the husky athletes for a second. Are Bobby and Ric really going to take-on the whole Belmont football squad? One of the jerks in front pushes me, another tries to trip me. I push back.

Oh, boy - here we go again...

No. Ric begins thumping. Gene and Steven follow the cue. They all begin rhythmically, hypnotically, hammering on a single, pounding power chord.

Cymbals crash and I turn. Huh? I'm surprised to see Dueg Provost behind me - playing Bobby's drum set.

I wonder where Bobby went?

And what about Cool Gene? He's gone too.

Steven signals Dueg as another galoot grabs me by the hair. Dueg gets a good footstomp going. Glancing right, I see Jeff Thomas slipping the strap of Ric's Fender bass over his shoulder. Now Steven disappears. Untangling myself from the grip of the big ape, I manage to roll away.

The song continues and the Belmont team, loaded to the gills, are baffled.

Later, back in Natick, Jeff Thomas tells us that none of the toughs seemed to comprehend "the old switcheroo" we just pulled on them. Fortunately for Slash, their group doesn't seem to release the same "who wants to fight me?" combative endorphins that I apparently do. Slash carried on with the dance and after Thundertrain vanished into thin air, nobody wanted to brawl anymore.

The following night, Thundertrain rolls into Monson, out near Springfield MA.

No gymnasium floor this time, we're set up on the auditorium stage at the high school. Same set as usual, same stage gear, same clothes. Nearing the midway point of the Thundertrain show I see a few of the girls begin to wiggle and giggle. Getting a bit over-excited. Minutes later, kids begin hurling themselves up onto the stage. A group of them go after Cool Gene. Another one wants Bobby. Steven has a flock of chicks tearing off his clothes. What the hell? We've never experienced mania like this. Even more kids, mostly girls but some boys too, are suddenly overcome by the wilding. They all go nuts too. I'm just trying to keep my pants on.

THUNDERTRAIN Mach & Steven. Photos by Lynn Ciulla

Mick and Jon push back the teeny-bopper tide to no
avail. Just like last night, there is zero security. No
authority figure to be seen. So we run for our lives.
Ric and Gene get cornered by a gang of screaming
sophomores in a locker room.
The rest of us escape, hiding in the stalls of the boys
restroom. That doesn't stop the frisky freshmen femmes.
They shove their way into our hideout, boost each other
over the stall-walls.
Gushing, screaming and grabbing at us.

We surrender.

Weird thing is, now that they've finally captured us,
what's a mob of confused 14 year-olds gonna do with us?
Nobody has a clue.
Sobbing, they slowly release their tiny grips and retreat.
Thundertrain makes it out of Monson alive. Gear intact.
Bruised, our stage clothes are in tatters.
But it was worth it.

{ 17 }

Hot For Teacher and Wooden Charlie
Bobby Edwards plays like a demon every night. Thundertrain is the main attraction for the crowds out front - but most evenings, Bobby stars in a sideshow of his very own.

Fedge, Bill Dill and their fellow drummers cluster by the side-stage. Carefully studying every flam, kick, splash and thump Edwards makes.

The lone athlete in our band, Bobby was a star baseball player at school and he's a lifelong Celtics basketball fan. Bobby's achilles heel is his near blindness. I don't think he ever wore eyeglasses but he owns some sort of contact lenses that he's perpetually in search of. How a guy with such poor vision can hit and field a baseball is a mystery. My theory is he developed lightning fast reflexes in order to cope with his disability. Once the ball finally became visible, inches away, Bobby would instantaneously smack or snag it.

The same trigger reflexes he uses to propel and punctuate our Thundertrain songs.

Bobby's other less-hidden talent is his growing-into-legendary schlong. I shouldn't really know much about this topic - except Bobby is quick to lose his pants whenever he isn't working behind the drums.

"Oh. Hi there, Mary. How are you tonight, Kathye? Don't mind me. My pants keep getting soaked...I have to wring them out."

If you think his drums are big, wait til you see his organ.
Photo by Lynn Ciulla

Christmastime 1975. Thundertrain is opening for Black
Sheep at the Mohawk, a big nightclub near Fort Devens
in Shirley. I don't know much about the headline band
except they come from upstate New York, they're signed
to Capitol Records and they just played in Boston the
other night, opening for that new band Bobby keeps
going on about, KISS.
We deliver another solid show and stick around to watch
Black Sheep. They have a good, churning, rock sound.
Built around a Hammond B3 and a singer with an

impressive anglo-voice and very frizzy hair. My
goldilocks look almost tame in comparison. Anyway,
after checking out their pro-sounding set, we're amazed
when the Mohawk management gives them a thumbs
down. Black Sheep are given the old *heave ho.*
The owner asks Thundertrain to remain and fulfill the
rest of the weekend entertainment duties.
Dejected, the Black Sheep crew tears down the gear.
I offer a few words of encouragement to their singer. He's
pretty good. He didn't deserve to get fired.
Just before they split, he tells me his name is Lou Gramm.

Thundertrain's reputation for hell raising spreads.
We display virtuosity when it comes to creating chaos.
A violent, piano-smashing riot at Marblehead high
school. Then, during another Thundertrain riot, a fan
gets flattened by a car leaving the parking lot at the Echo
Ballroom. Witnesses claim they saw a Thundertrain
member behind the wheel of the fleeing vehicle...

I keep finding myself at the wrong end of a gun barrel.
First, in Newport RI. The culmination of a weeklong
feud between the proprietor of a joint called Bourbon
Street, and yours truly.
"Too loud. Play some Aerosmith. blah,blah,blah."
Things worsen when Ric peers out the band house
window and sees someone stealing our truck battery.
Then some of Steven's cash goes missing. Turns out to
be an inside job. The thief is the club owner's flunkie.
On the final day of the Bourbon Street engagement, Ric
and I trash the band house. There's already plenty of

holes in every wall of this teardown - so Ric decides to make use of them. Returning from the bait shop at nearby Newport Harbor, our bassist stuffs chopped-off fish heads into all the wall cavities.

I can't top that. But I find a nearly-full jar of honey in the moldy fridge. I drip the sticky stuff up & down the staircase. House flies are swarming the place - so we beat it. Stopping at Bourbon Street, just to play the final five sets as contracted. As we finish the final song, the thieving flunky runs into the club, breathless.

"*They* did it. Thundertrain! They wrecked everything. They destroyed the whole band house!"

The boss stampedes out of his office. He stands on the dance floor, red in the face, finger-pointing and screaming accusations. I can't see the guy, because I'm standing center stage while the crew hurriedly shoves our gear down the back stairs. The stage lights are full, shining in my eyes. I can't make out the irate club owner. But I sure can hear him.

I retaliate. Berating the bum and his thieving toadie. I call them a bunch of filthy names. The rhetoric ramps up fast. We're both spitting mad.

Jon is trying to get my attention:

"Cool it, man. He's holding a gun on you."

What? I don't understand what the sound man is trying to tell me, so I continue barking rudely at the silhouette. Steven barges past me, tugs my arm and finally - as I stumble out of the focused par lamp beam - I see...

"*Shit.*"

The A-hole has a handgun pointed right at my melon.
Cleverly passing in front of me as they hoist some of the
largest gear off the stage, the Thundertrain crew play
"the old switcheroo" on pistol pete. They run
interference while I dodge through the backdoor and fall
down the staircase. Steven's already got his Mustang
revving. We burn rubber back to the state line.

Weeks later, Thundertrain is in Rutland Vermont,
playing the 19th Green nightclub. Completing the first
night of the weeklong engagement. We have to drive a
couple miles to the bad side of town where this week's
band house is located. The pay at most of these night
spots is so meager there's nothing left over for a motel
room.The club owners entice groups by offering free
housing in these grubby shacks.

It's around 3 a.m. when we finally find the lousy cabin.
"Damnit. Who's got the key?"
We all scrounge around, searching for the house key we
were given - to no avail.
"C'mon guys, check the windows."
Thundertrain piles out, inching our way through the
darkness, hoping to find one of the double-hung
windows left ajar.
"Hey. I got one."
I call to the others as I lift the heavy sash open.
I'm going in. Head first, into the unlit room.
My hands land on sticky linoleum. I wriggle my butt
over the sill.
Wham.

I feel cold steel. Pushed hard against my forehead.

"*Freeze.*"
Move one muscle and I'll blow your face off."
I'm halfway-inside, halfway-out, my ass is somewhere
in-between and suddenly I have a shotgun barrel
mashed against my forehead.

"Who are ye? State yer business but make it fast."

Ric runs over, introducing himself and the rest of us,
"We're the band. Thundertrain. We're supposed to be
staying here - but we lost our key."
I feel the gun pull away, the rifle barrel comes into view as
it lowers... and I finally find the nerve to look up.
My assailant is a cross between Aqualung and a garden
gnome. Toothless, bewhiskered, stubby and stinky.
I guess the little goblin comes with the property. Like a
hotel concierge. The rest of the band enter and flick on the
lights as I clamber to my feet. Rumpelstiltskin shoulders
his firearm. He's looks us over - very carefully.
Each one of us. Up & down. He licks the sores on his lips.

"Thundertrain, eh?
Hee-hee. I'll Thundertrain you boys!
Oh *yes* I *will*. Hee-hee."

Thundertrain welcomes 1976 by hosting our own New
Year's Party at the Stadium. We charge five bucks a head
and order a bunch of pizza and some cases of cheap
champagne. We're onstage, blasting through Let'er Rip, a

new bottleneck-barn-burner as the packed house begins to loosen up.

A proud looking guy, jumping forward from the crowd, presents Ric with a gift-wrapped box. Provost rips open his present and out pops a lengthy, crudely carved dildo.

"I made him for you guys. In shop class." beams the fan.

Ric is howling. Our bass-player loves his new toy and names it Wooden Charlie. Curious women on the dance floor can't wait to get their hands on splintery ol' Charlie. The knobby chap gets passed all around the Stadium. Charlie's almost as popular as the Thundertrain bomb.

Mach at the Thundertrain Mansion. Photo by Lynn Ciulla

Lynn is leaving our apartment for work when she catches wind that the downstairs tenant of the farmhouse is moving away. Vacating the ground floor. Crafty Ric applies for the downstairs apartment and ends up with the keys and a lease. Now, with the entire building fully in our possession, the farmhouse is re-named the Thundertrain Mansion (495 Old Connecticut Path, Framingham). Mick and Ric move into the downstairs bedrooms, the living room becomes our practice space. There's plenty of room to park the Thundertrain truck over by the covered porch. A large box truck, complete with a sleeper compartment. We bought it used, from a local sound company. Owning our own truck means freedom from shady Joe's early morning table & chair collection duties.

Bobby Edwards keeps fit at the Thundertrain Mansion.
Photo by Lynn Ciulla

The band meets with Bill Riseman back at Northern
Studios. We ask proprietor Riseman to recommend an
experienced producer to help us make the next single.
A couple days later we return to Northern.
The band is ushered into a backroom.
Here, waiting for us, are Nighthawk Jackson and
Earthquake Morton.
It takes me a few minutes to place the familiar looking
Earthquake - I finally recognize him as the singing bassist
from Duke and the Drivers.

THUNDERTRAIN 1976 with our Jelly Records production team.
Ric, Mach, Earthquake Morton (top), Nighthawk Jackson (below EQ),
Steven, Bobby and Cool Gene. Photo by AnneMarie Martins

Nighthawk turns out to be the younger brother of Drivers
leader Joe Lilly (aka Sam Deluxe), lead singer/guitarist on
the Driver's hit song, What You've Got.

Next day, James Isaacs, the columnist for the widely-read
Boston Phoenix weekly, recommends the ongoing Tuesday
night session featuring Mickey Clean and the Mezz.
They're performing at, of all places, the boring old
Rathskeller. *Really?* I gotta see this for myself.

Not many people here tonight.
It doesn't surprise me. The Mezz are onstage in their street
clothes. Small amps, zero production. The drum kit isn't
impressive like Bobby's. But I have to admit that Mezz
drummer, Howie Ferguson, is a natural.
Guitar player, Asa Brebner, isn't flashy either - he's just
good. The bassist, they call him Swine, doesn't look like a
farm animal, and he's really good too.
Overshadowing everything else is frontman Mickey Clean.
A cross between Jagger and Tom Terrific, he's dressed like
Soupy Sales. Clean's got wet lips, pop-out eyes, too many
teeth and a flip-flop of thick black hair.
No cover songs, no "remember to tip your waitress" crap,
no illusions of grandeur, forget about a drum solo.
Just a trio of cats rumbling while weightless Mickey floats
around the stage, rattling off stream-of-conciousness-
sounding tales about drifting and hillside walking. I can't
put my finger on why I dig it so much.

A few songs deeper, an even skinnier guy with a jack-o-
lantern grin and a rockstar haircut hops onto the
Rathskeller stage. His button-down shirt is open and I see
something scrawled in magic marker across his sunken
chest. He steps behind a well-stickered, electric keyboard.

The Mezz shifts gears as the keyboard man - he plays while standing up - sings his latest single, "Mass Ave."
This must be Willie "Loco" Alexander.

Willie Loco Alexander. Photo by AnneMarie Martins

Isaacs often writes about Loco in his essential Cellars By Starlight weekly column. Singer, songwriter, pianist. Willie is ten years my senior and he's done it all.

Willie's band, The Lost (Violet Gown, Everybody Knows) were stars of the mid-60's New England Teen Scene. Rocking the Surf Ballrooms and the original Boston Tea Party. Willie Loco was part of the "Bosstown Sound" blitz too. Singing and playing with the 10-man band, Bagatelle (ABC Records). Willie even tours Europe in Velvet Underground's final line-up.

Willie's charisma spills off the stage as the Mezz vibrate the walls. I'll never forget it.

May 16th. In New York City, Columbia Records releases the fourth Aerosmith album. They call this one "Rocks." Meanwhile, back at the Thundertrain Mansion, we're burning through our setlist. Nighthawk and Earthquake are both here too. Listening carefully, trying to pick a potential hit song.

Steven's lyrics don't always portray women in the best light. Of course I'm the one stuck singing most of Steven's audacious lyrics. The protagonist in Silva's ditties is either a peeping tom or some other perpetually horny dude, suffering from terminal blue balls. The women in Steven's oeuvre are either teasin'(I'm So Excited) cheatin'(Cheater) or leavin' the hero (me) behind, in favor of female companionship (Modern Girls).

Cool Gene, the Slade fan, prefers writing about teen rebellion: Hell Tonite, Readin'Riotin'Rock'n'Roll. Sometimes Cool even writes something mentioning the word "love" and the first number earning a thumbs-up from our production team is Cool Gene's *Love the Way (You Love Me).*

"What else ya got?" rumbles Earthquake after judging a
dozen of Thundertrain's original compositions.
Steven looks down,
"Well...I'm still working on this one... let's give it a shot."
By the time Thundertrain hits the first chorus, it's obvious.
Both producers are grinning.
The power tubes of the Marshall stacks haven't even
cooled down and Earthquake is already on the phone.
Booking studio time.

I think Willie Alexander's rollin' piano would sound great
on the new tunes we're about to cut. Alexander is the real
deal and his participation might even help Thundertrain
gain an ounce of credibility on the Boston scene.
Soon we're all in the studio, running through the changes
of Silva's latest gem. He calls it "Hot For Teacher."
Willie Alexander is taken aback at all the chord changes.
Steven's masterpiece, which brings to mind a Chuck Berry-
style rocker, is more complex than it sounds.

"So Willie, do you know your part?"
Willie: "Well, when I re-recorded the tape ya gave me, it
kind of slowed down to an F# and I haven't heard the
other song yet...and hey, I got an idea! Why don't you
punch me in the head to signal the chord changes?"
"Punch you in the head?"
Willie: "Yeah! It'll be a ga-ga effect on the 45."

We spend the first day cutting the Hot For Teacher rhythm
tracks and Loco turns-in a smashing performance. Steven

manages to fry both studio amplifiers after his own
Marshall 100 blows-up during the three-day session.
Bobby gets really upset when the producers advise him to
simplify the drum parts. Edwards opens the song with his
Ludwig Super Sensitive snare drum, executing a perfect
press roll. He peppers the number with palpitating bass-
pedal accents and ricochet-cymbal/tom embellishments.
Nighthawk shakes his head.

"Look, Bobby. You're a great live performer. All that showy
jazz works great on stage but you gotta tighten it up for the
record. Lose the cymbals and cut the kick beats in half.
Keep it simple. Chop wood on the snare and hi-hat."

Drama erupts. Bobby throws down his drum sticks. He
stomps out of the studio. Edwards races down the rusty
fire escape and bolts across the parking lot. Fleeing into
the night, cursing Nighthawk as he runs away.

About an hour later Mick and Jon finally locate the
disgruntled drummer. Back at Northern studio, Bobby
bites his lip and plays it their way.

Years later Bobby admits this track might be his best
sounding studio performance.

"Nighthawk was right."

During the session, I learn that Willie Loco has a new
single in the can, but no funds to press the thing.

Days later, Lynn Ciulla, Miss Lyn and I begin organizing a
"Boomland Benefit," hoping to raise funds so the new
Willie Loco record can be released.

Artist, Miss Lyn has taken over as editor of the Boston
Groupie News. A scandalous, typewritten one-sheet. The
BGN makes its first appearance one night in 1976, left on
the table tops of the Rat
Published anonymously.
When the eagerly awaited second issue of the Groupie
News fails to materialize, Miss Lyn takes matters into her
own hands. She writes Issue #2, she Copy Cops it and she
distributes it for free.
Thundertrain publishes our own free monthly "Photo-
Mag" that gets sent to our mailing list and handed out at
shows. Richard Nolan, Jon Macey, Marc Thor and Willie
Alexander distribute similar newsletters but Miss Lyn's
Groupie News leads the way, binding a disparate group of
"new wave" underground Boston rockers together.

Steven Silva is butt gazing. A beauteous brunette peels off
her flimsy panties. She toes the garment, flipping it across
the runway, over to where the guitarist is seated.
The peeler gives Steven the green light wink. Silva thinks
he's getting lucky but it's bad news for Thundertrain.
The bar owner is jealous. He's got his eye on the same
brunette and he wants her all for himself.
The rest of us are upstairs on break at the Three
Coppermen, a dual level nightspot in Lowell MA with non-
stop, rock'n'roll showbands upstairs while a bouncy T&A
exhibition grinds downstairs. Another five nighter for TT.
We'll be dispensing endless hours of penetrating rock each
evening and the owner already doesn't care for us.

We're here to make Mansion-rent and focus on new original material, we don't need any trouble.

We trick the audience by opening up with something they all know, tonight its Rock and Roll, from the untitled third Led Zeppelin album. Once we see a few couples glide onto the dance floor we segue into Cool Gene's new one, Hell Tonite or Steven's latest, Frustration. Bobby keeps the dance-beat groovin' and more dancers join in. We run-our-original-songs-into-each-other, in an attempt to keep the party on the floor rolling. Sometimes it works.

The sadistic club owner has everything timed perfectly. Steven's stripper only gets a break when Silva is busy rocking the upstairs. Just before Steven finishes his set, the boss puts the peach back on the downstairs stage to remove her clothes again.

I'm diverted from Steven's cock-blocked romance when I notice a slightly older, ruddy-faced dude sitting at the bar. He's wearing a Red Sox cap and he motions for me to join him. The guy introduces himself as Jim Harold.

Smiling, he hands me a cold beer.

"Those songs you guys just played, you wrote those, right?" I admit that we prefer playing our own stuff.

"Your band would be a perfect fit for my room down in Boston."

Okay, this is really weird. I'm usually arguing, or simply avoiding, these club owner guys. They're always hounding me to turn down or play some Aerosmith songs. Just last month, Frank Borsa and Thundertrain had to drag an Ipswich nightclub owner into small claims court after he refused to pay the $900 he promised us for four nights of

218

work. "They didn't play good songs" is his defense (we won).

"You run a rock club?" I squint.

"Yeah, I own the Rathskeller in Kenmore Square. These stage lights. Yours? And the sound system too?"

I nod. Jim smiles, and says

"We're gonna do some business together."

The Boston Phoenix, June 1, 1976

Cellars By Starlight by James Isaacs

Turning to the younger set, the hard rock band Thundertrain, the first nouveau outfit to be signed to a Jelly Records contract, encountered a few small snafus while waxing their debut single, "Hot For Teacher." Seems the group aspired to open the number with the familiar sound of a school bell, but finding one that was still in use nowadays was no simple task.

Train member Mach Bell (the surname is legit) and producer Greg Morton set up portable recording equipment and then lingered awhile in a hall at Framingham North H.S. After proving to a monitor that they did not require a special pass (the pair faced compulsory study hall), they were informed that the F.N.H.S. bells had gone the way of the Thom McAn Snap-jack shoe. Undaunted, Bell and Morton headed up the road for Cameron Junior High, where the principal told them in no uncertain terms that his bells were computerized and did not sound on Wednesdays. Taking matters into their own hands, they bribed a janitor with free records for his kids and the cooperative custodian disengaged the computer tapes and rang 'dem bells.

The pupils, surprised and bewildered, scurried out of their classrooms, assuming that a fire drill was taking place.

Among the first to air "Hot For Teacher/Love the Way" is a character named Oedipus. I think he's a couple years younger than me. Oedi is an extremely articulate rock fan with an ear for new sounds.

Oedipus 1976   Photo by AnneMarie Martins

There's this new wave coming out of NYC right now.
Blondie, Television, Wayne County, The Shirts, Richard
Hell, Mink De Ville, the Heartbreakers, the Ramones.
Oedipus spins their rarely heard records on his WTBS (the
MIT station where Joe Flash '71 recorded) Demi Monde
radio show.

Foppish, but very friendly, Oedipus gets rides from
AnneMarie, traveling to some of Thundertrain's local high
school and club shows where he enjoys doing our stage
introductions. Oedipus promotes our new record to the
young audiences and talks-up his edgy little college radio
show in the process.

A record he's spinning a lot right now is an Atlantic
Records compilation of Manhattan bands called
"Live at CBGB's."

Maxanne plays our new single "Hot For Teacher" every
day during her late afternoon shift at WBCN. We hear it on
our drive out to coastal Marshfield. Thundertrain is
playing the Ranch House tonight. A rustic road house with
a big dance floor, right up the lane from Green Harbor
beach.

A few hours later, we're on break when the stage manager
we just hired, a cool kid named Jimbo, runs backstage to
hand me a note:

"Care to buy a girl a drink?" It's signed Maxanne.
"She's here?"

I peek through the doorway and Jimbo points her out.
Grabbing an empty chair beside the star DJ, I thank her
for helping us and...sort of run...out of things to say...
I'm not connecting with Maxanne the way I did in my
dreams.

Bam. Steven plops down at the table and scores quickly. The radio personality goes all gushy. Now that my lead guitarist and Maxanne are hitting it off, I slink away.

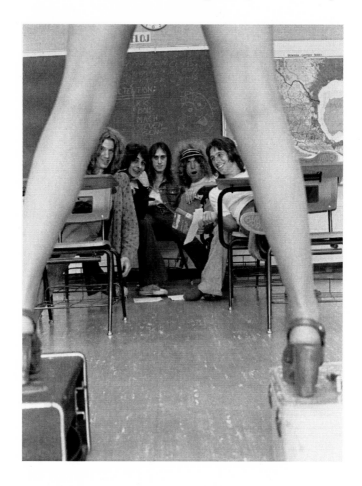

Walnut Hill School, Natick MA 1976. Thundertrain briefly used this classroom as a rehearsal space. The perfect setting for the "Hot For Teacher" 45 sleeve, photo session. Cool Gene's girlfriend played the teacher. We had to prop her up on amps in order to get the proper camera angles. Photo by Lynn Ciulla

On Sunday, July 11th, Manhattan's Max's Kansas City (213 Park Ave. South at 17th Street) features a Boston bill of Willie Loco Alexander & the Boom Boom Band paired with Reddy Teddy. As far as I know, they're the first from the 1976 crop of original "new wave" Rat bands to play the famed New York showcase.

On July 20th, Maxanne Sartori, Phoenix columnist James Isaacs and WTBS DJ Oedipus join me on the stage of The Club, hosting a bill that includes about-to-be-signed rockers The Atlantics, garage-rockers DMZ, wasted-looking Marc Thor, Third Rail (fronted by real-life mortician Richard Nolan), popular Boston DIY recording stars Fox Pass and rock writer Deborah Frost's profane punk-group the Bloody Virgins.

The Club,
832 Main St.
Cambridge MA

The Club, with two bars, a large dance floor and two levels of seating, boasts a slightly larger capacity than the Rathskeller. Maxanne and Oedipus do an excellent job getting word out over the Boston airwaves.

The Boomland Benefit is packed. A huge success.

7/20/1976 The Club, Cambridge. Oedipus, Maxanne and Mach at the "Boomland Benefit." Photos by Lynn Ciulla

THUNDERTRAIN at The Club in Cambridge

The $700 raised is enough for Willie to pay what he owes the recording studio and get the new record pressed. Closing tonight's festivities are the "Hot For Teacher" boys themselves. A packed house of urban dwellers gets to experience Thundertrain for the first time.

Green Circles by Jim Green Trouser Press Oct/Nov 1976
"Hot for Teacher" b/w "Love the Way" -
Thundertrain - Jelly JR 003
Could it be that Beantown's gonna cop the crown of
Energy Central from Motown? If one thing characterized
Reddy Teddy and Willie Alexander when I saw them live,
it was their high energy, and these guys have it in spades.
Both sides, particularly the B, with its MC5 voltage are
hot. "Love" has a tight, snappy arrangement, plus
smokin' solos and savage vocals, displaying a lot of
potential. Professionally recorded, too.

Three Minute Mania by David Barton
Rock - N - Roll News 9/3/76
WAHHAHGAHHH!! Rock'n'Roll!! Finally, its the
American Slade (and they don't wear funny leather bat
suits), roaring out of Massachusetts with two burning
sides of hot licks rock and roll, complete with blistering
lead guitar and screaming Noddy Holder vocals that give
the King of Screams a run for his money. Lead guitarist
Steven Silva's "Hot For Teacher" complete with clanging
recess bell at the outset, is standard rock fare about
Teacher teaching some things that weren't mentioned in
the catalog, but the delivery is a bit above average, high-
strung rock'n'roll that'll either have you writhing in
ecstasy or shrieking in pain.

Gossip. That's all it is. I hope.

Thundertrain is on Nantucket Island. We're playing a week
of shows at Preston's. Out by the airstrip. When we're not
rocking the tourists, we're living out back in a converted
henhouse surrounded by beach grass. Mick jumps off his
bunk to take a morning stroll. I flop around on my sweaty
pillow, stewing.

According to various sources, Steven Silva is looking to
jump ship. Our guitarist is trying to land a position playing
in Rick Derringer's touring band.

"I heard him at the Ranch House, that's what Steven was
talking about with Maxanne." claims one witness.

"At the Buttercup. I saw Steven on the phone. Trying to set
up an audition with Derringer." whispers another spy.

Our lighting tech returns from his hike, his legs dotted with blood sucking arachnids. From this day forward I call him Mick the Tick.

THUNDERTRAIN at the Rat '76. Photo by Lynn Ciulla

Thundertrain makes our "real" Rathskeller debut on Labor Day Weekend '76. Billed alongside a British/American power trio called Buck. They have an impressive line-up. Singer/songwriter/bassist Jamie Pease, a local guy, comes from Jon Butcher's popular club band, Johanna Wild. Drummer Mick Hough of Derby, England, is from a band called Flash. Steve Forest, a native of St. Albans, England, played lead guitar on the debut album of a major Thundertrain influence...Michael Des Barres' *Silverhead*.

Cool Gene Provost at the Rat. Labor Day Weekend 1976.
Photo by Lynn Ciulla

Before we finish our opening song - Chuck Berry's Around
and Round - the dance floor of the Rat is jammed. Mary
and Kathye are here. I see Pam Green, Eddie, Oedi,
AnneMarie, Earthquake, Lynn Ciulla and Miss Lyn...
Besides my Eddie Kent trousers, another Thundertrain
secret weapon is the robust hometown support we receive
from loudmouths Fedge and Bill Dill.

Both are drummers and both are fanatical when it comes to spreading the gospel about Bobby Edwards. They love Bobby and they aren't afraid to shout it out loud.

Steven's "Frustration" opens with lifting power chords that modulate higher as I snarl Silva's hand-wringing lyrics "Why does life treat me - so unkind?"
Cool Gene's "Love the Way" and my "Cindy is a Sleeper" are up next. Jim Harold beams from the back wall, watching his patrons erupt with shouts and sustained applause. I see the blonde bouncer, Dougie, strumming an air guitar during Steven's solo on Cindy.
During break I meet a sassy, shapely chick named Barb Kitson and an enraptured, bespectacled teenager named Eric Law. I meet lots of new kids, leaving me little chance to study the other band. When Buck finishes their second set we dash back out to finish the night.

The Rat is sweltering and full of cigarette smoke. The john in the men's room is clogged and a river of dirty water cascades from the bowl, soaking the bathroom floor and flowing out into the club.
No one cares.
Cool Gene's anthem "Hell Tonite" dials up the temperature further and by the time Steven and Ric dive into Hot For Teacher the place is generating steam heat. Our single is getting so much airplay this summer, it's a weird sensation opening my mouth and sounding exactly like the guy I hear everyday on WBCN. Wow.

Earthquake and I return to Northern Studios frequently to cut radio spots for upcoming Thundertrain concerts. I'm lucky to be in the control room during load-in for a "Live from Northern" in-studio concert that will be broadcast over a network of stations like WBCN.

I'm not familiar with this band, a progressive rock outfit from West Virginia called Crack the Sky.

I stick around for the show and they sound phenomenal. I'm even invited back for the next broadcast, featuring an artist I know a lot better, Tommy Bolin.

Tommy's group rocks for me and a couple dozen onlookers. He's promoting his newest solo record, Private Eyes. An inspiring set, but unfortunately it's the final time I'll see Tommy alive. The rising star will die at age 25 this December, while on tour with Jeff Beck.

Jim Harold decides to answer "Live at CBGBs" with a live record of his own. Following dates in Portsmouth NH and Bridgeport CT, Thundertrain returns to the Rat in September. We rock a multi-band "recording benefit" show on Sunday Sept. 26th and return on Wednesday the 29th to cut tracks in front of a live audience.

Harold takes whatever seed money he's got and combines it with the proceeds from the Sunday night benefit. It's enough to bring in a mobile recording truck. Eastern Sound from Methuen parks their studio out in front on Commonwealth Ave. The mobile is equipped with a 16 track mixing board and an Ampex 2" multi-track tape machine. Engineers run heavy snake-lines of cable from the truck, across the half-court-wide sidewalk and down the long staircase that leads to our cellarful of noise.

Eastern Sound mobile studio parked in front of 528 Comm. Ave.
Photo by Lynn Ciulla

The ten groups chosen for the record play an energetic brand of music. The Rat recipe varies but I think it boils down to a mix of punk, glam and rock'n'roll.

The Kids, who we gigged with last year in Natick, are now called The Real Kids. Low on glam, heavy on rock'n'roll, served raw with punk attitude.

DMZ are a more glamorous bunch with equal shots of punk and rock'n'roll folded into the batter. DMZ drummer David Robinson is another graduate of Jonathan Richman's group, the Modern Lovers.

Marc Thor provides some Warhol-esque, wasted decadence to the affair. Thor recruits a backing band for tonight's recording session, borrowing Thundertrain's Steven Silva and most of DMZ.

Also scoring points in the punk-rock department is undertaker Richard Nolan and his deviate looking Third Rail. Back on the glam side, we have lead vocalist Lee Ritter of The Infliktors. Ritter is blessed with sharply-chiseled facial features and his band rocks hard enough that Aerosmith's Steven Tyler occasionally joins-in when The Infliktors visit the Rat, adding his famous voice to their Kinks cover, Milk Cow Blues.

Another straight ahead rock'n'roll outfit is helmed by good guy Billy Connors. The Boize are on the younger side, they have a devilish look and a promising sound.

Ric Ocasek tries hard to get his band, Cap'n Swing, included on this recording but David Robinson (DMZ) is the lone future Car to make the cut.

Singer/writer Jon Macey, currently zeroing in on a major label deal for his group Fox Pass, turns Jim's offer down. So do Reddy Teddy, perpetually on the edge of breaking through to the mainstream. On Wednesday night (9/29/76) the recording begins and it will take several nights. Up first is Mickey Clean and the Mezz, followed by DMZ and Thundertrain. We brought our own producers, Nighthawk and Earthquake, they're out in the truck along with veteran rock engineer, Jesse Henderson. Each band is allowed 45 minutes to record in front of the live audience. No time for sound adjustments or playbacks. Hopefully the team out in the mobile will remember to hit the record button

Recording Live at the Rat. Mickey Clean, Mach Bell,
Mono Mann and Jay Jay Rassler.
Frenzy Magazine Archive

Jim Harold, owner of the Rat.

The first concert he ever attended was
Chuck Berry. Jim knows the good stuff
when he hears it.

Photo by Lynn Ciulla

Live at the Rat recording. September 1976. In the Eastern Sound
mobile. Back row: Ric, Mach, Steven, Bobby & Cool Gene of
THUNDERTRAIN. Front row: Nighthawk Jackson, Jesse Henderson
and Earthquake Morton. Photos by Lynn Ciulla

Steven Silva & Boston Groupie News
editor Miss Lyn at the Rat '76.

Mach and Earthquake Morton 1976. Photo by Lynn Ciulla
Courtesy of the Mark V. Perkins Archive.

{ 18 }

Thirty Days in Billerica House of Correction Yeah. It's me. Locked in a jail cell. Yup, I did it again. It's 2 am. Fluorescent lights are blazing and buzzing. I'm propped up, half-naked, crouched on this hard, cold, steel shelf that's allegedly a bed. In the distance I can hear police officers talking loudly, occasionally bursting into laughter. How'd I end up here? Could this really be happening?

48 hours after recording our contribution to Live at the Rat, Thundertrain arrives at our most anticipated concert yet. The October 1st date at Framingham South High is unlike any high school dance we've ever played.

Sold out. Way in advance. The tickets have been scalped to Thundertrain fans in Natick, Holliston, Boston...everyone wants to find a way inside. The drop-off area out front is packed with students, all hoping to score a ticket, or just hear a bit of our concert waft through an open vent shaft. Tonight's warm-up band is forced to quit mid-song when a dozen fans are discovered hiding atop the high school roof, peering down through skylights, hoping to catch sight of Thundertrain. The trespassers are removed from the rooftop and the red-faced Framingham principal has already had it up to *here* - and Thundertrain hasn't even begun playing yet.

I'm oblivious to all the rising emotion and commotion going on outside, inside and above. I'm sitting here peacefully, in our tranquil dressing room, a utility room halfway between the front lobby and the grand rock venue we're set to perform in, I think they call it the cafeteria.

Right now I'm half-dressed and half-glammed, rubbing some gunk on my eyelids. Whoops, I just remembered, Lynn is supposed to be here taking photos. I gotta go out front and make sure she makes it inside. As I leave to check on her, Bobby shouts,

"Keep an eye out for Pam, she left work a few minutes ago."

I pull on a shirt, wrap a towel 'round my neck and exit our dressing room. The hallway is a traffic jam. Kids are pushing toward the stage area, so I salmon - the wrong-way up the corridor - against the teenage tide. There's a barricade spanning the lobby with three different ticket takers, slowly allowing the excited customers inside.

I notice some older people, teachers, monitoring the box office activity. Scanning the horizon, I don't see Lynn but I suddenly spy Bobby's girlfriend, Pam, over at the last ticket booth. Moving her way, I can hear her speaking politely, trying to explain that she's with the band.

The ticket person scowls at her dubiously. That's when the hero, me, swoops in. Taking Pam by the wing, I guide her briskly past the ticket taker, escorting her toward our dressing area. Truthfully, that is how I recall the moment, although I'll admit the joint is packed and I might have rubbed elbows with somebody as I zoomed back to the safety of the Thundertrain dressing room with Bobby's girl.

238

I get back to work, doing final adjustments on my outfit, hair and cheap stage jewelry. The opening band's been off for a while now. Jimbo should be back here any minute to lead us to the stage...wait, that must be him now. The dressing room door bursts open and three policemen barge inside. Followed by the high school principal.

"That's him. Right over there. The blonde one. Arrest that man."

I'm doubled-over, arms stretched behind my back, wrists thrust into cuffs, crunched-down tight, tearing my skin. The patrol men prod and yank me out of the Thundertrain dressing room and push me down the high school corridor. It's hard to keep my balance. Children lean in for a better look. Like the Hunchback of Notre Dame in chains, I'm being trotted through the village square. The principal flutters around my captors, shouting allegations,

"I saw everything. He's an animal. He attacked one of my faculty members. He broke her arm."

Teenagers are plastered against the hallway lockers, gawking in disbelief. One by one they realize it's the lead singer of Thundertrain being hauled away. An officer keeps shoving my head down, so I can't really focus very well, but I can see enough. A hundred kids are standing out front in the turnaround as I emerge from the high school. The police herd me, full speed ahead. The Chief arrives. Sirens shriek as additional muscle shows up, the flashing-blues illuminate the faces of the inquisitive kids, now pouring from the building, hoping to witness the drama for themselves. The roundup pauses while an officer reads me my rights. Once again, I'm being arrested on assault and battery charges. The lead officer gives me a hard shove and I smack my noggin against the door jam before collapsing on the backseat of the police cruiser.

Silver-sheeny, Eddie Kent pants dangle extra low on my hip bone as lawmen circle round me in a back room of the derelict Framingham police station. Wrists still lashed behind my back, there's not much I can do about my descending trousers. Chief Martins interrogates me while another officer scrawls my responses onto a booking sheet. Behind me, a team of patrolmen carefully comb through my gig bag. So far, they're just holding me on an assault and battery rap - surely they can up the charges to include narcotics possession too.

"What's your occupation?" Demands Chief Martins.

I point to a Hot For Teacher single. One of the policemen just found it in my bag and threw it on the floor.

"I'm a rock singer. That's my new record."

The chief looks down and instructs the note taker, *"Unemployed."*

The officers moods begin to sour. At first they were laughing in my face, pointing at traces of fingernail polish and the Kohl eye goop I wear under stage-lighting. Not to mention my skin-rippin-tight attire. Sniffing the lining of my empty gig bag, these protectors of the peace are getting seriously pissed-off.

"Why would a guy go out in public, dressed like a broad?

"He must be high on speed or LSD. That's his only excuse... unless he's just a fag."

In disgust, the policemen prod me down a long hallway. Am I about to get my ass beaten by this gang of he-men? Relief comes when instead, they release the handcuffs, shove me into an empty cell, slam the door and turn the key.

At dawn I'm released into the custody of Ric Provost. My hearing is set for October 26th, twenty-five days from now. A few hours later I'm back at work, in another high school. King Phillip in Wrentham. Thundertrain is headlining here tonight and I do the show, absolutely traumatized and terrified after what happened to me last night. And what lies ahead.

Tables have turned, a couple months ago I was running a benefit for my friend Willie Alexander. It's October 13th and Thundertrain is back at the Rat tonight, playing a benefit to raise money for my own legal defense. Props to Bobby Dee, the kid loves Thundertrain and he loves WWF Wrestling. He personally throws $100 into the hat. After the legal fund benefit, we hit the road, playing back-to-back weekends in Mattapoisett MA and yet another high school in South Attleboro.

I'm beside myself with fear as the court date looms. Jail sucked, but serving a prison term, trying to survive amongst the general population, could be a tough road for this little blonde. My lawyer claims he's spoken with the teacher. The woman I supposedly assaulted. She remembers some minor contact as I rushed by her. The teacher is prepared to testify that absolutely no harm was done, it was all just a big misunderstanding. That's a relief but I don't trust the Framingham authorities. The last time I visited the District Courthouse, my dad and I were treated to a bribe attempt by the judge.

Five days prior to my court appearance, Thundertrain returns to Northern Studios for a few hours, running through a bunch of songs in the big room. Our producers record the set, hoping to zoom in on a candidate for a Hot For Teacher follow-up single. From Northern we journey directly to Hartford CT, for two nights at The Bull and from there, directly back to Kenmore Square. This time Th-Th-Th-Thundertrain is back at K-K-K-Katy's for a one-nighter. I can't eat, sleep or concentrate on anything. The pressure makes me physically ill. I have to clear my name.

On the morning of October 26th I arrive at 600 Concord Street along with Ric and Bobby. Standing in the marble foyer of the Framingham District Courthouse. I see my lawyer, he's dressed a lot better than me - thankfully - in his dark, conservative suit. I don't own anything like that but I dug up some relatively clean clothes and they cover all my parts. I already gave the lawyer a down payment and now he wants the rest of his $600 fee. I hand him the wad of cash we collected at the benefit, the needed balance was finally achieved thanks to a large contribution from Ric's quiet friend, Tim.

We file inside the cavernous forum and the flinty-eyed magistrate enters, ready to pass judgement. The case is called and my attorney is allowed to speak. He calls his first and only witness to the stand. The school teacher in question.

"Did my client, Mr. Bell...that's him sitting over there...did he assault you, ma'am?

"Well...it was such a busy night, it was hard to tell exactly. I'd say he swept past me rather forcefully. He pushed against my elbow...but no. It was definitely not an assault."

The judge is staring right through her. Waiting...

An out of order voice from the back of the room:

"Your honor, the streets of our town have become a jungle. The youth of Framingham deserve better than this. Drugs, juvenile delinquency, violence. That's what happens when we allow people - people like Mr. Bell - to roam our streets. Invading our schools for goodness sake! The court needs to do something."

The judge sits silently. Chief Martins hops out of his chair (also out of order),

"Your honor, the principal is correct. Following his arrest, the defendant was brought to my station house. A disgraceful sight. Who is this Mr. Bell anyway? Are we going to allow him to tear down our entire town? Smoking marijuana. Behaving like an animal. Perhaps a cage is what he needs."

Well, looks like that settles it.

The judge turns my way, clearing his throat.

"I hereby sentence the defendant, Mr. Bell, to thirty days in the Billerica House of Correction."

I choke. Ric and Bobby are stunned. Their heads spin towards me - just as an immense court officer yanks me to my feet. Another mammoth approaches me with the handcuffs. I pivot, looking over at my attorney. He's just sitting there, thinking about his lunch.

"What the hell?" I whisper-scream. *Do something."*

Waking from his daydream, Perry Mason rises, signaling a request to the bench.

"Yeah, what now?" intones the judge.

"On behalf of my client, I request a jury trial in Superior Court."

That stops the action for a moment. The judge confers with a nearby clerk.

"Request granted. In the meantime, I order that Mr. Bell shall remain in custody of this court, until a one hundred dollar deposit is paid."

The mammoth thrusts my wrists into the handcuffs. I definitely don't have a hundred bucks. Ric, still in shock, makes the universal "sorry man - no cash" gesture. I spin my head back toward the lawyer as they drag me away.

"*Pay him*. Use the cash I just gave you out in the lobby. I'll pay you back."

Time slows down right here...I'm escorted quickly across the courtroom in manacles. The lawyer thinks it over - for too long - before finally motioning to the clerk and producing the requested C note. Cash in hand, the judge brightens-up. He pockets the payoff, er..deposit, and proclaims,

"This case will be continued before a six man jury in Cambridge Superior Court. Release the defendant. Until that time, Mr. Bell... You are free to go."

Boston Groupie News item by Boston rock comic
Paul "Blowfish" Lovell.

During this time of award giving The B.G.N. has decided that certain me
bers of The Boston rock community deserve a special set of awards selecte
expressly for them and their outstanding actions in the last year! And no
here are The B.G.N. Awards For 1976...........

THE BABY TALK AWARD- To Willie 'Loco' 'Boom Boom' 'Ga-Ga' 'Ta-Ta' 'Momo' Alexander.

THE TEACHER BEATER AWARD- To Mach Bell for beating up one teacher,four substitutes and a PTA meeting.

THE PSEUDO INTELLECTUAL AWARD- To Reddy Teddy. Copescetic....holy shit!

THE BACK ROOM AWARD-(for the most time in a confined space.) To Jim Harol

DEPT. OF MOTOR VEHICLES AWARD- To Patty Forbes for commiting moving viola tions in parked cars.

XMAS IN HELL AWARD- If there's Xmas in hell then they're telling the thruth...To Dirt Magazine.

THE GREAT UNDERTAKING AWARD- To Richard Nolan for Tracks,which went under faster than one of his daytime clients!

THE PHOTO BOOTH AWARD- To Johny Barnes who almost flash fried himself get ting enough pictures for his single sleeve.

THE WATERGATE AWARD- To Oedipus for recieving and playing more tapes than Judge John Sirica

Even I had to laugh.

{ 19 }

Mink DeVille and Fred MacMurray

Mink DeVille and Fred MacMurray After listening back to the stereo two-track, live mixes, Earthquake urges me to consider letting Jelly Records release the Thundertrain demos just as they are, in order to quickly get an album out on the market. The Ramones debut album was recorded in similar fashion, costing a measly six thousand to produce - in an era where an Aerosmith album can cost over a million to make.

Back in the mixing room at Northern, EQ and I review the Thundertrain demos again. We edit and sequence the songs into a playing order. This thing actually sounds okay. My bandmates are taken aback when I tell them about about this scheme. Steven is convinced I've totally lost it this time.

"Why on earth would you want anyone to hear those half-baked tapes? It's career suicide." Ignoring Steven's objections, I push the the plan through.

Mink DeVille is house band at CBGB and one of the best groups featured on the "Live at CBGB's" compilation album. Oedipus arranges one of DeVille's first Boston visits, a weekend at The Club in Cambridge, alternating sets with Thundertrain. Singer Willy DeVille and his girl, Toots, look like time travelers from the doo-wop, wall of sound era. Skinny Willy piles his hair in a high pompadour and he has the sharpest shoes. I'm happily surprised to learn that DeVille's top musical influence is my friend from Tulagi, bluesman John Hammond Jr.

The DeVille band sounds great - they're playing right now. Ric and I slip outside for a quick breather. Our bands are trading sets this weekend, we headlined yesterday and Mink DeVille will close the show tonight. We're standing on the sidewalk alongside Main Street with a few other random groups of kids. Ric and I are shooting the breeze in the December night air when we hear the car. Approaching fast.

A Mercury sedan bombs past the Necco Candy factory and seems to be aimed right for us. The sidewalk onlookers scatter as the auto hits the curb, skims a light post and smashes to a stop, crushing into the rear fender of a car parked before us. Chunks of chrome, glass and plastic shoot past, ricocheting off the front wall of The Club and scattering across the pavement.

Startled, Ric and I take a step closer to the wreckage. The driver of the Mercury is still seated behind the wheel. Motionless. He looks dazed. A drunk in the crowd shouts something at the guy - but the driver remains frozen. Ric's eyes widen as the motorist finally, slowly, slumps forward. His forehead hits the steering wheel, setting off the car horn. That's when I see it. The handle of a butcher knife protrudes from the driver's back. The long blade is plunged deep into the victim's spine. The back of his shirt, it might be a uniform like a mechanic would wear, is caked with blood. Ric dashes to a pay phone just up the way and alerts the Cambridge police.

247

Just as Thundertrain begins getting noticed on the Boston/New York underground front, we're astonished to find ourselves sharing space with the Bay City Rollers and Donny & Marie in the pages of 16 Magazine. I was corresponding with Ramones manager Danny Fields a few weeks ago. I don't think I realized he's also taken over editing the celebrity teenzine, following the 1975 walkout by editor in chief, Gloria Stavers. During 1977 Thundertrain makes three or four more appearances in 16.

The flood of fan mail is beyond expectations, over 300 letters in the first week alone.

MEET MACH!

If you live around the Boston area, no doubt you've heard of that fantastic new group **Thundertrain**, and its sexy and sensational lead singer, **Mach Bell**. **Mach** is 18, with blond hair and blue eyes, and he loves to get letters from fans. "We answer all mail personally!" he says, and you can write to **Mach** in care of Thundertrain, Box 524, Natick, Mass. Be sure to say you saw his pic in **16**!

Following a good set and a great afterparty at U Mass Amherst's Blue Wall, Thundertrain returns to Kenmore Square. It's the first week of November and we're headlining the Rat again. Besides Willie Loco's Boom Boom Band, my current favorite is DMZ and they'll be opening these shows. Except for drummer David Robinson, the DMZ guys are younger than us. Peter and Jay Jay, the flashy/trashy guitarists, hold down the fort while their untethered frontman Mono Mann (Jeffrey Connolly) lunges back & forth between his Farfisa organ and a center stage microphone. When he's not busy being a nut case, Mono is a garage-rock historian.

Mach and Mono Mann (DMZ). 1976. Photo by Lynn Ciulla

The DMZ setlist reflects Mono's passion for pioneering punk groups like the Wailers, Sonics, Standells and 13th Floor Elevators, mixed in with his urgent, Stooges-influenced originals like Boy From Nowhere and Don't Jump Me Mother.

With years of non-stop club and school shows under our belts, Thundertrain has no problem showing the packed house who's boss tonight - but that doesn't stop me from leaping onstage to join Mono Mann and his DMZ bashers. I rock-along to their version of Riot on Sunset Strip. Thundertrain may rule the roost but my girlfriend Lynn decides she'd rather go home with DMZ guitar man Jay Jay. As Lynn explained it to me,

"Mach, when I saw you onstage with Thundertrain I thought it would be like dating Mick Jagger. But when I brought you home - you turned into Fred MacMurray."

Hours before the final night of the Thundertrain/DMZ engagement, Oedipus and AnneMarie meet us at the empty Rat on Sunday afternoon. DJ Oedi, who moonlights as a photographer, sets up a seamless black backdrop. AnneMarie arranges us, positions us in various ways, she hands us newspapers with prop headlines that blare *Teenage Suicide.*

Teenage Suicide Photos by Oedipus

Thundertrain 1977: Ric Provost (bass), Mach Bell (vocals), girl, Steven Silva (lead guitar), Bobby Edwards (drums), Gene Provost (guitar) in front with bomb.

The photo session continues the next day inside AnneMarie's Brighton apartment bedroom. A mirrored wooden vanity, something AnneMarie bought second hand, is carefully arranged with an ashtray, jewelry box, hair brush, rag doll and an open container of birth control pills. To the left of this array sits a framed photo of a middle-age couple inscribed "To our darling daughter - Love, Mom and Dad."

Dressed in a skimpy blouse, blonde hair disheveled, a model (the youngest Provost sister) takes her seat in a round-backed rattan chair. She faces the mirror that rises up from the back of the vanity. The mirror reflects the whole scene - almost the whole scene. I'm called in and handed a lipstick. I scrawl the word *Thundertrain* across the top of the large vanity mirror. Now AnneMarie gets down to business, applying heavy theatrical make-up to the model's left arm. Using a waxy substance, AnneMarie creates a deep laceration that slashes across the child's wrist. Raised and bruised, the wound is further embellished with drippy gushes of blood.

Oedipus sets up his Nikon, shooting from behind the girl's seemingly lifeless form. Reflected in the mirror we see her, the dying fan, head drooped to one side after scrawling her final word, *Thundertrain*. It's only when the viewer's gaze shifts down, to the bottom left of the tableau that the grisly suicide finally becomes apparent.

I came up with this novel Teen Suicide idea while lying around, staring at AnneMarie's second hand furniture find. She'd been carting the mirrored vanity around from apartment to apartment for awhile now.

The concept of putting a beat-up teenager reflected in a mirror on a rock album cover has been done before. In 1973 by Silverhead (!) *16 and Savaged*. I attempt to kick their concept up a notch, implying that our frustrated kid, grounded on the night of the big Thundertrain show, has chosen to end it all.

Suicide is a taboo subject. A word rarely heard in public. I've never heard the words *Teenage* and *Suicide* combined - who ever heard of a kid committing suicide? Thundertrain records for a tiny regional label with a meager ad budget, so I figure a dose of old fashion shock-rock might help get our debut album noticed.

Jim Harold has taken ownership of the entire property at 528 Commonwealth Ave. A battered brick building with four levels. The rear, service doorway, topped by a Budweiser sign, opens out to a large, shared, parking lot bordering the noxious Massachusetts Turnpike.

Out in front, the Kenmore Square sidewalk is extra deep, almost like a plaza, and a row of six pay phones stand to the right of the funky front facade. A sign over the entry reads "Rathskeller Drinks - Music." Walking inside you have the immediate choice of continuing straight ahead into the (free admission) upper bar, or making a quick left & right, leading you down to the underground (paid admission) level - the Rat. Where the hottest rock groups on Earth play nightly.

In the 60's, most of the Rathskeller live music happened in a back room of the upstairs bar, which today includes a full kitchen and a raised balcony area.

The street level, back room (now gone) is where most of the 60's rock bands, like the Barbarians and The Lost, entertained. Apparently the basement space originally opened for music (briefly) in 1965 to accommodate overflow crowds attracted upstairs by Barry and the Remains (Don't Look Back). In 1974, the venue (known for a while as TJ's) finally reopens the basement space, turning it into a rock showroom with a legal capacity of around 200.

It's the very last night of 1976. America's parade-happy, red, white and blue, Bi-Centennial celebration is finally over. Thundertrain is in Kenmore Square at the Rat, playing the *Rat New Year's Party 1977* on a three-band bill with Reddy Teddy and Willie Alexander's Boom Boom Band. In six months time, we've successfully maneuvered ourselves into the thick of things here in the city.

Once again, the Boston rock recipe of glam/punk/ rock'n'roll is on the menu tonight.

Reddy Teddy play rock'n'roll in a bouncy, upbeat way. Bandleader Matthew MacKenzie wears a floppy newsboy hat over his puffed-up, auburn mane. A constellation of band promo-buttons decorate his guitar strap. Playful Matthew radiates a magnetism that reminds me of the Lovin' Spoonful's animated guitarist, Zal Yanovsky.

Meanwhile, Les Paul slinger Billy Loosigian, guitarist for the Boom Boom Band, is the lone player from this "Live at the Rat" pack to graduate with honors from Truth University. Billy's licks are true to professor Jeff Beck's lesson plans. Loosigian laces his delicious Brit-licks through-out Willie's infectious, heartfelt, bohemian compositions.

Speaking of Willie Alexander, WA personally provides all the required punk and glam elements needed for this Boom Boom pie. Hot out of the oven their presentation contains equal measures of each vital ingredient.

Thundertrain's strange brew favors the glam and rock'n'roll flavors. Steven Silva throws a tantrum whenever he hears Thundertrain associated with the word punk.

In my book, that makes Steven a punk.

{ 20 }

Dead Boys, Teenage Suicide and Phil Lynott I had two really exceptional years in my music career. 1977 is one of them. Thundertrain is back in Boston on Thursday January 6, loading into the Rat for the first show of a four night engagement. In his office on the top floor of the 528 building, Jim Harold tells me the opening band just drove 700 miles from Cleveland. They're downstairs in the club already. The Dead Boys.

Neither of us has ever heard of them.

Not expecting much, I go down the back stairs to an amazing sight. Sprawled out across the stage, spilling out onto the dance floor, are the hungriest, skinniest, sickliest looking bunch of long-hairs I've ever seen. Glammed-out in shiny pants, pointy boots, scarves and mascara. Damn, they might be even cooler looking than my own band.

I move closer, they seem eager to meet me.

Cheetah Chrome, the lead guitarist, introduces himself. He's very familiar with Hot For Teacher and he asks me all about the record. After buttering me up, Cheetah asks if his Dead Boys can play through Thundertrain's gear tonight. They've driven to Boston, squished together in a sedan with only their guitars. No drums. No roadies. They don't even have a bass player. My fellow Ohioans seem pretty cool, so when Bobby, Ric, Cool Gene and Silva arrive, they agree to share their gear.

Jon calls for sound check. Drummer Johnny Blitz sits down behind Bobby's Ludwigs and explodes into action. Blitz has plenty of muscle, a Tasmanian devil on the skins. Guitarist Jimmy Zero is mild mannered and resembles actor Christopher Walken. Gaunt and articulate. Turns out Jimmy shares my taste for Universal and Hammer monster movies. Mr. Zero tells me how he corresponds with Forrest Ackerman, editor of Famous Monsters of Filmland magazine and how Zero has his own collection of monster stuff, including an actual Dracula ring from the Bela Lugosi estate.

Rounding out this troupe of delinquents is frontman Steve Bator. I find the singer sitting in the corner of the dimly lit Rat dressing room. Looking intelligent in his reading glasses. Steve is quietly going over band expenses in a little book. It's up to us rock singers to keep track of details in our little books.

The Dead Boys recently changed their band name. Steve tells me they formerly went as Frankenstein and that's when I realize I've run across them before. Frankenstein shared a page with Thundertrain in a recent issue of Rock Scene Magazine.

Today - as the Dead Boys - they're on a quick swing thru NYC and Boston, testing foreign waters. When Bator is called to the stage I'm taken aback again. The mild mannered bookworm and his friendly guitarists suddenly mutate into the most viscous, callous creatures I've ever seen stalk a stage.

A Thursday night in January. Maybe a hundred kids show up to watch Thundertrain and catch the Boston debut of these unknown Dead Boys. In the crowd I see Jonathan, the stalwart Thundertrain fan from Wellesley, Eric the excited teenager and sultry Barb. After an intense four sets, Steve and I make a pact to do it again. Another Thundertrain/Dead Boys double-bill. Soon.

We're back at the Rat the following night. Opening our show for the rest of the weekend is electric-debris artist turned punk-rocker, Alan Vega. He calls his band Suicide (there's that word again). Vega is an older guy, Willie Alexander's age at least. He struts in wearing a motorcycle jacket and tears into a rockabilly-tinged set of soulful noise. The weekend crowd is a lot bigger, augmented by our underage girl following, led by Mary and Kathye. The regulars aren't sure what to make of this impassioned Alan Vega. But I see he's got at least one tall fan, looming above the crowd, bopping his head to the beat. Ric Ocasek.

Thundertrain runs into Ric Ocasek a few nights later (1/17) in Biggy Ratt's hometown, Medway MA. We're at the Hungry Lion, booked at this "agent's showcase" which is an old Indian word meaning "no pay."
I feel bad for Ocasek. I know how much he wanted to get his band, Cap'n Swing, included on the Live at the Rat compilation. But man, look at them...Too short, too tall, one wears glasses...These guys just don't have an image.

Speaking of look, I notice Ocasek's sound man perk up as he watches us blast thru our set. His eyes are on stalks, seeing our female fan club crowd the dance floor while Steven spins across the stage. I talk with the Cap'n Swing sound tech later. He's the roommate of their lead guitarist, Elliot Easton. He says his name is Alan Kaufman.

Blondie is another popular group that started out at CBGB. Oedipus knows them well enough to arrange a Thundertrain/Blondie weekend at the Rat. The singer, Debbie, and her guitarist Chris will stay on Beacon Hill at Oedi's apartment. The rest of the band will crash at AnneMarie's flat on Comm Ave. in Brighton. I'd love to tell you the rest of this sizzling story but a blinding snowstorm hits the Tri-State area on the eve of our big double-bill. The Blondie station wagon gets stuck on I-95 and the entire engagement is cancelled as the blizzard advances on Boston, taking down power lines as it approaches.

Jimmy Carter becomes the third US President of the Thundertrain era. Gerald Ford steps down on January 17th as Carter takes his inaugural oath.
Returning from weeklong stints at the blotto Black Sheep club in Newburyport and Whitinsville's PunJabs, Thundertrain returns to Kenmore Square to headline two nights. Jim Harold has hired a new kid, a friendly gorilla named Mark, to work the busy back door.
Mark turns out to be a helpful ally, and he's from Natick.

The Dead Boys are back. Their group fits right in with
Thundertrain's philosophy of rock. Lots of power and
swagger. Sharp clothing, but not too-much clothing.
Buckets of sweat and angst. We both have type A
drummers and the Rat still has a wide, parquet dance floor
both groups can fill with frantic bodies. Tough guys stand
back at the bar chanting and egging us on.
The Dead Boys perform Syndicate of Sound's "Little Girl,"
we rock the Standells "Dirty Water." We both draw heavily
from garage-rock and glam bands like the New York Dolls,
Alice Cooper and the Stones. While Thundertrain's Steven
Silva plays lead guitar in the Johnny Winter/Chuck Berry
style, Cheetah Chrome is a Johnny Thunders/Wayne
Kramer-type player.
The Dead Boys have strong original material too. "Sonic
Reducer," "I Want You To Know What Love Is" and "Dead
Boy" are straight out of the Doll's mold.

Thin Lizzy suddenly materialize at the base of the Rat
staircase. I'm right in the middle of our closing set on
2/9/77. The Dead Boys have already finished for the night
and Thundertrain is joyriding through the rare Ric Provost
song, "Feels Like This."
It's not really the whole Thin Lizzy, just their band leader,
Phil Lynott, and one of his guitar players.
Brian Robertson, I think. They came straight to Kenmore
Square after rocking for thousands at the Boston Garden
tonight.
Opening for the UK quartet, Queen.

Not their first time at the Rat either, the entire Thin Lizzy
was here a few months ago at a Johnny Barnes show. The
Thin Lizzy guys push past onlookers and balance their
beers atop a section of the pony-wall that separates the Rat
main bar from the seating area. Ric offers Phil Lynott the
use of his Gibson Thunderbird and minutes later Phil and
Brian join Cool Gene, Bobby, Steven and me onstage.
"What do you guys know?"
Lynott suggests "Hard Drivin' Man," a J.Geils hit.
Probably because this is Boston and also because he knows
the lyrics. The joint is really jumping now. I join-in for the
choruses and Steven trades licks with the hard-driving
visitors from Dublin.

Steven Silva (Thundertrain) and Phil Lynott (Thin Lizzy) at the Rat in
Boston 1977. Boston Groupie News Archive

Just a week later Max's Kansas City sends the Rat one of their favorite glam bands, The Fast (Boys Will Be Boys), led by Miki Zone. A visually arresting band wearing pop art fashion and playing catchy, concise songs.
Like Thundertrain, The Fast have been around. They were stars of the Mercer Arts Center scene that also spawned the New York Dolls. The Fast arrive in Boston atop so much media juice, even the mighty Thundertrain find ourselves second-billed during the two-nighter at the Rat.

Teenage Suicide, Thundertrain's debut album, is released on Jelly Records during the final week of February '77. The packaging is jarringly superb.

Oedipus's black and white photo of the suicide scene graces the record's front cover. The back of the LP jacket shows the same girl (alive) as she nestles against my shoulder, surrounded by her favorite band. Over on the left, Cool Gene can be seen with his hand balanced on the nosecone of the Thundertrain bomb. Earthquake Morton surprises everyone by including a big, glossy Thundertrain poster inside every album. It's another great photo by Oedipus, with Thundertrain brandishing and reacting to the newspaper headlines. Adding to the fun, Jelly presses the initial 300 copies on clear vinyl.

The *Live at the Rat* double LP hits the record racks only days later. I think Jim probably shopped the tapes to the majors before opting to start his own Rat Records, operating out of a spare room right next door to his office on the top floor at 528. Thundertrain lands two songs on the long awaited compilation. Leading off Side Two is our live version of Steven's "I'm So Excited."
Strikingly, Teenage Suicide and Live at the Rat both close exactly the same way.
With Thundertrain's live version of a hot new song Steven wrote, with some additional lyrics I contributed.
The lone difference is the way the track is listed.
Somehow, the typesetter at Rat Records misspelled the song title as "I've Got To Rock."
The song - destined to become one of Thundertrain's greatest hits - is spelled correctly on the back of Teenage Suicide.
I Gotta Rock.

Clearing a pile of old junk from the new Rat Records headquarters, Jim discovers some old food service items. On my arrival this morning I see them sitting in the corner near his desk. A tall, red popcorn machine encased in plexiglass and a smaller, stainless steel hot dog steamer. The machines look beat but both still function.

I'm thinking... Monday nights are slow for Thundertrain. Even super agent Frank Borsa struggles to root-out bookings on the first night of the week.

I propose a plan to Mr. Harold. I'll shine 'em up and install the machines at the end of the downstairs main bar, near the cigarette machine. If Jim will spring for some popping corn and a few packs of Fenway franks, I'll do the rest. Having two record albums hitting the market simultaneously is all well and good, but my new Monday night gig, as the Rat's hot dog & popcorn vendor, will ensure at least one square meal a week for this rocker.

Rat Dogs and Kong Korn are an overnight sensation and the club even mentions my bill of fare at the bottom of their weekly newspaper ads.

Kong Korn is great. Courtesy of the Mary Johnson Archive

THE RAT

BOSTON
ROCK & ROLL
528 COMM. AVE.
BOSTON, MASS 02215
617-247-7713

"Home of
Boston's New
Wave of Rock"
Thurs.-Sun.
Thunder-
train
and
Dead Boys
from Cleveland Ohio
LIVE RAT LP
DOUBLE ROCK —
$8.95 — 75%
handling • $9.74. Rat
Records "A" • 528
Comm. Ave., Boston,
MA or come to the
Rat and buy one
signed by the bands.
Kong Korn is great

{ 21 }

Let's Go to the Rat with the Runaways, Iggy Pop & David Bowie

March 16th. Almost three years have passed since I returned east from my Sunset Strip expedition. Surveying desolation boulevard beneath the giant billboards, neon lit marquees and swaying palm trees. Watching dune buggies and gassers race past hustlers hawking Maps to the Stars Homes. Circled by glittering SoCal kids crowding in front of the Rainbow and Rodney's. Cracked Actor and Baby's on Fire blaring across the sidewalks. That was the glamorous L.A. vibe I attempted to import and infuse into my nightly performances with Thundertrain.

Tonight the Rat plays host to Cherie Currie, Lita Ford, Sandy West, Jackie Fox and Joan Jett. Five teenagers straight off Hollywood's Sunset Strip. The Runaways. Thundertrain gets the plum assignment, opening for the Queens of Noise, which is the title of their second album, released two months ago on Mercury.

Thundertrain shares common ground with the visiting group. Stage clothes, image, attitude & showmanship. Show-stopping guitar solos punctuated by crashing drum breaks, teen anthems and lots of hair. The Runaways main influences include Jeff Beck, Gene Simmons and David Bowie. They're as hard-rock as we are...

...but like Thundertrain, the media lumps them into the punk-rock category. We're still trying to define what that term even means.

For the past few years the editors at Creem Magazine have been awarding their Punk of the Year award to Steven Tyler. Does that qualify Aerosmith as punk-rock? Growing up in the 60's, I thought singers Reg Presley (The Troggs), Sean Bonniwell (Music Machine) and Sky Saxon (The Seeds) were punks. At this moment, The Ramones probably fit the profile best. Four long-haired stoners sporting identical uniforms. Marlon Brando-style motorcycle jackets worn over ripped-at-the-knee blue jeans.

Joey Ramone sings about sniffing glue and bopping people over the head - but Johnny Ramone's chord structures sound more like surf music or Shangri-La girl pop.

Sharing the compact Rat dressing room, squished between the quintet of L.A. music-biz starlets. That's the tantalizing vision that's kept me at attention for the days leading up to this big night. I sure hope Bobby doesn't bum out the visiting covergirls, greeting them with his log hanging out. My fantasy is harpooned the minute we arrive at the Rat.

"Dressing room is all yours tonight guys." beams back-door Mark.
"Huh? What about the Runaways?"
Mark laughs,
"Their road manager won't allow the girls anywhere near you pervs. They're upstairs, getting dressed by themselves, in the Rat Records office."

This is one of the many nights when the Rat's official capacity is simply a recommendation. Every inch of the club is packed, I'd estimate 350 easy. Mike lets the Duck Sisters perch on the back bar for a better look. Elaine, Barb, Jonathan, Mary, Kathye, Eric, AnneMarie, Rayboy, Annie Rock'n'Roll, Trixie, Oedipus, Bill Tupper, Miss Lyn, Bob Colby, Eddie Kent and hundreds more are readying themselves for the extravaganza. Upstairs, bouncers Rick and Dougie work the door, collecting four bucks a head.

The Rat has been forced to make major infrastructure changes these past couple months. National touring bands like the Runaways require house sound and lighting. Contract riders demand specific stage dimensions. Up until recently, Jim has been anchoring his weekend bills around established draws like Reddy Teddy, Orchestra Luna or Thundertrain - bands who travel with their own pro sound and lighting systems. Once the anchor band is in place, Jim can co-bill a traveling Dead Boys or Boston fave like DMZ, outfits who rock but lack their own production equipment.

Jim Harold hires Jon and Mick of the Thundertrain road crew to widen and extend the Rat stage further out into the room. The expansion comes at the expense of the dance floor which is more-than-halved in the process. Mick rewires the performance area, upping the circuits to handle newly installed stage lighting and a house sound system. Granny, an Aerosmith roadie, is hired as full-time house sound tech. The most visible change is the sign...

A garage-door-sized backdrop emblazoned with a rodent now spans the entire back wall of the stage. The sign bears the slogan, *The Rat – Boston Rock & Roll.*

Ever since Cherry Bomb was released (around the same time as our Hot For Teacher) I've been hearing plenty of Runaways music over at AnneMarie's apartment. The debut album, and now the new one, blast from Annie's stereo on a regular basis. Good records. But I've heard about the shenanigans behind a lot of these L.A. groups. Its probably just the same session guys who played most of the tracks on the Turtles, Beach Boys, Byrds, Monkees and Raiders records I was raised on. These Runaways are almost ten years younger than Thundertrain.

GOTTA ROCK: *here are Thundertrain's Mach Bell and Steven Silva back in the day, rockin' up a storm.*

The girls' image is unbeatable but I doubt they can actually replicate the solid sound of their records.

We make our entrance. Look out, here we come. Charging out of the Rat dressing room, a cramped utility room, wedged between the back bar and the rest rooms. We worm our way through fifty feet of pressed-flesh, eventually nearing the stage. Top rock manager Dee Anthony always warns his groups "Never, never, *never* walk into a crowd without applause - always have announcers." Well, Thundertrain can't afford to carry a Master Blaster of our own, so in lieu of an announcer, Jon Read cranks up Blues Theme.

The Provost Brothers in front of the new sign. Photo by Lynn Ciulla

Hitting the stage, Ric and Cool Gene plug in, creating an instant whirlwind of feedback while Bobby batters all four of his mounted toms. By the time Steven and I leap aboard, the audience is adding to the din, screaming and stomping. Silva slices into the opening chords of Frustration and Thundertrain is off and running.

My Eddie Kent designer originals are wearing thinner by the day. I'm crammed into a pair of bronze colored strides tonight and I've been messing with hair dye for the first time. My 'do is sometimes referred to as dirty blonde but in honor of our tinseltown guests, I've lightened-up a bit. The crowd shakes to the rhythm of Cool Gene's "Love the Way," one of the few Thundertrain songs that actually bears a resemblance to Aerosmith music. We continue building from there, feeling invincible by the time we release the set's final ringing chord to a hail of salutations.

THUNDERTRAIN at the Rat in Kenmore Square 1977.
Photo by Lynn Ciulla

We're recovering, back in the dressing room when I feel the atmospheric pressure change. Kenmore Square quakes as the back hallway is cleared and the Runaways make a grand entrance.

The outfits these guys wear make me gulp in envy. Not the ragtag duds Thundertrain decorates ourselves with. I treasure my Eddie originals but the rest of the goofy stuff I wear comes from my sister's closet or the sidewalk sale bins in front of the Dress Barn and Fashion Bug.

Runaway lead guitarist, Lita, stuns in her high-heeled, silver leather boots rising to the knees. Tight black short-shorts, silver-zippered up the front are paired with a matching-but-contrasting white sleeveless top that spotlights the same silver zipper-front. Lita is the juiciest of this troupe so her neckline is lowest, with an X-marks-the-spot silver necklace dangling just so.

Singer Cherie, is Barbie dolled-up in a tight silver space-suit accented with black stretch-panels running along the inseams. Viva la *Barbarella*. Her boots are similar to Lita's but shiny black. Cheri's form-fitting suit evaporates into a halter at the shoulders, allowing her spaghetti arms (surprisingly white for a Valley girl) to stick out.

Not in Boston to be ignored, Joan Jett, principal songwriter, jets into the Rat wearing a crimson jumpsuit. Even tighter than Cheri's and with the front zipper half undone. Jett's black shag cut and heavy eye make-up draw cheers. Damn, the wardrobe alone looks like it cost a million.. Much more impressive than my frayed King Kong t-shirt. But can these L.A. guys really play?

The Runaways have been together for two years, actually less I think, because outside of Joan and drummer Sandy, the balance of the line-up has gone through a few changes. Last year was extremely busy for the Runaways. Recording and releasing the first LP and immediately going-out on big concert tours, supporting Tom Petty and Van Halen among others. The Runaways are slated to begin a headlining world tour in just a month or two.

Their backline equipment is pretty much the same as ours. Over-sized drum kit, Ampeg SVT bass rig, Marshall and Orange guitar stacks. I see Lita has a copy of the Live at the Rat album leaning up against her speaker cab. They plug in, Gibson Les Paul (gold top) for Jett, Gibson Thunderbird bass (white body w/black headstock) for Jackie Fox, Gibson Explorer for Lita (black with white binding). Kicking off with "Queens of Noise" and....
the sound of three hundred and fifty jaws dropping.

Whoah. They sound a whole lot better than the record. Fully-formed, heavy and rock hard. Next up is "California Paradise" Sandy is supergirl on the skins, mesmerizing and muscular. "Waitin' for the Night" Lita amazes with her nimble fingered, gnarly-toned riffs. Cherie and Joan are the stars but I think bassist Jackie is the sexiest. The music is great and there's a lot to look at.

Now my blood is boiling. I dig the Runaways, the Dead Boys, Reddy Teddy and Willie...but when it comes to business, Thundertrain is all business. We live by a credo, a slogan oft repeated in our dressing room, wherever it may be. After adjusting our dime store wardrobe as best we can, we assume formation, all tuned-up and ready for

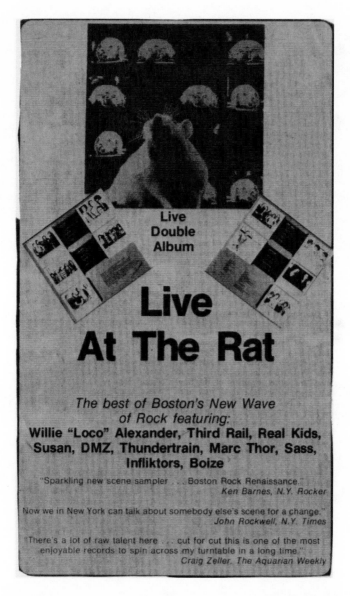

Live Double Album

Live At The Rat

The best of Boston's New Wave of Rock featuring:
Willie "Loco" Alexander, Third Rail, Real Kids, Susan, DMZ, Thundertrain, Marc Thor, Sass, Infliktors, Boize

"Sparkling new scene sampler . . . Boston Rock Renaissance."
Ken Barnes, N.Y. Rocker

Now we in New York can talk about somebody else's scene for a change."
John Rockwell, N.Y. Times

There's a lot of raw talent here . . . cut for cut this is one of the most enjoyable records to spin across my turntable in a long time."
Craig Zeller, The Aquarian Weekly

the second show. Round Two. Coach Ric delivers his famous rallying cry once again.

"Okay boys, let's get out there and *blow 'em off the stage.*"

Vaulting back to my SM58, nothings gonna stop us now. We've been challenged and we shall meet the challenge. Bashing madly into Let 'er Rip followed by I'm So Excited. Audience members fist-pump along to the music, others climb atop their tables. Taking it higher with Hell Tonite, a potent track off the new Thundertrain album that's already scoring airplay. Deep into the song, I'm killing it, leading the crowd, everyone chants the refrain... *ZAP.*

The air is suddenly sucked out of the Rat. Pressure drop. Heads turning... Turning away... Away from me?

What the hell is everyone looking at?

A cat fight? Groupies groping each other on the floor? Ripping each others clothes off?

If it's a fight - somebody better be dead - because I don't dig being upstaged. I scramble atop the tall, side-fill monitor to get a better look.

Shit.

David Bowie just walked into the Rat.

Here's the low down. Tonight's show at the Rat, crowded as it is, might've been even more packed except for another landmark show in Cambridge, across the river, where Iggy Pop is making his first USA appearance since the break-up of the Stooges. Iggy is singing over at the Harvard Square Theater and I know that theater very well because during the week it's a 24-hour movie house, playing double bills of cult & classic films. Admission is two bucks, so it's an affordable place to crash for the night if nothing better comes up. Iggy is touring behind his debut solo record "The Idiot" (Funtime, China Girl) and he's got his producer, David Bowie, playing keyboards. The Iggy concert lets out just in time for the headliners to catch a Boston Taxi, cruise over the Mass Ave. bridge and around the corner into Kenmore Square. So, here I am standing on this speaker box as Ziggy Stardust and Iggy Pop stroll into our party.

"*Steven*! I Gotta Rock...I *Gotta* Rock!" Silva fires off the opening riff to the song that closes Teenage Suicide (and Live at the Rat).

I've been playin' the dance halls from town to town, tryin' to get you off your seat before they shut me down.

Like in that Cecil B. DeMille movie, the red-faced sea of Boston rockers parts, allowing visitors Iggy Pop and David Bowie prime viewing space behind the soundboard. Tagging along behind the stars is the singer from Blondie, Debbie Harry. Her band opened the Iggy concert. Blondie have a record out too, called X Offender, I don't think WBCN plays it, but I heard it on the Oedipus college radio show.

I Gotta Rock escalates into a tornado of lead guitar before parachuting back down to the scorched stage. Bobby breaks-it-down to a bare groove, Ric's bass bubbles up. This is my cue to begin preaching. I begin by telling David Bowie (and everybody else in the room) the true tale of an average guy, a guy just like me, who watches the Charlie Chan late show while eating a Patio Mexican TV dinner, all the while praying for some real rock'n'roll to come on the radio. He spins the dial...searching...Frustration rising when all he can find is Debbie Boone's "You Light Up My Life" and Barry Manilow's "Copacabana."

Mach Bell preaching at the Rat. Photo by Lynn Ciulla

Lobbing my off-the-cuff tale into this voracious crowd of fans, writers, photographers, drunks, musicians, students, DJs, vagrants and rock stars, I feel myself lifting off, into some sort of out-of-body experience. Realizing, just for this golden moment, that I've achieved the goal I set for myself as a 15 year old. To have my music playing on WBCN and to be rocking the hottest venue in Boston. The Tea Party is a distant memory but on this particular evening the Rat is the hottest venue in the world.

The Runaways close the night with a popping "Cherry Bomb" and they deserve all the accolades they receive tonight. It's the final night of their three night stand (Real Kids and Reddy Teddy were openers on the previous evenings). The teenagers from Hollywood take Boston by storm, selling out every show, proving beyond any doubt that they're true rock'n'roll animals.

Mach Bellがインタビューの冒頭で語っている「77年、(Thundertrainが)RATでRunawaysと共演した時」の現場写真。左からOedipus(*WTBS DJ)、Sandy West(*Runaways Dr)、Mach Bell、Jackie Fox(*Runaways Ba)。
Thundertrainのファン・クラブ会報誌『Thundertrain Photo-Magazine』77年夏号に掲載された一枚。同号のフォトグラファー・リストにはAnneMarieの名前も見られる。

Jim Harold is on the phone ordering Pu Pu platters from Aku Aku down the street. And a dozen pitchers of White Russians from the bar. Elaine piles everything on trays and totes it all upstairs to the Rat offices. Jim's after-party is a swirl of laughter, famous faces, egg rolls, whispers, jumpsuits, exposed skin and high hopes for whatever tomorrow brings. I don't get to talk with Ziggy, he's the most dressed-down of this bunch of rebel rebels. Clad in a simple plaid, flannel shirt. Bowie smiles at his disciples and takes a long drag on his cigarette. I'm inflated because Thundertrain held our own tonight - and also because I really like sitting next to Runaway Jackie Fox.

Time Magazine, sensing a scoop, flies reporters out to the Rat the very next night. The Runaways have left the building but Thundertrain is still holding court. We're onstage blasting another cut from Teenage Suicide, "Modern Girls," when the journalists descend the steep staircase that leads to the Rat. Welcome to Night #1 of the marathon Live at the Rat Record Release Party. This shindig will rage for the next two weeks in two different cities. We're paired with the Infliktors tonight. The next evening it'll be Thundertrain with Willie Alexander's Boom Boom Band and the night after that its DMZ, Marc Thor - and yours truly, Thundertrain.

I'm over at the bar, talking with Mike the bartender, Rick Coraccio, the bassist from DMZ, and AnneMarie. We're watching the Infliktors set. I hear a commotion and glancing back, I catch a glimpse of Rick Derringer, producer Jack Douglas and the singer from Aerosmith, as they enter the Rat and slink through the crowd.

Steven Tyler stops in his tracks, staring my way before moving to a back table with his friends. Minutes later, waitress Elaine swoops in, telling AnneMarie that,

"Steven wants you to join him at his table."

Poof. She's gone. I remember when I first met AnneMarie. She was a Barbra Streisand fan and - incredibly - she'd never listened to rock. The poor kid never heard of the Rolling Stones. Forget about upstarts like Aerosmith. To me it was bizarre, but she was the oldest kid in her family. Lacking an older, trailblazing sibling, someone to lead the musical way, can impede a child's cultural growth.

Mr. Tyler has his work cut-out for himself though, because AnneMarie is currently dating Tom Jones. I mean, Tom hasn't given her a ring or anything like that, but the pelvis-thrusting Welshman is a regular headliner at the Chateau DeVille where Annie is one of producer Jerry's "Angels." Tom Jones and AnneMarie share a bed whenever he's in town. Five or six years ago, when we started dating, I remember AnneMarie told me about the life-size Tom Jones poster that used to hang on the back of her bedroom door in Holliston. She was only eleven at the time. A girl with big dreams.

So that's What's New Pussycat.

Time Magazine is here to cover the current music/fashion/ lifestyle craze, "Punk-Rock" in a photo feature that won't actually see print until July. Suave-looking Lee Ritter of The Infliktors and sickly-looking Dead Boy Stiv Bators are among those pictured in the article. Thundertrain is name-checked prominently.

Time Magazine 7/11/77
Buzz and Blast. Up on stage can be found a numbing
variety of groups and soloists whose names dramatize
the nihilism and brute force that have inspired the
movement: Clash, Thundertrain, Weirdos, Dictators,
Stranglers...Four letter words are not spared. And
when Thundertrain bawls,"I'm hot, hot, hot, hot for
teacher," there is no missing the point.

THUNDERTRAIN Photo by Lynn Ciulla

{ 22 }

Thundertrain Go NYC
CBGB at 315 Bowery in lower Manhattan hosts Week #2 of the Live at the Rat Record Release Party. This is my Big Apple debut and Thundertrain is booked to rock the NYC hotspot for the next three nights. While Jimbo, Mick and Jon load-in the gear, Cool Gene and Ric venture up to Music Row on 48th Street between 6th and 7th Avenue. You never know what might be hiding on a back shelf at Manny's.

Bobby and Steven gallop up to 42nd Street. Trying out for the chorus of the latest Broadway show? Nah. You see, the world has really changed since I got my first Zim Gar electric. Back then, the glimpse of a bare bum or breast in a Playboy Magazine was enough to set off smoke alarms. Movies, even the seedy drive-in features I prefer, were relatively modest when it came to sex.

American culture swerves into the ditch in June 1972, the day Deep Throat premieres at the World Theater in Manhattan. The purple picture pulls in millions. Deep Throat is followed by equally rough stuff, the Devil in Miss Jones and Behind the Green Door leading the charge. Dirty movies suddenly begin playing on Main Street in towns across America and the crowds keep coming. Upping the ante, X-rated theaters here on 42nd Street are currently running Live Sex Shows between films.

Weary-looking couples drag a mattress out onto the movie house stage every 40 minutes or so, right in front of the movie screen. They hump while the projectionist threads-up the next reel. I came along with Steven and Bobby but only for the popcorn.

I've already moved into my room in Brooklyn. Well, the bedroom actually belongs to Annie Golden, the multi-talented singer for top CBGB headliners The Shirts. Jim Harold made a clever swap with CBGB owner Hilly Kristal. For the duration of the NYC Rat Record Release Party, Jim has The Shirts headlining back in Kenmore Square at the Rat. He also manages to get the key to The Shirts four-decker, brownstone band house in Brooklyn. This is where Willie's Boom Boom Band and Thundertrain will be staying. Besides fronting The Shirts, I hear Golden is in rehearsals for a Hair revival, set to open on Broadway this fall. There's a big poster of Debbie Harry, clad in a sheer blouse, hanging on the bedroom wall and right below it, plopped on the floor, eyes stained with tears, sits Willie Loco's weepy girlfriend, Angie.

Showtime. I pass beneath the famous awning...that must be Deer France working the door. She nods hello. I've seen her face before, probably in cartoonist John Holmstrom's Punk Magazine. She wears her hair like Nico.
The nightclub is on the ground floor, sidewalk level. Kinda feels like a shotgun shack/lemon squeezer at first, crushing past the main bar on the right, every stool occupied, but then the room opens up into a much wider showroom. No dance floor. Cocktail tables and chairs

cover most of the floor space. The 350 capacity nightspot has a really big sound system that frames the oddly angled - but large - stage. Finally I get a close look at the club's signature, antique photographs of 19th Century glamour girls and cowboys (Tom Mix?), blown up life-size and propped along the right end of the stage. Nearly a hundred years ago this room was the saloon of the Palace Lodging House. Maybe the images are left-overs from those days or maybe club owner Hilly Kristal picked them up at a flea market. Wherever they came from, the ghostly visages can always be spotted in live photos taken onstage at CBGB.

9 BOSTON BANDS

WILLIE LOCO ALEXANDER & THE BOOM BOOM BAND,
THUNDERTRAIN,
MARC THOR,
THE REAL KIDS,
THE INFLIKTORS,
SUSAN, DMZ,
THIRD RAIL,
THE BOIZE

APPEARING AT
CBGB's
MARCH 23rd · 27th
315 BOWERY
AT BLEECKER STREET

"Mach, come with me. You gotta meet some people." Danny Fields totes me around to several tables, introducing me to scouts from a half dozen major record labels. Everyone's here to find out what the noise coming out of Boston is all about. We're up next.

Thundertrain opens with Hell Tonite and we hurtle through both sides of Teenage Suicide, streaking to the finish line with Hot For Teacher.

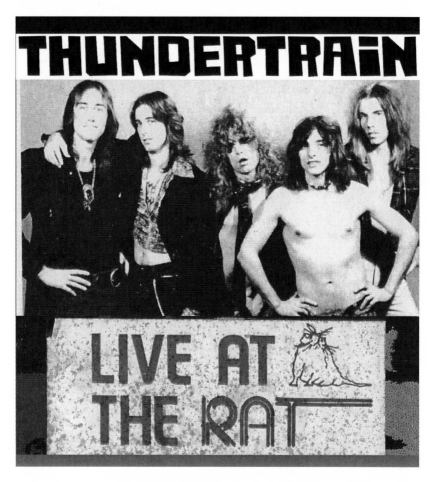

THUNDERTRAIN Photo by Oedipus

The headliner of this party, Willie Alexander and the Boom Boom Band, follow us with their pulsing set. Drummer David, bassist Sev and guitarist Billy underpin Willie's antics and recitations with a surprisingly old-

284

school, hard-rock approach. Take Willie out of the
equation and what's left resembles the James Gang.
Tasty, Jeff Beck-inspired riffage, served hot over a
relentless, booming, tribal beat. While other rock vocalists
harvest the same lyrical row that Willie Dixon and Bo
Diddley extensively hoed, Loco sings about getting a hair
cut. Bimbos, gin, B.U. babies, Jack Kerouac...These are the
topics Boston's "pedagogue of punk" will lecture on
tonight.

Exhausted, but pleased with our Manhattan debut,
Thundertrain subways back out to Brooklyn. Our house
comes with a caretaker and he's right where we left him,
lounging in the front parlor, seated on a sidewalk-find
recliner, staring at the dented, black and white TV set.
Rabbit ear antennas covered in twisted tin foil, the set is
propped on a gold-toned, roll around stand. The walls are
patched and water-stained, the wallpaper is peeling. Feels
like we've walked onto the set of the Honeymooners TV
show.
Upstairs in my room, Willie's girl is right where I left her,
still bawling. I have no idea why she's here and I can't
understand Angie's words through all her blubbering.
Can't tell if its sorrow or booze or pills... Anyway, she's
rolling around on the floor in a Marilyn Monroe-style slip-
dress, moaning in agony that Willie drinks too much -
which she thinks is causing him to ignore her.
Doesn't add up.
Willie just tore up CBGB's. I'm sure he had a shot or two,
but he was in fighting form. I don't share my assessment
with red-eyed Angie - she's totally invested in her sob-
show. I pass out to the sound of whimpering.

Abe Beame, the mayor of New York, publicly acknowledges a serial killer is on the loose. The rash of shooting deaths began last July and the .44 Caliber Killer, also known as Son of Sam, is on the loose in Manhattan. Sidewalk peddlers offer T-shirts emblazoned *Son Of Sam. Get Him Before He Gets You.*

Billy Connors and The Boize are already onstage when Thundertrain arrives back at CB's for the next night of this Live at the Rat Record Release Party. Of all the rockers who pass through 528, Billy might be the closest with Rat owner Jim Harold. Connors and his band play efficient party-rock with lyrics that come straight to the point. One of their offerings from the new Rat album is titled *I Want Sex.* It's not just their lyrical genius that appeals to Jim. No. He and Billy spend a lot of time together around the corner from the Rat. Sitting in the stands at Fenway Park. Red Sox fans, both of 'em.

Variety
Thundertrain(5) Songs 40 Mins. C.B.G.B & OMFUG, NY Hard-driving, unabashed rock'n'roll is being served by Thundertrain in their first New York visit. And, the Natick, MA Combo, ages 21-23, have the power and youthful stage appearances to have impact. Quintet, together for about two years, has an exciting vocalist in blond Mach Bell, who powers his way through a strong original program. Lead guitarist Steven Silva is another exciting performer. Valuable work is turned in by Ric Provost, drummer Bobby Edwards and rhythm guitarist Gene Provost, the bass guitarist's brother.

*With product on Boston's Jelly Records, Thundertrain
also doubtless is a good rock dance band as their high-
decibel rock never lets up. They could have commercial
appeal for youths. - Kirb.*

It's Friday, CBGB is even busier, following good notices
from last night's showcase. Danny Fields points out some
of the faces for me. Dick Kline from Atlantic, Mark Spector
of CBS Records and Arista's Stu Fine. They all watch
closely as The Boize finish their set to rousing applause.
Showcases are different from regular Thundertrain
performances. On a regular five-nighter, somewhere out in
the suburbs, we'll mess with arrangements, ride around on
the bomb or argue with audience members. Gene and Ric
will pause to break into hysterics. Bobby and I will switch
places - I whack the drums while Edwards croons Route
66. All that merriment is ditched when performing at a
Runaways show or playing for the majors in New York
City. Tonight it's just the facts, ma'am. Thundertrain is
proud of our repertoire and that's what we offer tonight.
The music stands on its own, no gimmicks needed.
Some of the Ramones are backstage tonight, as is
Runaway Jackie Fox. I touch base with her for a moment
and she tells me The Runaways will be jetting out in a few
weeks, for a tour of Japan.

Saturday is Thundertrain's last showcase at this seemingly
never-ending record release party. A few of the Rat bands
will stay in NYC for an additional night, but by the time we
come off stage tonight, we're confident we've completed
our mission. Preceding our finale, while moving-out of my

bedroom at the Shirts house, I see Angie is still curled-up in the corner, blubbering. It's confusing because I thought Willie was supposed to be crashing at this same address all week, but I don't think I saw him here once. Teary-eyed Angie is still wearing the same peach-colored slip, booze-stained, reeking of cigarettes and cheap perfume.

Girls are funny.

Following the CBGB showcase, record deals are awarded to DMZ (Sire), Willie Loco Alexander and the Boom Boom Band (MCA) and the Real Kids (Red Star). Our friend Rayboy's band, The Atlantics, who chose not to participate on Live at the Rat, get scooped by ABC Records. Thundertrain is overlooked.

Earthquake calls us with some good news. Jem Imports of South Plainfield, New Jersey wants to distribute our Teenage Suicide record nationally. Our album's unusual cover art is what caught their eye. Jem has been around since 1970. Whenever I search the record shops for a hard-to-locate, phantom track by the Kinks, the Who, the Yardbirds or some new UK band like the Damned or the Stranglers, I always head to the back of the store and check the "imports" bin.

Most of the imported rock discs, on foreign labels like Track, Parlophone and Immediate, bear the circular Jem Imports sticker. Earthquake has struck a unique deal with Jem. Thundertrain will now be distributed in the States by the importer. This is the first time a domestic group will be handled by Jem.

Thundertrain races back to the showband circuit to grub up some gas and rent money. We rock for ten nights straight, split between Lunenburg MA and Manchester NH. Finally, with a night off, I hitch a ride down to the Rat. Selling our singles through the mail, for a buck or two each, I occasionally receive a dollar from a celebrity. One of the first to purchase Hot For Teacher was Martha Davis, vocalist for West Coast band Angels of Mercy, who later become The Motels. Another early Thundertrain record buyer is Dee Dee Ramone.

It's April 17th and walking down the dark companionway that leads to the Rat, I can hear soon-to-be recording artist, Mono Mann, shouting Mighty Idy. After DMZ leave the stage, The Ramones take over.

Regardless of what my lead guitarist says, this Queens-based quartet knows just what they're doing and they're doing great. Dee Dee (Rockaway Beach, 53rd & 3rd) is the main songwriter and bassist. Following a very brief but dynamic set and a couple beers, I need to do cowboy beeps. Its not advisable doing beeps in the dank, putrid Rat restrooms, so I race past back-door-Mark, down the service staircase and out the steel reinforced rear doorway, making tracks to the ever-present, nearby dumpster. I'm back here doing beeps like a cowboy in Springtime when I notice a cat to my right, doing the same thing. Its so dark I can barely make him out, he's wearing a black motorcycle jacket and then I realize,

"Hey - Dee Dee! Great set. They loved your new song."

"Thanks Mach. Yeah, its okay. I mean its pretty much always like this when we play CBs or in Boston...but...hey man. I don't get it..."

"What don't you get, Dee?"

"I don't get you Thundertrain guys. I just don't get you. I heard you at CBs a few weeks ago. I mean...I get why *I* always play that place, and why the Ramones play dives like the Rat everywhere we go...but *you* guys..."

Dee Dee gazes at me in wonderment before continuing.

"I mean...*you* guys should be playing the big places...with Hot For Teacher and all those guitar solos and your drummer and everything. Ramones are doing good but Thundertrain is...well...I dunno...you guys should be *really* huge like...like....*Uriah Heep*."

The very next day I get a call from Stiv (formerly Steve) in New York. The Dead Boys have moved into their own place in the Bowery. They're quickly building a following in New York City. A record deal is being talked about. Bators makes me an offer. If I can set up a Thundertrain/Dead Boys weekend in Boston, he'll put together a Dead Boys/Thundertrain bill in the city. My parents have recently bought a place up in Maine, so their house in Holliston, 25 miles outside Boston, is often empty. I have an idea. I tell Stiv that I'll pitch a return gig at the Rat to Jim Harold. The Dead Boys can crash at my parent's house for a week. Thundertrain's really anxious to see our pals again - but we're in for a shock....

When the Dead Boys return to Kenmore Square for
soundcheck we can't believe our peepers. We truthfully
don't recognize the guys at first. They've chopped off all
their long hair. Gone are the shiny glam pants and scarves.
Replaced with dog collars, buzz cuts and spikes. In the
space of a few weeks they've totally altered their
appearance. Jeff Magnum is a full time Dead Boy now, on
bass guitar, and they're acting like a bunch of New
Yorkers. Direct and hardened. The Thundertrain crowd at
the first show, Thursday April 21, doesn't know what to
make of this odd looking, shorthaired rock band.
They sure sound good though.

Mach Bell and Dead Boy Stiv Bators at the Rat in 1977.
Photo by AnneMarie Martins

Later, back at my parents' house along with a dozen of my girlfriends plus the security and bar staff from the Rat, Stiv pulls me aside. We're in my old bedroom. Bators unwraps some 45 rpm singles he's managed to obtain from England. Most of them are on the Stiff Records label. One single has a funny, nerdy guy pictured on the sleeve.

"Elvis *Costello*?" I choke.

"No way! This has got to be a joke.

"It's for real. He's actually good." Stiv assures me.

Then he pulls out another 45, called "Anarchy in the U.K." by the Sex Pistols. I'm dumb-founded.

"This is what my band is gonna do." Whispers Stiv.

He shows me some more photos of the Sex Pistols. Now I can see where the Dead Boys got the idea for the strange new look...

Fundamentally, Thundertrain has parted ways with the Dead Boys. We're both still loud and outrageous - but Thundertrain is a hard-rock outfit with an eye towards the arenas and the long haul. The Dead Boys have turned themselves into a self-destructive, punk-rock band.

The underground club scene in the cities is evolving fast. More and more bands seem less concerned with good times. The vibe is turning darker. Stiv's violent antics will make headlines – and attract a rougher crowd. I'm a little freaked out by it all. During our Thundertrain set, the girls still push to the front, bopping to the beat in whatever space they can find. During the Dead Boys set, most of the girls retreat as a swarm of salivating guys push to the front, gobbing phlegm, and hurling mock-insults at Stiv and Cheetah.

{ 23 }

Off the Rails
In June, Thundertrain gets another taste of the future. We're headlining the Notre Dame Arena and our opening act is Ric Ocasek's newly refurbished Cap'n Swing, re-named The Cars. Complete with a stream-lined sound and greatly enhanced stage image.
My friend, the DMZ drummer David Robinson, is one of the more dashing-looking characters from our scene and he has been added to The Cars line-up.

Kilsyth Manor is the Reddy Teddy band house. Located on Kilsyth Street, right on the town line between Brookline and Brighton. The big Victorian has plenty of room for the tipsy afterparties that start right after the Boston rock bars close - between 1 am and 2 am.
I'm in the kitchen with Elliot Easton, the easy-going, left-handed lead guitarist for The Cars, talking about the show we both played last weekend. The party begins to really pick-up around us - as often happens at this address.
After consuming a tad more liquor than usual, I go outside to vomit in one of the bushes that surround the stone foundation of this stately Boston residence.

It's dark out here and other inebriated invitees apparently had the same urge as me. I have to poke around for a minute or two to find an unused bush.

After purging myself, I notice Winkin' Blinkin' and Nod
have just landed on my right shoulder.
Yawn.
Gee, I could go for a nap right now.
I pass-out beneath one of the Boxwood bushes flanking the
front porch of this fine New England home. Time passes.
I'm awakened from a sweet dream by warm, gentle rain.
The sprinkle turns into a torrent and that's when I realize
I'm being pissed-on by another blotto - but satisfied -
Kilsyth Manor party guest.

The following weekend Thundertrain books into the Paris
Theater, a movie house in downtown Portland Maine.
Co-billed alongside us is another good band from the Live
at the Rat LP, called Susan. Packing the Rat with
underground rockers is never a problem back in Kenmore
Square - but the Boston smoke signals have yet to reach
Portland Maine - the theater is more than half-empty.

July 28th & 29th, Thundertrain headlines at the Rat with
the Dead Boys opening.
The first night of the summer two-niter is a great success.
Except for one thing. Back at my parents' house in
Holliston, where the Dead Boys are once again bunking,
Stiv Bators and I leave the party and go upstairs.
Guitarist, Cool Gene Provost, Thundertrain's de facto
accountant, joins us.
Cool has the night's door money.
Our pay is a shoebox full of ones. We count it out. Five
hundred bucks. Split between the two bands.
"I don't understand it," says Stiv, looking calm and
studious in his reading glasses.

"Every time we play the Rat the room is packed. The place must hold 200 or more. They charge 4 bucks at the door. There should be a lot more money here." Bator's words unlock the floodgates. For all the work we put in, all the records we sell, the fans we attract...the truth is, we're dead broke. Just to put gas in the truck and keep the gear patched-up takes every penny that comes in.
Money earned by rock musicians, through admissions or record purchases, passes through many sticky fingers before the band ever sees it.
If there's anything left to see....

Stiv and I stay up all night. The Saturday show at the Rat is the hottest ticket in Boston. All the record and radio people, the press – everybody's gonna be there.
On Saturday night at 7 o'clock, only hours before showtime, I call 247-7713, Jim Harold's office hot line at 528. I inform him that neither band will perform unless our demands are met.

Both groups end up playing the Saturday (7/29/77) night show, but it will be Thundertrain's final Boston gig with the Dead Boys. It will also be the last time Thundertrain sets foot inside the Rat for a very long time.
The Boston Phoenix covers the scandalous story, headlined "Thundertrain Smells A Rat."
The Dead Boys and Thundertrain refuse to go on stage unless Jim Harold takes his people off the door and allows the bands to collect the cover charge themselves.

It's late when we finally take the stage, playing short but intense sets. In the end we collect more cash than we'd seen the previous nights - but the stunt is a terribly sad way to end our relationship with the Rat.

Jim Harold, who until this evening, considered me a friend, is deeply hurt by my accusations. Jim has done a lot for me, our band and hundreds of other independently minded rockers, I regret my decision almost immediately.

THUNDERTRAIN on the roof of the Rat in Boston.
Photo by AnneMarie Martins

Teenage Suicide is selling pretty well and on August 2nd
Jem Records releases a sampler LP featuring Thundertrain
and a bunch of the other acts they distribute. I haven't
heard of all these bands but they include: The Jam, David
Coverdale, Elvis Costello, The Saints and the Sex Pistols.
In fact, this LP is the very first US vinyl appearance from
Stiv's inspiration, the Sex Pistols. Thundertrain closes out
Side One of the disc with our famous Hot For Teacher.

Duke and the Drivers pack the Cricket Lounge in Ashland
for four nights with Thundertrain second-billed. A few
days later Northern Studio and Worcester's WAAF-FM
team-up, presenting a live-over-the-airwaves Duke and the
Drivers concert. Bill Riseman invites me and a hundred
other Duke enthusiasts to attend. The party is
momentarily derailed when we get word that the King is
dead. Elvis Presley just passed away.

Thundertrain rocks the suburbs four or five nights a week
and in the city we move our base of operations across the
Charles River to The Club in Cambridge.

Hilly Kristal, manager of CBGB, phones me. The Dead
Boys are taking Manhattan by storm. Kristal is now their
manager, he just landed them a deal on Sire Records. Hilly
says Stiv wants Thundertrain to drive down and play a
weekend at his room with the Dead Boys. Stiv even offers
to put us up at the band apartment. Mick, Jimbo and Jon
load-up the truck and Thundertrain returns to NYC.

Arriving on skid row, we find the Dead Boys apartment.
It's obvious why they enjoy visiting my parents suburban
home so much. This dingy walk-up is in a beyond-sketchy
Bowery neighborhood. You enter directly into the kitchen,
where a bath tub, full of suds, sits smack in the middle of
the linoleum-floored room. No shower curtain or
anything. Bare-ass drummer, Johnny Blitz, is plopped in
the tub, eyes slammed-shut, bleaching his buzz-cut in the
kitchen tub.
Roaches run for their lives from these Dead Boys. The
place stinks. Stiv Bators hangs-up the phone to greet us.

"Hey Mach, welcome back to New York! That was John
Belushi, he showed up at CB's last night and played drums
with us for two songs. He's coming back tonight. We're
gonna have a blast!"
I'm impressed, but the truth is, Thundertrain hasn't had a
Saturday night off in three years. I've yet to actually see
Saturday Night Live or this John Belushi cat in action.
Animal House won't be released for another year.
The apartment is full of Dead Boys news clippings from
American and British rock magazines. Their debut album
"Young, Loud and Snotty" is about to be released. People
are in and out of the flat and the Dead Boys phone rings
constantly. They've come a long way, since the January
afternoon we met, just seven months ago. That's when I
notice scars on Stiv's chest and arms.
A strange, foreboding fear comes over me.

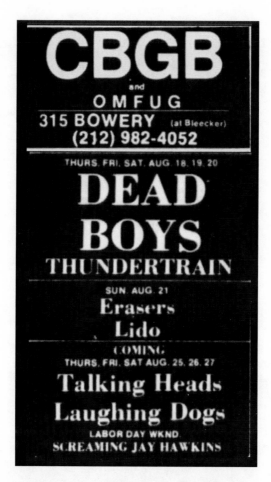

This really is their moment. August 18-20.
The Dead Boy gig is the absolute talk of New York. In our
dressing room, nearly midnight, waiting to go on, I can see
Seymour Stein and Bob Feiden (the heads of Sire and
Arista Records) chatting ringside.
SNL stars, Gilda Radner, Jane Curtin and Lorraine
Newman are at another nearby table. Danny Fields,
writers from the New York Times and the Voice, members
of the Ramones, Television, Blondie – you name it, they
just keep crowding in the door.

Thundertrain hits the stage hard, but I have to wonder,
doing my thing in the spotlight, what this industry crowd
is thinking. Looking out at all the trendy Manhattanites I
suddenly feel like a longhaired hick from Holliston.
One guy, waiting for the Dead Boys to start, sits at his
stage-front table, nose buried in the Village Voice while we
entertain. Steven Silva retaliates by cannonballing off the
CBGB stage, power-chording his Stratocaster mid-air
before crash-landing onto the startled guy's lap.

Steven Silva onstage at CBGB. Photo by AnneMarie Martins

THUNDERTRAIN
at CBGB. Photo by
AnneMarie Martins

The gallery is amused - and we exit to a decent ovation.

How are the Dead Boys gonna top that?

We find out soon enough.

Bators minces out to thunderous applause mixed with punky jeers. They launch a full frontal attack. Writhing across the stage, face twisted in what appears to be pain. Stiv and the Dead Boys definitely look and sound like America's answer to the Sex Pistols. Zippers, pleather, spiked hair and nasty attitude. Then things get weird. Guys push to the front, spitting at the stage. Stiv flips-off the entire audience and proceeds to gob on the front row. The crowd gobs saliva back at the singer. Someone throws a bottle. It smashes against the drum kit. Bators dives into the broken glass, a la Iggy. Bleeding, Stiv crashes backwards into Blitz's kick drum. Cheetah jerks into the next song. I look around, feeling that everything is on the edge of going totally outta control. The faces of the crowd bother me. They don't seem concerned at all. They're digging it. Stiv picks up another glass shard, stabs his arm and slashes the skin wide open.

{ 24 }

Counterattack

Thundertrain heads for the hills. Literally. We load up the truck and take gigs in the Berkshires of Western Mass, Vermont's Green Mountains and New Hampshire's White Mountains. Spending the balance of 1977 rebuilding from the ground up. Writing, rehearsing, performing and further honing Cool Gene and Steven's latest material. "Readin'Riotin'Rock'n'Roll," "Schooldays Rock'n'Roll" "Counterattack" and "Afterschool."

Disco Fever continues to spread, running rampant and gobbling-up venues that formerly booked rock'n'roll acts. Our ever-evolving showstopper "I Gotta Rock" becomes an anti-disco rallying call heard across New England. Jon Macey of Fox Pass was the first person I ever heard utter the words "disco sucks." He said it onstage back in 1976. Macey seemed to dismiss the slogan, so I grab his motto and run with it.

Thundertrain's hot-wired version of the Standells nugget "Dirty Water" is another crowd pleaser that we rework and supercharge. Gene comes up with a Thundertrain power ballad, "Got Past You." We don't usually go in for pretty singing or stacked harmonies, but Steven and Gene work on ways to blend their voices with mine to help define our melodies and add color.

The biggest adjustment is made by our incredible drummer, Bobby.

Bobby Edwards Photo by Lynn Ciulla

Bobby Edwards inventive beats are the hallmark of the Thundertrain sound. As dance floors fill-up and I stomp atop Ric's bass cabs, our songs accelerate. The crowds dig it but the tempo variations don't translate very well to our debut vinyl. Bobby takes control of his meter and we hear our sound getting thicker, heavier and more arena stomp-worthy.

A pair of students attending Harvard Business School have taken over the reins of Thundertrain management. Now that we've assembled a second album's worth of fresh material, Thundertrain is sent back to New York City to land the big record deal.

This is our first time at Max's Kansas City.

The venue, located at 213 Park Avenue South, is about a mile uptown from rival CBGBs, and just across the street from the David Whitney Gallery. A dude named Mickey Ruskin opened Max's way back in 1965 as a steak house. Adopted as a hangout by the art crowd (Roy Lichtenstein, Leo Castelli, Robert Rauschenberg) poets (Allen Ginsberg) and jet-setters (Edie Sedgwick). Eventually rock musicians get added to the mix when the Velvet Underground starts exploding inevitably at Max's Kansas City in 1970 and the venue suddenly becomes the most exclusive club in town. After the Mercer Arts Center gets condemned (the front of the hotel building collapsed in 1973), the New York Dolls adopt Max's as their new base of operations.

Aerosmith get signed to Columbia Records by Clive Davis after their showcase here in August 1972, but the music actually stops for awhile, beginning in December 1974 when the Max's building becomes campaign headquarters for mayoral candidate, Ed Koch. Max's re-opens in 1975 under new ownership, with Peter Crowley employed as house talent booker.

Max's Kansas City really stands-out on the block. The lengthy, jet black awning stretches from the front door all the way to the sidewalk curb.

Emblazoned "upstairs at max's" in neat white type.

A jet black marquee, equally impressive, juts from the
upper floors of the large-windowed, shiny black building.
The marquee is lettered with the same typewritten white
script:
"Max's Kansas City steak lobster chick peas"
The building itself appears similar in size to our own Rat,
back in Boston.

Merry (Joe Flash) beneath the famous awning. Photo by Lynn Ciulla

Max's street level restaurant is white with black accents. The tables are small with white tablecloths and clean looking silverware. I don't have enough bread to get steak so I order cheese and crackers instead (two dollars). The walls of the restaurant, which probably seats 80 or so, are lined with large, framed, black and white photographs of Nico, UltraViolet, Lou Reed, Alan Vega, David Johansen, The Fast, Andy Warhol and other faces I'm not cool enough to recognize.

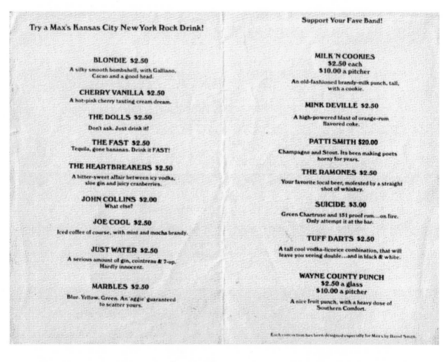

Upstairs at Max's is where the rock'n'roll happens and the vibe is campier than CBGB. This level is basically a standard black box. The ceiling is hung low and once Thundertrain hits the raised stage, I think Ric might graze his head on the ceiling tiles. Lighting and sound is good but not as stellar as the CBGB system. No dance floor, the viewing area, roughly the same size as the Rat, is a maze of cocktail tables, pushed right up to the stage.

I'm dressed down tonight. No point in trying to dazzle the Manhattan crowd with the New York Dolls-style trousers I used to wear at the Stadium. Ric is dressed all in black. Cool Gene looks sharp in a crimson velvet jacket worn over blue jeans. Steven, freshly permed in response to Frampton Comes Alive, is wearing the ultra-femme, black spaghetti-strap top he stole from one of his girl's closets. All I brought to the party is an Idiot's Delight t-shirt and some tight Levis.

Opening with Hell Tonite, our sound is a lot more powerful than last time we hit NYC. Bobby's tempo-control has rerouted some of our wild energy. Superfluous noise, previously backfired out the exhaust pipe is now channeled back into the manifold and turned into extra horsepower. Tonight (10/11) we open for Max's regulars The Fuse Band (Action, Glad to be Alive) with singer Tommy Bell and drummer Niki Fuse. The following night we get co-billed with The Fleshtones, a garage band from Queens.

The Great Gildersleeves is a brand new venue in the run-down Bowery, at 331. With a capacity of 500 and much cleaner bathrooms than CBGB, it's hard to believe both clubs are on the same block. Thundertrain is here on a bill with the Bonnie Parker Band.

Itsy-bitsy Bonnie sings and plays her big Fender bass in the Suzi Quatro style. Parker's been a mainstay on the club scene ever since the days of Biggy Ratt. Tonight (10/25) we rock Gildersleeves and it's a really nice room but lacks the indefinable CBGB magic.

November '77 is a blur except for the evening of 11/21, the night we go to the recently opened Paradise Theater in Boston to see Cheap Trick for the first time.

After the mind-blowing concert, I'm out in the front bar, admiring one of Ron Pownall's color photographs of Joe Perry that hangs on the wall. There's a bunch of other Boston music stars, framed and displayed but Joe is by far the coolest. He's onstage, wearing the tallest cowboy boots with circular tug-holes cut into the tops. I'm just gazing and grazing, nibbling the free Chex mix.

Suddenly a horrifying alien hand swoops-in over my shoulder, it snatches the food right out of my hand. The creature turns out to be one of those gripper, extension grabbers, with a claw on one end. The food-grabbing toy is operated by a devilish-looking Rick Nielsen.

The impish Cheap Trick guitarist escapes before I can properly introduce myself.

New York City welcomes Thundertrain, yet again, the very next week.

We're at Max's Kansas City for two more nights, this time we're paired with Alex Chilton.
As lead singer for the Memphis-based Box Tops, Alex hit the Billboard #1 spot in 1967 with "The Letter."
He was only 16 years old when he hit the top.
Teenager Chilton and his Box Tops continue racking-up Top 40 gold with Cry Like a Baby, Sweet Cream Ladies and my favorite, Neon Rainbow.

Later, in 1971, Alex formed the power-pop trio Big Star (When My Baby's Beside Me, In the Street) with Chris Bell.
I totally missed-out on Big Star but they're one of Ric's favorites.
Tonight at Max's, Alex Chilton favors a more primitive, punk-rock approach.
Opening the show is Peter Holsapple (the dBs, R.E.M.) and his group H-Bomb.

Draw the Line finally comes to market the day after we get home to Boston. Aerosmith have been working on this thing for what seems like a decade. The title song is built around one of Joe Perry's best riffs yet.
A charging slide-guitar line, played on a clear-bodied Dan Armstrong guitar.
Another interesting track, Bright Light Fright, also penned by Joe Perry, not only sounds like punk-rock, it even times-out at a Ramones worthy 2:19.

Mama Weer All Crazee Now, a 1972 recording by Slade, is one of the cover songs Thundertrain is best known for. Even though we're an original act, we usually pepper our set with songs by other artists.
We can play just about anything from the Kinks Greatest Hits.
We open many shows with Around and Round, the Chuck Berry number that also kicked-off the debut album from the Rolling Stones. Silver Train, also by Mick and Keith, is a Thundertrain standby.
Lots of nights we'll encore with Born To Be Wild.

It's our version of the Steppenwolf rumbler that catches the ear of various Hell's Angels, Huns and Devil's Disciples, making Thundertrain the go-to entertainment choice for a variety of motorcycle club functions.
These soirees include a lost weekend where we get hired to perform for random colors attending an international biker rally, held in a sandpit just south of Montreal.

After completing the second day of near non-stop
rocking, Thundertrain is brought to the nearby, hidden
clubhouse.

Whiskey bars are set-up on either end of the concrete-
floored shed. A satin-lined, open casket sits on an
elevated platform in the center of the room.

I'm captured by some of the surliest bikers and stuffed
inside the coffin.

I try to appear calm as the casket lid is slammed shut.
Claustrophobic and terrified - am I about to be buried
alive? Several long minutes pass before the drunks let
me out, having apparently passed the club initiation.

Thundertrain stars at an even worse motorcycle gang
event, held in an anonymous warehouse near
Worcester. Ric is at the wheel of the "jumbo transport,"
a '73 Plymouth Fury III he recently purchased especially
for ferrying the group around. The trunk of this monster
holds six guitar cases, plus all our luggage. There's
plenty of room for the five of us in the cabin - groupies
too - if we want company.

It's already pitch dark on a late December afternoon.
Ric skids over crusty patches of snow, trying to locate
the secret entrance to the Devil's Disciples MC 1977
Christmas Party.

We see a pack of leather jacketed thugs collecting
weapons at the door. Inside the cold steel structure a
fistfight is already in full swing.

More like a beating. One poor rider gets the tar whipped
out of him. They smash his bloodied head against one of
the long planks, supported by barrels, that line the

periphery of the quickly-filling hall. The victim passes-out as holiday beer pitchers are slammed on top of the makeshift bar.

Thundertrain is set-up over near the Christmas tree. Festively decorated with empty pill bottles, arrest warrants and - topping the tree - a big Nazi swastika. None of these hog ridin' revelers seem very jolly, on the contrary, the dead-eyed, meth-heads are just waiting for the next opportunity to whack somebody.

Time to spread some cheer. Thundertrain opens the show with our popular version of Born To Be Wild. Nobody claps but at least they don't murder us.

Thundertrain continues the show but about three songs later, the Disciples instruct us to sing Born To Be Wild again.

We do as we're told as the spiral-eyed goons press against us. At this point it becomes a game of chicken - with bikers demanding we repeat the Steppenwolf hit over & over & over again.

Scared-stiff but still rocking, Steven and I take refuge behind the ampline as we regurgitate the song for the head-butting horde of criminals.

This goes on for what seems like hours.

Get your motor runnin'...

{ 25 }

The Beatles, The Stones and Donald Duck
New Year 1978 arrives and Thundertrain is back at The Club in Cambridge for three nights. Our fan, Jonathan from Wellesley, has changed his name to Johnny Angel and along with another early Thundertrain acolyte, Barb Kitson, they form one of the first New York-style, Boston punk groups - Thrills (Hey! Not Another Face in the Crowd). Thrills open these shows and they'll go on to become a popular, local headliner themselves. It's snowing and it continues to snow for the rest of January.

The day after my 25th birthday the great storm blows in. Riding winds over 80 mph. We've already got nearly two feet of old snow on the ground when this new dump arrives, blanketing the state with an additional 30 inches. Over January and February Thundertrain loses six weeks of work due to snow cancellations.
I get a call from Cap'n Swing's ex-sound man, Alan Kaufman. The enterprising kid immediately puts me to work at the Park Street subway station, hawking official looking parchment certificates he printed-up overnight, that proclaim *I Survived the Blizzard of '78*.

While Thundertrain waits for the snow to melt, Aerosmith is in sunny Ontario California playing to 350,000 at California Jam II (3/18/78). The event, promoted by Wolf & Rissmiller Concerts, also features Mahogany Rush, Ted Nugent, Heart and an old acquaintance, Lou Gramm, and his group Foreigner.

THUNDERTRAIN visits the Boston Public Garden, 1978.
Photo by AnneMarie Martins

Spring finds Thundertrain gnawing on pricey sirloin at Newbury Steak House.

Alan M. Kaufman, a couple years my junior, hosts the fabulous meal while laying out his master plan, detailing our futures together. Former roadie Alan is now boss at AKtive Talent Productions/Management Inc.

His office has an impressive address. 79 Milk Street, near Post Office Square in Boston's financial district.

He's already hired Earthquake Morton as his assistant and he has top groupie Helanie answering the phones in the reception area.

As I understand it, Kaufman comes from a New York family heavily invested in one of the top frankfurter brands in the country. I think our new manager's old man might have helped get this ball rolling. Alan immediately nabs Thundertrain a slot *this* Thursday at the recently opened Paradise Theater. Owned and operated by top promoter Don Law. Located at 967, just a couple miles up Commonwealth Avenue from the Rat and a block from Boston University. Law's new showplace is the hottest venue in Boston. It includes a large front bar and a great stage complete with real dressing rooms. It seats nearly 1000.

For our first show at the Paradise (5/25/78) we open for Reddy Teddy, who are about to call it quits after a six year run. Actually, it's good we're just the warm-up because the moment we get offstage, Alan whisks us across the river to The Club where he has us headlining an after-party show to celebrate AKtive and his new association with Thundertrain. Alan insures a huge crowd by offering a free open bar to every attendee. One of the kids I run into at the open bar is the singer, bassist for a group called Rage. Like Thundertrain, Rage works the suburbs surrounding Boston.
I recognize this guy from a wild photo in Eddie Kent's fashion portfolio. I didn't recognize him without the Ziggy foil space suit, Danny Hargrove.

The Cars stun the rock music world on D-day June 6th, with the release of their debut album.

Thundertrain is back at the Paradise, headlining with another new-to-the-Boston scene band, called the Nervous Eaters opening the show.

Alan waves his wand, and manages to convince Jim Harold to allow Thundertrain back inside the Rat.

Entering the front door for the first time in a year, we're met by a handsomely slick, middle-aged gentleman in a sharkskin suit. His thick, greying hair pushed straight back, smiling behind dark shades.

Mitch is his name. He's been put in charge of the busy front door since we left. The jukebox in the upstairs bar is still loaded with singles from all the local bands. "Loretta" is playing right now, on Rat Records from the Nervous Eaters, they're catching on like fire. The Real Kids and DMZ are still going strong but some of the other Live at the Rat bands have already faded away. Thundertrain's return to 528 is a four-nighter. We alternate the headline spot with the Romantics (What I Like About You), a power-pop group from Detroit.

Cape Cod Cable travels up to Boston, hoping to videotape Thundertrain's added, Sunday afternoon performance. I've never seen a portable video camera before. It's massive and filming requires a ton of light. The Rat regulars have never been subjected to such blinding illumination, it rivals the high-wattage light towers at Fenway Park. While the TV crew dodges dancers - we mess around onstage, jamming on a Dave Clark Five nugget.

That's when I spot them. Moving through the crowd. Sitting down at a corner table.

John and Paul.

I never thought I'd see The Beatles here at the Rat. Figures they'd walk in now. I'm right in the middle of singing "Catch Us if You Can" a hit by their rivals, the

DC5. Calling for a quick break, I scamper back to where the Liverpudlians are seated.

Nearing The Beatles table, I'm flummoxed.

The Beatles look different up close, I mean...wait. What?

Paul introduces himself as Mitch.

"Mitch Weissman."

John turns out to be David Leon.

The mop tops are here on a brief visit from New York City where they're currently starring in *Beatlemania* at the Winter Garden Theatre. A look-alike, sound-alike thing. Produced by Aerosmith managers Leber and Krebs. Beatlemania is advertised as "Not the Beatles, but an incredible simulation."

Opening on Broadway in May 1977, the hit show runs for 1,006 performances.

When we're not onstage, managers Alan and Earthquake have us in the recording studio. June and July are spent at Triton Productions in Brighton. Tracking new songs from Cool Gene: Anything Money Can Buy and Young and Krazy. We head north for more shows in Quebec, then it's out to Longview Farm. At the Farm, one of New England's premiere studios, we begin recording Counterattack, an exciting new one penned by Steven Silva.

Meanwhile, Ric and Bobby are cutting rhythm tracks for Thundertrain's cover version of Dirty Water and Cool Gene's rock ballad, Got Past You.

Julia Channing (the new receptionist at AKtive) just
walked into the Rat accompanied by our newest crew
member. A dude named Oh Bob.
This is my chance to get to know Julia a bit better.
After receptionist Helanie called in drunk, Earthquake
told Alan about Julia. She's just off the boat from
London and Earthquake thinks she'll fit in at AKtive.
It's hard for me to understand her, she speaks softly and
talks in an upperclass British-way. She says lots of
words and phrases that are foreign to me.
I impress her a little bit, I guess, because she accepts my
invitation to the next Thundertrain show. Tomorrow
night up in Lowell at the Commodore. Our first date.

"The Rolling Stones are playing the Paradise."
That's the rumor going around Boston. The marquee at
967 reads: Dr. J. Jones and the Interns.
Our manager manages to scrounge up tickets and I can't
wait to finally see my favorites, the Stones.
I have to admit, I'm a bit deflated when the mysterious
Interns turn out to be Aerosmith.
I haven't seen our local rock sensation perform in a
really long time. Has it really been seven years?
And boy, have they changed.
They don't seem to be playing on the same team
anymore and I can't recognize any songs - just
unidentified sound waves roaring off the stage.
Aerosmith used to be so tight and fresh, tonight they
sound mushy and burnt out.

Duke & the Drivers are doing a New England tour and they've added Thundertrain as opener on lots of the shows. Earthquake Morton is back on bass guitar and Nighthawk Jackson rocks the lead guitar.

THUNDERTRAIN with the Drivers at Foley Stadium Worcester MA 1978. Photo by AnneMarie Martins

On a night-off I head to Paul's Mall (733 Boylston St.) where the Drivers are headlining. Turns out to be one of the very last nights before the famed twin venue - The Jazz Workshop/Paul's Mall - closes its doors for good. My dream comes true when Cadillac Jack calls me up to the Paul's Mall stage . Here I am, singing lead on Duke & the Drivers biggest hit, "What You've Got."

Thundertrain feels that with our songs, our stage show, our diehard supporters and the dues we've paid, we're bound to be the next big thing out of Boston.

Radio plays us, the press follows us and we keep getting cool gigs. We're miffed when a local band called New England gets discovered by KISS's Paul Stanley and signed to Infinity Records.

Next up, a phantom band called Boston lands a deal with Epic. Nobody we know has ever seen or heard of this group before.

Meanwhile, the latest Thundertrain demo submission has actually passed several levels of A&R scrutiny at Atlantic Records. Ultimately, the label sends Thundertrain another "regretfully, we have decided to pass" notice. I'm crushed.

Watching Thundertrain's rejection letter-pile grow to haystack proportions, I'm getting more than a feeling that we've somehow missed the boat. By 1978, we're feeling like the perennial bridesmaids. Still, the gigs are steady and Alan has us back in the studio cutting more demos: Afterschool, Moth to the Flame.

The big signings from the Live at the Rat campaign fail to catch fire with the public. Willie Alexander and the Boom Boom Band (Radio Heart, Kerouac) release two strong records on MCA and land an opening slot on the national Elvis Costello tour. DMZ (Don't Jump Me Mother, Mighty Idy) come to market at the same time with their Flo & Eddie-produced debut on Sire Records. Local faves, The Atlantics (One Last Night, When You're Young), tour with Roxy Music and have product out too. Their album Big City Rock, is on ABC Records. None of the maverick, underground Rat bands make a dent in the charts.

Meanwhile, New England's first single (Don't Ever Wanna Lose Ya) breaks into the Top 40.

The debuts from Boston (More Than a Feeling) and The Cars (My Best Friend's Girl) will both go multi-platinum.

Van Halen makes a splash this summer.
The California quartet released their debut LP eight months ago and it jets all the way to #19 in Billboard. An increasingly rare feat for a guitar-powered, hard rock, glam-band. Alan secures Thundertrain the opening slot on a Van Halen show by sending VH's management a Thundertrain press kit. Complete with a copy of our claim to fame, "Hot For Teacher."
Off we go to Ohio.

We're booked to rock the Cleveland Agora. Thundertrain hopes our big break has finally arrived. Earthquake has a connection at the local powerhouse, WMMS-FM, where Duke and the Drivers received a lot of support. Top jock, Kid Leo, allows me inside "the Buzzard" where I make a quick on-air pitch about our Agora debut.

Returning to the venue we're flattened to find Van Halen has scrubbed the date (9/5/78, they open for Black Sabbath in Maine instead). The only saving grace is our Cleveland show will still go on. Thundertrain rocks the Agora, but without David Lee Roth or Eddie Van Halen. In their place the venue brings in a hard working Indianapolis group called Roadmaster.

Oh well, at least Van Halen got a free copy of
Thundertrain's "Hot For Teacher" out of the deal.
The Neighborhoods are a really young band. They're
opening for Thundertrain this weekend at the Rat.
David Minehan, the teenager who leads the trio, sings
and plays guitar. David tells me he was inspired to start
his group after seeing Thundertrain at Lakeview
Ballroom.

Mach and Bobby with
THUNDERTRAIN at
Lakeview Ballroom,
Mendon MA.

Photos by Lynn Ciulla

A couple days later its back to the Paradise. We're opening this time for The Dictators. Prior to the show, I'm at yet another recording studio, Soundtrack, over by the Boston Garden, adding lead vocals to all the tracks the guys have been laying down. The talented engineer on this session is named Michael Golub. By the time October rolls around the mixdowns are finally complete. A week later, on October 14 we all go to a wedding. Our guitarist Cool Gene Provost gets hitched.

Cool Gene Provost at the Thundertrain Mansion.
Photo by Lynn Ciulla

Counterattack, one of our best new songs, premieres on WBCN while Thundertrain is working in Troy NY.

A rousing call to arms, Counterattack opens with both Thundertrain guitarists harmonizing a soaring dual-lead line over a hurtling bass & drum cadence.

The vocal melody is strong, with Steven's best-yet lyrics:

I've been waitin' so long to play for you
I've been hopin' you'd really want me to
The feeling's so strong - I can't wait too long
I can see you, thousands of miles away
I can hear you, thousands of miles away
The feeling's so strong - I can't wait too long
The fools will fill you, full-up with rules in school
I'm here to tell ya, the fools can be overruled
Fight back, Fight back, Fight back, Counterattack
The fools will tell you their way of life's ideal
But to us, their lives just seem so unreal
The feeling's so strong - I can't wait too long
Soon you'll see, that all of your fears are gone
To hell with them, We ain't doin' nothin' wrong
Fight back, Fight back, Fight back, Counterattack

First to air the new Counterattack demo tape is WBCN's Charles Laquidara, star of the top-rated Big Mattress Show. If Charles plays it, it must be okay.

Thundertrain gets even more spins from the new hire, Mark Parenteau. Worcester-born Mark, starts out at WORC-AM at age 15. The deep-voiced announcer gains a Detroit following at WKNR and WABX before moving back east, working first at WCOZ-FM and then taking over Maxanne's top-rated afternoon 'BCN drive-time shift.

Another new DJ at WBCN who pushes the Counterattack demo is our old ally, Oedipus, now with his very own air shift at the Rock of Boston.

By the time Thundertrain returns from New York, competitor WCOZ-FM has also begun playing the Counterattack tape.

Our timing is a little off, now we're headed down to DuBois PA where our demo tape is receiving zero airplay. We'll spend another week rocking anonymously at the Hitching Post while bunking out back in a haunted toolshed.

Lucky for us the new song has legs. Returning to Boston we hear the guitar harmonies of Counterattack spill from the radio in Ric's jumbo transport.

Alan has us at the Paradise Theater tonight (12/9) with an even younger punk-band called "Unnatural Axe." Then it's back to Albany for a showcase at Hullabaloo. Our first time here and we're paired with Capitol City sensations, Zachariah, a nice bunch of well-seasoned, rowdy rock players.

We'll finish 1978 down the road apiece in Troy NY. Dudley Do Rights is the club, we play here regularly. I even have a fan here, a smiling teenager named Joanie. We're still here at Dudley's when New Years Eve rolls around. We've been headlining all week but tonight we play second fiddle to a

resuscitated Iron Butterfly. Butterfly show up late to the party with zero gear.
We end up letting them use our equipment but Thundertrain doesn't own an electric organ.
In A Gadda Da Vida with no organ?

Following the psychedelic Iron Butterfly set - straight outta 1968 - Thundertrain exits quickly and heads back towards Boston. 1979 is here and Steven is starving. Pulling off I-90, somewhere near the Massachusetts state line, we find a 24 hour supermarket. A big place, like a Purity Supreme or a Grand Union. The five of us are the only food shoppers at 3 a.m. Some guy is waxing the floor and another lady is stocking shelves. We all grab a candy bar or some crackers. Bobby wants yogurt. He goes searching while we line-up at the check-out.

Purchases made, we head back outside to the jumbo transport. Wait. Where's Bobby?
We look back and *shit* - he's being questioned by a security officer. We run back into the supermarket where the cashier and the officer are examining a spoon. Not just any spoon - this spoon has a dumb looking plastic duck-head stuck on the end of it.

Bobby just got busted for stealing a Donald Duck spoon. Another security guy joins the scene at the register. About a half hour later, they release our drummer. Making our getaway, the thief spills his guts...
"All I wanted was a stupid yogurt. I didn't have a spoon. So I looked in the ice cream aisle, searching for a wooden one.

Y'know, like those flat ones that come free with Hoodsie cups... I couldn't find a wooden spoon so I tried to find a plastic one. There was nobody around to ask...and you guys were already leaving...So I ran down the aisle and that's when I saw the duck spoon. I think it's supposed to be for a baby because it was with the Gerber stuff. Anyway, Donald Duck was the only spoon they had, so I stuffed it in my pocket."

If not for WBCN and their frequent airings of Thundertrain music, we'd be sunk. Man the lifeboats, it's 1979 and suddenly the survival of WBCN is in doubt. Hemisphere Broadcasting takes over the operation, putting Michael Wiener in charge. Weiner's mission is to bust the union that represents all the station staffers. He pink-slips more than half the WBCN employees, including new hire Oedipus. In retaliation, everybody walks off the job, even the high-profile jocks.

Despite biting cold, a union (United Electrical, Radio and Machine Workers of America Local 262) picket line forms out front of the 52 story-tall Prudential Tower where WBCN occupies the top floor. Scab talent is elevatored-up to the booth by Hemisphere and suddenly 'BCN is broadcasting all these strange voices - talking to us as if nothing's out of the ordinary.

Support for the strikers quickly spreads to city venues like the Orpheum (formerly the Aquarius), where Private Lightning, The Fools, Sass, Pousette-Dart Band, James Montgomery and Robin Lane and the Chartbusters perform in support of the WBCN walk-out.

Thundertrain headlines one of the first WBCN Strike benefits, at the Rat with Charles Laquidara hosting.

The strike is ultimately successful - Oedipus and the rest of the regular jocks return and all the terminated staff members get their jobs back. Mr. Weiner will later use WBCN as the launchpad for Infinity Broadcasting.

WCOZ-FM broadcasts from atop Boston's other major skyscraper, the John Hancock Tower (200 Clarendon Street). Boston Beat is a weekly radio program dedicated to local sounds, hosted by Leslie Palmiter.
Leslie convinces her radio station to get behind the release of "The Best of the Boston Beat - A Collection of Boston Rock & Roll." The 1979 compilation includes tracks from Jon Butcher's Johanna Wild (Suzanne), The Fools (She Looks Alright in the Dark), The Atlantics (I'm Hooked), The Stompers (This is Rock & Roll) and Luna (Hollywood).

Luna features one of my favorite drummers, Joe Pet.

Ms. Palmiter is prescient with her musical selections. All the bands listed above will continue on to major label contracts. Thundertrain closes out Side One of the album - with our updated version of the Standell's "Dirty Water."

THUNDERTRAIN Photo by Lynn Ciulla

Dirty Water becomes one of Thundertrain's most-played recordings. Originally cut at Longview Farm, our cover of Ed Cobb's song features a greasy slide-solo from Steven.

The resulting Dirty Water tape is sent out to labels as a demo and gets solid radio play on all the New England rock stations.

For the WCOZ album, Alan sends Earthquake and me to Intermedia Sound Studios (331 Newbury St.) to re-cut my Dirty Water lead vocal.

This is my first time inside the studio where Aerosmith made their first record. Joining me in the control room is old friend James Montgomery. Earthquake trades a six-pack of Heineken for a harmonica solo.

After a few healthy swigs, bluesman Montgomery whips out a harp and starts riffing. Montgomery's musical addition replaces half of Steven's original guitar break. Later, after the album comes out, Steven wonders what-the-hell-happened to his carefully constructed solo.

Leslie Palmiter goes on to present a full one-hour Thundertain concert on WCOZ Playback (2/7/79). Recorded just a week earlier (2/1) at the Summit Room, a motorcycle club hangout in Peabody MA. The recording is made by the Starfleet mobile and it will be the last time Thundertrain records together.

Thundertrain returns to Hullabaloo in Albany where we open for my current favorite band, the David Johansen Group (Funky But Chic, Girls).

Then it's back to NYC where we showcase for A&R man Paul Atkinson at "the rock disco" Hurrah (36 West 62nd St.) Mr. Atkinson was formerly the lead guitarist for British band The Zombies (Time of the Season, Tell Her No, She's Not There).

THUNDERTRAIN   Photo by Lynn Ciulla

Massachusetts is about to raise the drinking age.
First to 20 (on 4/16/79), and soon back to 21. Overnight
Thundertrain's core audience is locked out of the clubs.
The final evening of teen drinking happens during a two
night stand at the Main Act in Lynn. The huge venue is
packed with noisy juveniles. The following evening, with
the drinking age raised by two years, Thundertrain is all
alone, playing to the bar staff and our road crew.

So much confusing stuff is happening to rock'n'roll right now. Led Zeppelin just broke up. KISS takes off their make-up. Joe Perry leaves Aerosmith.

Thundertrain limps along, trying to appeal to college age (and even older) crowds but most of them act like they've outgrown our high octane sound and wild escapades.

Fueled by growing financial pressure and doubts about our musical direction, long simmering feuds between me and lead guitarist Steven Silva erupt.

After five glory-stomping years, Thundertrain calls it quits.

{ 26 }

Thundertrain Speaks
*The following Q & A is reprinted from the booklet
that accompanied a 2002 CD re-issue of
Thundertrain - Teenage Suicide.*

STEVEN SILVA Q&A

What made you want to play rock'n'roll?

"Pullin' birds." The preceding spoken with the true Scouse accent of my earliest influence - The Beatles. Right, me and about a gazillion other musicians. So much for artistic expression; the creative imperative; blah, blah, blah. As a young lad, it always comes down to sex, right?

Were you in bands before Thundertrain?

I was in the requisite number of cellar bands - the New England version of garage bands - before landing in Thundertrain. All pretty unspectacular.

What was the inspiration for Thundertrain?

Inspiration? Please refer to preceding birds/sex response. Later, we also had a somewhat political (or anti-political) agenda. Mach and I would give interviews against the powers-that-be, and my songwriting, while preoccupied with school-type situations (there's those darn schoolgirls again!), would at least attempt to slip in some slight, innocuous anti-establishment suggestions about maybe burning down the school etc. Alice Cooper songs were a good template for this type of teen-angst.

Why did you choose the band name Thundertrain?

The name "Thunder Train" was coined by Bobby, I believe. I think Ric wanted "Hot Chrome" (gasp!) and I was pushing for "Show Biz Kids" (gack!). Our second rehearsal space was afternoons in the back of a club that had railroad tracks about ten years behind it. Every hour or so, the building was rocked by passing trains. When we realized that we were louder and more rockin' than Amtrak - and my suggestion of making it one word "Thundertrain" (Aerosmith and all that) was accepted - the legend began!

How did Thundertrain fit into the scene around the Rat in Boston?

In the beginning, we didn't fit at all, and that was perfectly fine by me. The first time I set foot in the Rat, Mach had brought me down to see the song stylings of one Mickey Clean & the Mezz. I was aghast. His set consisted pretty much of three-chord songs (always the same three chords) and him falling off the stage. Fleeing as soon as the set was over, I announced to Mach that he was nuts if he thought we would go over with this crowd. As far as I could tell, they were all art-damaged trendies and scenesters, and we would be looked at as a bunch of hay-sticking-out-from-behind-our-ears suburban rubes. And with that I stomped off into the night. Well, even though the tragically hip never really embraced us, our high-energy shenanigans wowed the college kids, and we became one of the biggest draws at the club. We truly kicked ass and left a footprint.

Lead guitarist/songwriter Steven Silva of Thundertrain.
Photo by Lynn Ciulla

Did you feel alienated by punk?

Yes, I must admit I never acquired a taste for punk. Just not my cup of meat. And as an aging rocker, I realize I'm on thin ice when I paraphrase Lenny Bruce:

"There's nothing sadder than an aging punk."

What did you think about Van Halen's "Hot for Teacher" when it came out?

Well, I lifted the title from the back of a paperback stroke-book that advertised such uplifting entries as Teacher's Pet, After School, Teenage Tease, and other onanistic classics. I'm sure Dave Roth saw our album, and had the same reaction I did: "Wow, what a cool title!" So he in turn lifted it from us. Creativity was ever thus.

Can you tell me about "Modern Girls," your tribute to lesbian ladies?

"Modern Girls" was written about my first menage-a-trois. (Merry and Beth, where are you today?) It was an unmitigated disaster. I felt like a completely unnecessary appendage. Although to this day, that's still my favorite lyric:

I know the times are changin' Romance rearranging,

Call me old fashioned if you like.

But like the little Dutch boy, when the tide was turning

I have to do my duty, and keep my finger in the dike.

How long did the band continue after the LP was released?

We continued for awhile, buffeted by increased indifference from the record companies and changing tastes from Boston audiences. Punk! New wave! Disco, for chrissakes! Timing is everything. We saw bands that opened for us become superstars (The Cars). Unknown local bands rocket to stardom (Boston). Good, better, best, bested. That was our declension.

We quit at the perfect time.

We had run out of 8 x 10s. The dream is over.

What's up with you currently?

I'm still rockin' l.a.m.f. every night. Too young to die, too old to tour.

GENE PROVOST Q & A

What made you want to play rock music? What are your early influences? Were you in bands before Thundertrain?

Girls, girls, girls were my major motivation for playing rock. And it lived up to all the hype and then some. My earliest influences, once I figured out how to play the instrument, were the British blues players like Clapton, John Mayall, and Peter Green. And that turned me on to the black roots of B.B. King, Albert King, etc.
I always felt that blues was at the base of all our songs. My brother Ric and I played in several bands before Thundertrain. The Provost Brothers Band, which had Phil Provost on drums, was a combination of blues and country-rock. I took a break from playing while in college, then Ric started a band called Doc Savage. We put it together through ads in the Boston Phoenix, and it was a short-lived, kick-ass, hard-rock band. Didn't get around to any originals, though.

When did Thundertrain get together?

Thundertrain came about when my brother Ric and I were in the process of putting another band together after Doc Savage. We saw Mach and Bobby in a band called Biggy Ratt. We thought they looked cool and seemed to have the attitude, so they hooked up with us. Steven answered an ad. We were more interested in his looks and stage presence than his guitar virtuosity, but he brought both. The purpose of TTrain was quite simple: Have a great party, get babes, and make a fortune, if at all possible. And oh yeah, make music. Most important was having a good time that the audience could feel.

When you released Teenage Suicide in 1977, punk-rock was beginning to dominate the underground. Did you feel alienated by punk, or did you feel like Thundertrain was part of it?

The punk scene allowed us to enter into a vibrant time, even though we were technically not punk. Our manic stage show and obnoxiously loud approach got us lumped into the punk rock category. We wanted the punk energy and attitude, but with well-constructed songs and some degree of quality playing. Punk was too raw for the mainstream anyway, but cutting-edge stuff usually is. Remember Blue Cheer leading the way into high volume and attitude? Do you ever hear a Blue Cheer song now? And my favorite band of all time, Slade. Talk about being ahead of their time. Quiet Riot gets the hits 15 years later. Never hear Slade today, though.

I think we felt like part of the scene, not alienated, but we also felt that we wanted to be taken a bit more seriously as musicians and songwriters than most of the punk bands.

Cool Gene Provost. Guitarist & songwriter with Thundertrain.
Photo by Lynn Ciulla

How long did the band continue after the LP was released? What led to the band parting ways?

The band lasted about two years after the album. I was the first to leave. I guess I felt that we had peaked and it was getting time to make a decision regarding the future. Take a chance and keep rocking, or go the straight route. There are times I regret not continuing.

It's hard to leave that excitement behind. I just lost some of my motivation. We had a short-lived band called The Hits, after Thundertrain, that was a 90-degree switch from Train's style. Pop music.

I knew that Mach and Steven would continue in the quest for success. I think Thundertrain could have been successful if a strong manager and producer worked with us to refine the sound a bit. We were working on it ourselves but you often need an outsider's influence. We cut a few demo tapes that were much more polished sounding, but I guess the thrill was waning at the time, at least for me. One thing that stayed even to this day, is our love for each other. No matter how hard things got, we got along extremely well. When we get together today, which isn't that often, we still have a great time partying.

Can you tell me about your musical activities after the end of Thundertrain?

I guess I was the only member of the band to not continue playing. I went into the banking business and became a dad. Once I felt that I wouldn't be playing in front of a crowd, I lost my desire to play altogether. It appears I was more of a performer than a musician.

 Even with all the great things of kids and family. I can assure you that no time will ever compare to my years in Thundertrain. Not even close.

Playing with a bunch of great guys like we had was beyond belief. It's the greatest feeling in the world, sometimes even topping sex.

RIC PROVOST Q & A

What made you want to play music?

To get laid, paid, create a scene, and raise hell - have a wild time every night, see the world not as a tourist but as a participant, and to be the epicenter of all the action.

What bands influenced you early on?

The Shadows of Knight, the Standells, Richard & the Young Lions, the Animals, the Five Americans, Barry & The Remains, the Beacon Street Union, the Blues Magoos, the original Velvet Underground, the Other Half, the Grateful Dead (first album), J. Geils, Big Star, the Stones.

What was behind the formation of Thundertrain?

Five guys who saw absolutely no future in the boredom of routines working straight white or blue-collar 40 hour-a-week jobs. I was still reeling from barely missing the draft for Vietnam. I didn't believe in the American way - there was no security or trust in the establishment. We were five guys who felt we knew better. What did we have to lose by shooting at the moon? We were five guys who had the balls, determination, intellect, and imaginations - plus we all needed freedom of life - five distinct reasons for success. Ask each one and you'll get a different response.

Ric Provost, bass player, writer, driving force and principal architect of Thundertrain. Photo by Lynn Ciulla

Why did you decide to do your first single on your own, rather than look for a record deal?

No record company would sign such a wild-card, loose-cannon bunch. We were difficult to categorize, and we didn't have that standard New England rock-and-roll look: thick black shag hair, Magnum P.I. macho mustache, Jimmy Page pose. We had real angst and we let it show. We were truly over-sexed, over-energized, anti-establishment guys who weren't going to take any corporate crap, with a take-no-prisoners attitude. What chickenshit A&R flunky would dare pull us in when you could safely attempt to launch bands like Starz, Bad Boy, and Roadmaster? You could take their image home to mom - but not ours. We were extremist politically and sexually - nothing sacred. Just the way I loved it!

When Teenage Suicide came out in '77, punk-rock began to dominate the rock underground. How did you feel about the punk thing?

In my opinion there were no real punks, except for the Dead Boys. Most of the bands around at that time were misfit pussies who bought biker jackets, couldn't play their very marginal instruments, but subsequently found a niche and a way to finally get their dicks sucked. The real punks weren't playing at the Rat - they were stealing the tires off your car, or raping your chick in the car park behind Kenmore Square. We were a big part of the Rat scene. Our road crew rebuilt the Rat stage, expanded the room, and rewired the place so it could handle a real sound system and lights. We were in the thick of it, if not leading the pack most of the time.

What did you think when Van Halen's "Hot for Teacher" came out in the 80's.

I was in shock, because when that came out we were fighting to climb the Boston rock ladder again. Thundertrain had broken up. And there was some really good new blood on the scene. I'm sure Van Halen heard of the song, as well as our band, but didn't give a rat's ass who did what. They had big corporate bucks - and what a great title! What guy didn't choke the chicken at least once over a teacher?

Can you tell me about your musical activities after the end of Thundertrain?

The Hits (1979-80), Mag 4 (1981-82), Johnny Barnes Back Bay Beat (1982-84), Ric & Phil Provost (1984-85), UK Union w/ Bobby Edwards (1989-90), New Thundertrain (1991), British Yankees (1992 - xx), who released the CD Legendary Knights in 2001. I've also been employed as an optician for almost twelve years. I had to get a real job!

BOBBY EDWARDS Q & A

What made you want to be in a rock band? What were your early influences? What bands were you in before Thundertrain?

Girls, girls, girls! The Beatles, the Stones, and the D'Angelo brothers (the Joneses, Mad Angel) influenced me. Before Thundertrain, I played with a band called Biggy Ratt.

When did Thundertrain get together, and what was the inspiration for the band?

August 1974. Testosterone (girls!).

How did Thundertrain fit into the Rat scene?

We owned the scene.

Drummer Bobby Edwards of Thundertrain. Photo by Lynn Ciulla

Was it through playing at the Rat that you got Willie Alexander to play on your second single?

No, it was cheap wine and girls - the only reasons to play rock'n'roll.

Because of the time, you often got lumped in with punk-rock bands. Did you feel Thundertrain was part of that scene?

The industry thought we were part of it, but we knew better.

How long did the band continue after the Teenage Suicide LP was released?

We were together five years, and then we got tired of the Punch'n'Judy show between Mach and Steven.

Do you think Van Halen knew about Thundertrain's Hot For Teacher?

Oh, please!

Can you tell me about your musical activities after the end of Thundertrain?

I played with The Hits, Mag 4, Velocity, and did a lot of recording to no avail. I'm not currently with a band.

{ 27 }

Circus Vargas 1981
While Thundertrain is in the middle of our final band meeting and splitting up, some bastard is stealing our equipment. Most of our gear has been left stacked near the pinball machines in the back of the Rat. That's where the heist goes down. Ric amazes me yet again - I had no clue he'd taken out an insurance policy on all our gear - guaranteed through Lloyd's of London no less!

When the dust settles, and with new equipment, the Provost brothers, Bobby Edwards and I will carry on as The Hits. Influenced by the current chart success of acts like Graham Parker, the Romantics, Joe Jackson and the Knack, we streamline our sound and play live shows as a quartet. This is a full revamp, we don't perform any Thundertrain material.

Alan M. Kaufman and Earthquake Morton of AKtive Talent Productions continue to represent us. In the studio our quartet is aided by Billy Loosigian, the fabulous lead guitarist for Willie Alexander's Boom Boom Band (and soon, Robin Lane and the Chartbusters).

With Steven out of the picture I feel more confident about writing songs again. Cool Gene continues to crank out good ones too. But it's a powerful number that Ric Provost and I pen together, a dramatic thing called *Storm Brewing* that suddenly takes off for The Hits. Both mega-watt rock stations in the city, WCOZ and WBCN play it daily.

A promising omen for 1980, but no - too late, Cool Gene leaves us, to begin a full-time job in finance.

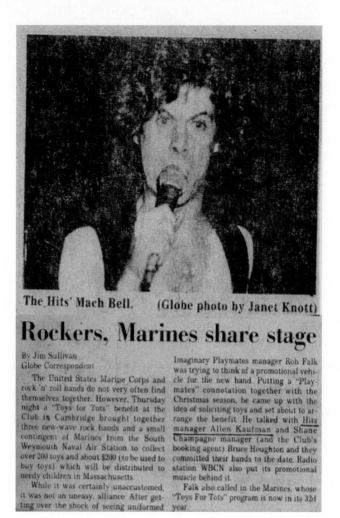

The Hits' Mach Bell.   (Globe photo by Janet Knott)

Rockers, Marines share stage

By Jim Sullivan
Globe Correspondent

The United States Marine Corps and rock 'n' roll bands do not very often find themselves together. However, Thursday night a "Toys for Tots" benefit at the Club in Cambridge brought together three new-wave rock bands and a small contingent of Marines from the South Weymouth Naval Air Station to collect over 200 toys and about $200 (to be used to buy toys) which will be distributed to needy children in Massachusetts.

While it was certainly unaccustomed, it was not an uneasy alliance. After getting over the shock of seeing uniformed

Imaginary Playmates manager Rob Falk was trying to think of a promotional vehicle for the new band. Putting a "Playmates" connotation together with the Christmas season, he came up with the idea of soliciting toys and set about to arrange the benefit. He talked with Hits manager Allen Kaufman and Shane Champagne manager (and the Club's booking agent) Bruce Houghton and they committed their bands to the date. Radio station WBCN also put its promotional muscle behind it.

Falk also called in the Marines, whose "Toys For Tots" program is now in its 32d year.

Airplay and gigs are still coming our way but The Hits ain't no Thundertrain. I mean, we're basically the same guys, but now I'm realizing the power a "brand name" wields. Struggle we did, but the Thundertrain name carried cachet, a mystique I never fully-valued until now.

I miss being lead singer of Thundertrain terribly, and a lot of our fans take the dissolution of the brotherhood really hard. Our identities are interwoven with the Thundertrain name and legacy. Anytime The Hits are mentioned, it's accompanied by "former Thundertrain members."

Now it's 1980, Steven is playing in a cover band. I go over to Bunratty's (186 Harvard Ave.) to check it out. His group is nothing to write home about, the main thing I remember are the expensive looking red leather pants Steven is wearing. Bobby and I convince former Biggy Ratt colleague Big Bill to join our Hits. I'm writing some really strong songs and Jon Read records us with studio gear he's assembled. We play gigs locally, but somehow the thrill is waning. The path forward is unclear.

Bobby and I decide to strip this thing down even further. He's been learning to play guitar and he's okay. Just for kicks we scrounge up some acoustic guitars and compile a bunch of cool tunes we can harmonize on. Eddie Cochran, Stones, Elvis Presley type-stuff. I sing lead, Bobby harmonizes. Sometimes he strums, sometimes he keeps time, paddling on the body of his guitar like a bongo drum. We call our little act The Beat Brothers. Maybe this duo idea came about subliminally, I'm not sure, but one thing about The Beat Brothers - we're extremely compact, built to travel light.

John Lennon is murdered in New York City on December 8th. Reeling, Bobby and I take the senseless tragedy as some sort of sign. Time for us to take a chance, a crazy gamble. On what? Not sure about that.

We just need to shake things up. Real good. And it's starting to get cold in New England.

We book a cross-country ride on a Trailways bus for $99 each. Bobby and I end up joining a three ring circus out in Phoenix Arizona. Circus Vargas. We'll travel with the show for a couple months, working under the Big Top.
What do you do after your rock band breaks up?
If you're me, you join the Circus.

Here's the diary I kept while traveling with Circus Vargas.

Monday Jan 12, 1981

"Life is grand" offers Bobby as he polishes off the Jack Daniels, 40 miles west of Harrisburg.
Big sendoff at Natick Trailways. Mother, Bobby's aunt Marjorie, his brother Elliot and Mary Beth.
Bill Dill bids us farewell via phone.
2 acoustic guitars. 2 back packs. 2 bedrolls. Bobby's bag 'o tricks. A sack of vegetables. A bit more than a pint of Jack Daniels in Dr. Ric's farewell travel kit. The bus line is running a "See the USA for $99" deal, a ticket good for a whole month of travel anywhere on the mainland.
Left MA at 1 pm. Zero degrees on a sunny day. Worcester, Hartford, Manhattan. Stop at Port Authority. 2 onion burgers. Bus driver looks like Homer Bedloe. Board St. Louis bound bus at 6:15pm. We get the last seat in the rear, next to the john.

Broke out the medication at 8:30 pm, outside
Philadelphia.
Eileen, a student, lends us her bus schedule. We party for
awhile and rap. Next stop Pittsburgh 3 am.

Tuesday Jan 13

Route 70 west. The Beat Brothers eat some grub at 3:30
am in Pittsburgh. Bus stops are in the funky area of most
cities. Lots of action at the White Castle at quarter to 4.
Homer Bedloe splits and the meanest man in the world
takes over at the wheel. As we pull out at 4:30 am ("fifteen
minutes late" grumbles Bobby as he peruses Eileen's
schedule) the driver announces
"No playing musical instruments."
Shit man, just what we planned to do at 5 am.

We sleep through the tip of West Virginia and hit a snow
flurry stretching through Ohio. Bobby and I begin new
careers as contortionists. Only 12 people on this Trailway
Silver Eagle, so I move to another duo-seat.
The Beat Brothers attempt to sleep. Fifty miles east of
Columbus. I check on Bobby who appears to be dead.
Since nothing can be done with his remains right now, I go
back to sleep. Next stop Columbus.
"Most snow we've had" claims a liar.
Bobby rises from the dead, thanks to Doc Provost's
medication.
Sitting in Terre Haute, Indiana. Met up with a bunch of
new passengers we picked up in Columbus.

Andrew - who looks like Richie Cunningham - his little sister, and the mom. All are re-locating to New Orleans. The Mad Inventor is carrying a suitcase full of stuff he supposedly patented. He sizes up the Beat Brothers as a couple of ex-cons. He actually is one himself. The Mad Inventor proceeds to explain to me how he rode for six years on just one bus ticket. Liar.

We stop outside Indianapolis and discover that some of Bobby's secret whiskey is missing. Dig into some McDonalds chow and enjoy the sunny 35 degree temperature. A heat wave compared to Pittsburgh last night. Somewhere near here the time zone changes. Dunno if it has yet. We're feeling a bit baked after our first 24 hours of riding.
Back on the bus heading for St. Louis on I-70.
A conman named Richard is threatening to stuff Andrew (Richie Cunningham) into a pillowcase and drag him behind the bus.

We speed through Illinois and cross the Mississippi just after sundown. The Beat Brothers applaud the Archway. Stop at the St. Louis terminal where I hang while Bobby purchases some hootch. Back on the road, heading south through Joplin and Springfield where we say good-bye to the Cunningham family. The ex-con has turned into a pain in the ass. We're happy when he splits in Springfield. The bus rolls through the Pan Handle state on Route 66. We try to sleep.

Wednesday Jan 14

No more snow and the temperature is rising. We meet a
lady with a cute tot. They just returned from Las Vegas.
She shows us a pile of coupons she'd been handed on the
street for free food and other junk. Anything to get the
tourists into the casinos. Maybe we'll give that town a go -
later on. I listen to my transistor radio. A killer cold snap is
wiping out the Florida citrus crop. 5:10 am Oklahoma City.
The beat Brothers decide to take a more southerly route.
We load our stuff off the Silver Eagle and wait for the 8 am
Dallas bus. No room for our guitars and luggage on the
Dallas coach - so our gear gets thrown onto another bus
that leaves 15 minutes ahead of us.
9 am. Heading down into Texas. Green grass and a nice
clear day. We plan to layover in Dallas this afternoon.
Change our shirts, wash and hopefully write a hit song.
Lots of cattle and oil derricks. Bobby snoozes while I watch
the scenery roll past.
Bobby wakes-up and I talk about jetting home in glory
later this Spring. We're both feeling good. While we're in
town I want to visit the grassy knoll and meet all the
Cowboy cheerleaders.

Dallas is great. We get off the bus, locate and locker the
gear. Then it's off for a sightseeing walk. Shirt sleeve
weather, its even sweaty! Look at Texans and try some B-
B-Q at Laidback Lenny's. A cold Coors beer knocks me out.
My brain is sizzled from lack of sleep. We head over to city
hall and play a few Beat Brothers tunes on our guitars. Our
debut outdoor show and our first show in the west. A guy

with a Super 8 films us singing. Zapruder? We find a
grassy patch on the other side of City hall where we lie in
the sun. I can see the book depository building.
Bobby sleeps for a bit. We head back to the bus terminal to
check our bags onto the 6 pm Los Angeles bus and wait
around. I write postcards.
After we get back on the road fatigue sets in and we both
crash. Westbound, I think we're on I-80 now but soon
we're on I-10 heading for rangelands.
Sometime after midnight the coach develops a
transmission problem. In Odessa a bus is waiting and we
all transfer. It takes about 45 minutes, then, like Duke and
the Drivers, we're Rolling On.

Thursday Jan 15

I wake up an hour before dawn to see the scruffy trees
disappear and the desert begin. Cactus, sand, mountains,
wind erosion. This is really the West. Slowly the bus wakes
up and we all stare out the windows at the landscape. An
occasional abandoned stone building. Mine shafts.
7 am. Breakfast in Van Horn TX. A real cowboy town.
Just a strip with some adobe-style restaurants, a theater
and a beauty salon. The Beat Brothers eat a good
breakfast. I go next door and buy some celery, carrots,
oranges and crackers for the next stretch. Bobby and I gaze
out at the strangeness as the coach pulls out. Leaving
town we see a character with a heavy pack strapped to his
back. Heading west on roller skates. Where the guy's
headed - who knows? There's nothing but miles and miles
of zilch ahead of him.

Lunch stop in El Paso. The Beat Brothers walk in the hot sun. The mud architecture is funny to us. This town looks more Mexican than USA. We check out the snail-shaped convention center. Magazine racks only have romance, True Story-style mags. No rock mags. We also see stores that only sell soap opera-type books. Due to the transmission breakdown last night, our new driver has to make-up time. We blast through a corner of New Mexico and cross into Arizona.

The terrain gets more amazing. Balancing rocks, barrel cactus, paddle cactus, sagebrush, tumbleweeds, prairie dogs and cattle scattered out over the range. Entering Tucson we see military jets doing Blue Angel-style tandem maneuvers. Really wild. Tucson is beautiful, ringed by mountains dotted with pretty little parks. Girls too. A huge "Chicago Music Store" indicates a healthy local music scene. The Beat Brothers agree that Dallas and Tucson are winners.

The sun sets and we zoom the last 120 miles north to Phoenix. We hit town, feeling totally burnt. Happy but a bit nervous as we get off the bus. This is a heavily policed city. We hope it's not gonna be a big hassle. We check into the "Luxury Motel," peel off our socks, brush our teeth and shower for the first time in four days.

Friday Jan 16

We can't afford to live in luxury for more than a night. In the morning we check out, grab our stuff and wander down the street. Low riders rocket past us. Some slow

down to shout at us or wing an empty bottle our way.
Eventually we come to the local shopping mall. We hear
music playing. Not rock. Sounds more like a brass band.
Then we see an elephant walk by. An elephant with a sexy
babe riding in the crook of its trunk.

Turning the corner we see it.
Right in the middle of the mall parking lot. A huge four-
pole circus tent, gleaming blue underneath the Arizona
sun. Twice the size of the Carousel. Flanked by smaller
animal tents, a snake house, a rolling box office and
various food concession trucks.
The elephant with the girl on top tails-up to thirteen other
elephants and more glittering women, posing outside the
backdoor tent flap - waiting to be introduced to a youthful,
noisy crowd inside the Circus Vargas Big Top. Bobby and I
want to get a closer view of the showgirls, so we hustle
closer to the tent. Above the entrance I spy a metal sign:
"Young, Strong Men Wanted. Join the Circus.
Talk to Horse."

We watch the pachyderms march into the darkened tent as
the band begins a safari-style theme song. Judging from
the ovation, we can tell the crowd is loving it.
I'm intrigued.
"Wadda you say Bobby? Let's talk to Horse!
We can join the show!"
Bobby isn't so sure, but... if it means a place to keep our
gear safe and a roof over our heads...why not?
Horse turns out to be a big galoot from Walpole MA.

Not the town, the State Prison. Horse killed the guy who married his ex-wife. Horse says the guy deserved to die because he was abusing Horse's kid. The murderer has us both sign some papers, then he tells us both to get inside the tent and watch the afternoon show for free.
After that, we're to report to wardrobe and begin working at tonight's performance.
We're with the show!

Saturday Jan 17

Last night Bobby and I stayed in Cell Block 8.
No, I haven't been sent to jail again. The Cell Block is an old travel trailer with 8 bunks. Newbies are sent here I guess. Cell Block 8 is parked way-out on the farthest edge of the lot. Near the smelly horse-meat trailer and the

roaring generators. I can see the empty trucks that carry the canvas and bleachers from town to town. The circus performers and executives all have their own sleek RVs, parked much closer to the Big Top.

Fish is the den leader in our stinky bunk house. There's just enough room for our guitars and packs. I even have a filthy window next to my mattress. Another Cell Block inmate, a teenager named Shorty, is impressed with our guitars. He immediately becomes our new little buddy.

Shorty. Inside Cell Block 8. Circus Vargas 1981

Circus Vargas will present two performances today. An afternoon and evening show. Bobby and I got fitted for tuxedos yesterday, after we watched the first show for free. There's one part in the middle when the lights go down and this big white, winged horse - a pegasus? - canters-out and waltzes around the center ring under a blue light. It sure looks real but I'm not sure if the horse actually has wings.

I don't quite understand it yet, but we're supposed to be ushers today, helping customers to their seats. Then, when the people complain that their seats suck, we're supposed to up-sell them to better parts of the stands
 - a ticket upgrade.

Sunday Jan 18

Our final night in Phoenix. Immediately after the evening show the crew tears everything down and packs up. Even before the last of the excited customers exit the front of the tent, the bleachers are already being collapsed and dollied-out the back door via two extremely well choreographed forklifts. With the seating out of the way, the elephants join us and begin collapsing the shorter tent poles that push-out the sides of the tent. This is done using chains. The large animals enjoy helping with the heavy work. The three rings are dismantled and removed along with the lights, the rigging and sound. Our circus employs almost 200 crew members. Some are busy loading the electrical truck, the pole and stake trucks, food service and office equipment wagons. Besides Pegasus, we have regular horses, zebras, llamas, dogs, lions, tigers and elephants. Each with their own handlers, enclosures and special vehicles. The putrid smelling horse-meat truck provides big meals for the big cats.

Bright moon tonight, things quiet down on the lot. I follow several of my co-workers as they clamber up to the apex of the Big Top. The canvas is released from the 4 main tent poles and it slowly deflates. We remain up top, chugging beers and enjoying the long, slow ride back down to Earth.

Monday Jan 19   Yuma AZ

I was fast asleep when Fish hitched Cell Block 8 to a truck cab and rolled us out of Phoenix. Rising this morning in the midst of a grassy field. We're parked on the Yuma Fairgrounds. Right next to the military base. Jets will be screaming over my head for the next three days.

Bobby and I are dressed for summer in our jeans and t-shirts. Our tuxedos get returned to the wardrobe truck every night after the final performance. Two over-worked women are trapped in there, bent over sewing machines in a trailer full of racks, draped with an impressive variety of bejeweled, elasticized, sequined, triple-stitched creations.

Clifford E. Vargas is the truly bigger-than-life guy who started this whole show. Cliff lives in Beverly Hills, but whenever "America's Big Top Giant" hits the road, so does he. Mr. Vargas has what I'd call a Las Vegas look. Think Wayne Newton, Elvis, Liberace. Vargas has a George Hamilton tan, dark glasses, semi-pompadour haircut dyed a shade too-dark, a perfectly groomed moustache and ultra-bright, white-capped-teeth.

Clifford founded this circus in the mid-60's with just three trucks and no animals. By 1973 he'd grown it into the "world's largest, classiest and most superlative traveling circus." Circus Vargas offers something for everyone with its fantastic wild animal acts and beautiful, youthful performers, average age 25. Six of the more alluring showgirls on display are called the "Vargettes."

I can hear Horse yelling.
Then I see a bunch of guys in the field, a few are from Cell Block 8. They're all pounding stakes into the ground with sledgehammers. Long, hefty, iron tent stakes. I scan the horizon and notice a wobbly pile of folding chairs.
I make a bee-line for the pile.
Horse is yelling at everyone to load-up with more iron and keep swinging. Bobby joins his fellow musclemen and hoists a sledgehammer over his head.
"Where the Hell is Bell? curses Horse.
Then he sees me, off in the distance. Dragging a plastic chair across the grass.
I wave back at Horse.
Bobby Edwards is a macho guy and he's really strong.
He races ahead of the other brutes, holding out his arms, calling for more iron.
"Load me up. Load me up."
I keep my head down and arrange folding chairs. Horse keeps screaming at me to grab a hammer. But I think he knows I'm not cut-out for hammering stakes into the dirt. Lucky for me, David, the seating superintendent, walks by and gives me a bit of direction. David is impressed that I took it upon myself to start moving the plastic chairs.

"Bell has initiative."
Hopefully I can continue messing with these rickety seats at every stop from now on. Bobby and his pals can swing sledgehammers for Horse.

Circus boy Mach Bell. You can see the Big Top behind me.
Photo by Bobby Edwards

Tuesday Jan 20

The Vargas crew and the circus animals have already turned this lovely grassy lot into a dirty, muddy, dustbowl. It'll get even messier when the hordes begin arriving in a few hours. I check the donniker. As usual there's a line forming near the rear of the show's only bathroom trailer.

Everyone is waiting for a shower. The donniker only has
two shower stalls for the 200 crewmen on this lot.
No matter how dirty and stinky I get, at 2 pm I simply
head over to wardrobe and get handed an immaculate,
dry-cleaned monkey-suit for the day's performances.
Even if I'm covered with sweat and grime, I feel a lot more
respectable after wiggling into my crisply pressed tuxedo.
Off the circus lot, in Washington DC, Jimmy Carter steps
down and Ronald Reagan is sworn in today as the new
President of the United States.

Wednesday Jan 21

Air Force jets take off every 5 minutes. Right over the tent.
The horses try to kick out of their rings as the roaring
fighters zoom overhead.
This Circus is a spectacle with top quality acts throughout.
Fierce lions and roaring Bengal tigers open the show,
baring their teeth at a brave Tarzan-guy inside a caged
enclosure within the center ring. To the beat of African
drums, the big cats make their entrance, racing through a
steel chute that stretches from the cat trucks parked at the
"back door" of the tent, straight into the center ring cage.
After being sufficiently tamed, the lions, tigers and brave
Tarzan exit the Big Top.
Ringmaster Joe Pon introduces a dozen young aerialists.

Ropes are lowered into all three rings. Scantily-clad
women are spirited skyward to perform an aerial ballet.
On the lot we call this act "the web."

Meanwhile, in the darkness below, the Rex Williams crew tears down the big lion cage. The clowns divert attention, doing some quick business along the ring curbs before "a captivating collection of college-bred canines" come yapping into the center ring.

Then we present "perch pole perfectionists" from Poland. Followed by a trio of juggling teams, simultaneously working in all three rings. The juggling families hail from Holland, Mexico and Italy.

Next, we have a magician with his lovely assistant.

Spoiler alert. The magician actually has two lovely assistants - identical twins. Very helpful when making a girl disappear, only to re-appear a second later, locked inside a chrome cage suspended at the very apex of the Big Top.

I've never seen the two golden twins together at the same time, but Presto and the identical sisters all live together in a late model RV parked right behind the ticket wagon.

Lots of juicy rumors about what goes on in there...

Thursday Jan 22   El Cajon CA

When I wake up, Cell Block 8 is parked in the middle of a huge shopping mall parking lot in a suburb of San Diego. A textbook southern California spot, ringed with hills.

Friday Jan 23

Between shows I wander through the adjacent shopping mall and meet a rather sultry dish named Kathy. She sells sausages at the Swiss Colony Store.

We talk and laugh for a bit and make a plan to meet-up later. But I never hear from sausage girl again. My hoped for birthday date is a flop.

On my birthday, animals dine while we begin setting up the circus tent. You can see the four 56 foot center poles in the distance.

Saturday Jan 24

I've squirmed my way into a couple of the circus acts. I've been leading a haltered llama around the three rings during the mid-show Circus Parade.

I also got asked to fetch runaway hounds from the stands during the "College Bred Canines" dog act.

Sunday Jan 25

I'm finally beginning to understand why they invited me to
"help out" with the dogs. I'm not really retrieving
runaways. These trained animals are totally in on the joke.
Every time I dash into the bleachers after one of the
"escaped" pooches, the mutts get the better of me.

I'm racing through the stands, tripping all over myself,
trying to catch these college educated dogs, while the
audience howls with laughter at me. Even the dogs are
chuckling at the confused little dude in the tuxedo.

Payday! Bobby Edwards and the Vargas Big Top.

Monday Jan 26

We pick up our first check at the pay wagon. Joe is General
Manager, he tells us we can cash our check at the
Company Store. Lots of guys join this show with no dough
in their pockets. No dough is no problem at the Vargas
Company Store. They will gladly provide you with
cigarettes and sandwiches *on credit*. A thin, Wonder Bread
and olive loaf sandwich goes for five bucks. Cigarettes are
three bucks a pack. Almost 6 times what they sell for at the
gas station up the street. This makes me very happy that
Bobby and I had a few bucks for eats and beers during our
first week of employment. We owe nothing to the
Company Store, so we collect our weekly salary in full.
Lots of these Vargas employees will never get out of debt
to the Company Store. It's just like the old Tennessee
Ernie Ford song "16 Tons"
"I owe my soul to the company store."

Tuesday Jan 27 Carlsbad CA

I'm arranging folding chairs in the box seats while Bobby
and the rest of the real men pound tent stakes into the
blacktop at another shopping plaza parking lot.
A bigger than usual mall here in Carlsbad. A double-
decker. I can hear homicidal Horse shouting at my friends
to work faster, pound harder.
As usual there are plenty of onlookers, including several
yellow busloads of innocent school children on a circus
field trip. They stare as our hungover crew of ex-cons,

cheats and brawlers turn the empty parking lot into an enchanted city of painted canvas, music and wild animals.

Wednesday Jan 28

Carl joined Cell Block 8 the other day. At the end of every evening show he hands around free buckets of popcorn to the rest of us. Seems like a friendly thing to do. Until I catch him during our post performance clean-up chores. I see Carl underneath the stands, sweeping dirty popcorn into little piles and scooping it into discarded cardboard pails.

Friendly Carl

Thursday Jan 29

Shorty discovered a fantastic rope swing out in the forest behind the Carlsbad Mall. We rack up some good rides before the afternoon show. The smell of the eucalyptus and California sunshine is intoxicating.

Friday Jan 30 National City CA

This town sits on the USA/Mexico border.
Circus Vargas is king all over Southern California.
For years, Johnny Carson has been making jokes about Clifford's flashy circus during his opening monologues on the Tonight Show. Vargas spends a fortune on TV ads in SoCal, saturating all the major stations. We'll be in National City for five days. Ten shows. Every single one will be sold out. They used to call it a Straw House.
That's when the crew scatters straw on the ground in front of the bleachers for extra seating after all the real seats have been sold.

Saturday Jan 31

I have to admit it. I stink.
The showers are always busy. Long lines. Even at 3 am.
It's no use. So I bathe in the donniker sink, that's about it.
It's tough, living on unpaved lots like this one. Nothing but dust, mud and filth. It gets worse with each performance.
We're set up in the middle of a pasture - flanked by a warehouse zone. Nothing but anonymous buildings and sprawling car dealerships line the boulevard.
No fast food. No bars. No rock.

Sunday Feb 1, 1981

What's up today? Two more big shows, that's what. It hadn't really occurred to me when we signed up for this job that there would never be a day off, no holidays...just circus, circus, CIRCUS.

Fist-fighting doesn't sound like fun to me, but a lot of my co-workers really enjoy ending their circus day by rolling in the mud with towners who come to our lot looking for a scuffle. V.C. is the boss canvas man and he makes it clear that he doesn't allow his crew to brawl on the lot.

"You better not let Mr. Vargas catch you guys fighting."

Monday Feb 2

The man who owns the Serpentarium just hired me to set-up and take down his exhibit at every stop. His reptiles travel inside a steel trailer.

Serpentarium

There's a bunch of panels that fold-out, hoist-up and chain-into-place. Once un-folded, the trailer looks about twice as tall and a lot longer too. The panels are painted with all kinds of frightening Godzilla and Ghidorah looking creatures that you can supposedly see inside for 50 cents. I didn't see anything like that in there.

Just a two-headed snake inside a cardboard box.

I'm getting paid $25 per stop to set this contraption up.

Tuesday Feb 3

What a bloody mess.

A new electrician joined the show yesterday. I didn't meet him myself, but I heard that he was an okay guy. Tonight is our last show at this too-long, National City engagement.

Horse is screaming at us.

"Get these people seated before the lion and tigers begin."

I'm busy pointing kids in the right directions when I hear an actual "blood curdling scream" for the second time in my life.

Rex William's crew of animal handlers race in through the back door of the tent. A fire blanket is tossed over a body. Additional crew follow with a bale of straw and sawdust pails. The windjammers on the bandstand lurch into action. Honking a vigorous "Stars and Stripes Forever" - the universal emergency signal for circus workers - while the widening pool of blood gets sopped-up and the blanket-covered corpse is removed.

A moment later - spotlights up - safari music, Tarzan enters the big cat cage to enthusiastic cheering and shouting from the audience. The lions and tigers go through their paces innocently.

According to Rex Williams,
"My animals can be trained but never tamed."

Looks like the crowd totally missed the mauling, the gore
and the confiscation of the carcass. Entering a darkened
circus tent, full of color, motion, noise and hundreds of
people, patrons are busy finding their seats and keeping
track of their kids. None of tonight's ticket holders seem to
be aware that a killing just occurred.
Over by the tiger chute.

We rip through the performance.
I rarely see Clifford Vargas inside the tent during the show.
Tonight he's impossible to miss. Cliff's top guys are with
him too, Jack, Gary, Kenneth...
Finally, the elephants tail-up and do their dance routine.
Satisfied throngs flood out of the Big Top.

Now it's our turn to line-up.
Clifford stares each of us straight in the eye.
"As you all know, something unfortunate happened here at
my circus tonight.
Everything's been taken care of.
Nothing more needs to be done.
Nothing.
If anyone asks you anything...Say nothing.
Nobody here saw, heard, or knows ANYTHING about what
happened tonight. Is that clear?"

Wednesday Feb 4 Riverside CA

Rolling up the California coast in Cell Block 8. I think this is my favorite part of circus life. The sound and feel of our trailer home as it glides through the night air.

Nobody can sleep. It was the electrician. A young Spanish speaking guy, working his very first show with us.

He got within a few feet of the tiger run. A Bengal tiger, waiting for the act to begin, reached out between the bars of the steel tunnel. Fish says it looked like the tiger was just giving the new guy a playful swat.

Fish: "But then the Bengal's claws dug in.

Through the guy's shoulder and back. Real deep.

The cat just tore him in half."

Shorty whispers that Jack and Joe from the office sent some of the toughest crew members to lose the blood-soaked evidence and handle the body removal.

I'm tuned to my transistor radio, clutched to my ear, wondering if there'll be any news reports about the grim event.

We're pulling into another shopping mall parking lot.

Thursday Feb 5 Riverside CA

Dead tired. No sleep last night and then double duty, setting up the Big Top and the Serpentarium. Followed by two performances. At least we're back on a paved parking lot, away from that dusty, dirt lot in National City.

This is a nice mall with a food court.

Friday Feb 6

The elephants, lions and tigers are all owned by Rex
Williams. He's about 60 years old and he still travels with
the show. He lives with his animals. The handlers
employed by Williams are a mean, unpleasant bunch.
Not to the animals, no, they're sweet and patient with the
animals. The animal handlers treat the rest of us humans
like shit.
"Hey. You. Bell. Scram! Stay away from the elephants."
One of the William's guys is screaming in my direction as I
wander back home to Cell Block 8.

During our performances I get to spend plenty of time
with the elephants. I feel a close kinship to them. Like
humans, these animals started out in the wild, and like us,
it's obvious how much they appreciate having a protected
home for their families. A safe place where they can rest
with their clan, get watered and dine regularly.
Before man invented heavy machinery he had elephants -
and the Vargas pachyderms take great pride in their jobs.
A continuing legacy of helping-out us weak humans.
The elephants perform the heaviest tasks on the circus lot.
Struggling with a tent pole, a team of musclemen is bested
whenever an elephant takes over.
Show business is in these animal's blood. Just like me.
I wasn't around for the Cleopatra days (69-30 BC) but I'll
bet you a cookie that even back then, elephants were
parading, standing on their hind legs and trumpeting to
the delight of thousands.

Circus Vargas carries 14 elephants, a team of horses, camels, llamas, zebras, dogs and a winged pegasus.

Like me, these performers feel at home around large crowds. They respond happily to applause and human joy. They tail-up (create a chain by linking their tails and trunks) whenever they hear their theme music cue up. When Joe, the largest bull, lifts a Vargette into the air with his tusks - everyone can see the proud twinkle in his eye - and every audience erupts into applause.
Support your local, hard working, performing elephant!

Saturday Feb 7

Next week we're playing the Hollywood Bowl. I've never been to the Bowl myself but I saw pictures of The Beatles playing there in 1964. Seventeen years ago.

Bobby and I are getting a little antsy to run away from this circus life.

But there's a big problem.

When we joined the show back in Arizona, Horse had us both fill out paperwork that included addresses for our final paychecks to be sent. If you quit this show you don't just grab your cash on the way out the door...no, they hold onto your earnings for a week and then mail the check to whatever address you provided the day you signed on. In our case, the checks will end up back in Massachusetts at our parents' houses.

Getting ready to raise the canvas.

The only way to leave Circus Vargas with all our earnings, is to get fired.

Sunday Feb 8

Somebody made a major Big Top gaffe by opening one of
the tent flaps right in the middle of this afternoon's
performance.

A shaft of California sunlight pours into the darkened Big
Top just as the show's fourteen elephants, tailed-up, begin
thundering around the three rings.

Attracted by the sudden bright light, one of the elephants
breaks formation and escapes from the tent. Jumbo is
running loose. Hoofing straight for the Riverside shopping
mall. This isn't one of our compact elephants either, this is
a full size pachyderm on the lam.

I leave my post long enough to watch a bunch of William's
team go chasing after the scared beast. Shoppers are
screaming, car horns honk. The elephant is heading
straight for Woolworth's.

The handlers catch up to the confused animal. They flank
the bull and using wooden prods, they manage to slow him
down. Jumbo is relieved, seeing all his buddies. He allows
them to guide him back to the safety of the circus.

Monday Feb 9 Montclair CA

New town. New mall. No food court this time though. As
usual, our show commandeers at least half the parking
area with our trucks, trailers, RVs, the Big Top, several
animal tents, the Serpentarium and other structures.
While I set up the snake-house I see a bunch of unfamiliar
big rigs pulling onto the lot.

Wardrobe trucks, lighting trailers, mobile dressing rooms, camera trucks... is someone shooting a movie here?

Tuesday Feb 10

CBS is filming a circus-themed, made-for-TV movie *Leave Em Laughing* on the lot while we present our usual two shows a day.
The film stars Mickey Rooney as Jack Thum, a real life Chicago area clown who raised dozens of homeless children. 37 of them over the years. When the grown-up kids discover Thum is terminally ill, they all come back to the circus to visit the clown one last time.
Anne Jackson plays Rooney's wife, Shirlee.
Red Buttons, William Windom and other familiar faces are in the cast. Former child star Jackie Cooper is the director of this tearjerker.

Wednesday Feb 11

I'm trying my best to cast myself into this TV movie.
This could be my big break. The film crew is shooting constantly, throughout all our performances, so I try to be anywhere I see the cameras pointed.

Thursday Feb 12   Hollywood CA

This is it. I've made it to the Hollywood Bowl.
Well, not exactly. We're actually in the Hollywood Bowl parking lot on North Highland street. The legendary venue, built into a hillside amphitheater, is right over

there. Off to the left of Cell Block 8. Traffic on the
Hollywood Freeway 101 rushes past me on the right.

We get to work, setting up the lot as usual. Boss canvas
man, V.C. plots the exact placement of each element. The
four, 56' center poles are raised first, using a combination
of winch, forklift and elephant power.
There are 136 additional support poles to drag into
position and 500 tent stakes to pound into the blacktop.

Once the skeleton is erected, the canvas is rolled out,
cabled and raised. Unfurled, our fireproofed, midnight
blue Big Top canvas measures 90,000 square feet.
Back in 1956, Life Magazine predicted the end of this
American tradition, the traveling Big Top circus, after
Ringling Bros. folded up their tent for the last time in
Pittsburgh.

Tent circuses have been on the decline ever since a deadly
1944 Ringling Bros. Barnum & Bailey tent fire injured 682
and killed 167 during an engagement in Hartford CT.
Thousands of children and their parents, trapped inside
the inferno, stampeded toward the tent's nine exits.
Some doorways were blocked. The show's four water
trucks were all a quarter mile away, carrying water to
animals and spraying down the dusty lot.
The circus tent had been waterproofed with a mixture of
1,800 pounds of paraffin wax and 6,000 gallons of
gasoline. A giant Molotov cocktail waiting to be set off.
Safety measures had been ignored or overlooked.

Civilian manpower was scarce during World War II. The
circus was badly understaffed. So was the city inspectors
office and the Hartford Fire Department.
The cause of that massive blaze has never been
determined.

Shorty and the author outside the Circus Vargas tent. A very rare pic
of Cowboy wearing a cowboy hat. Photo by Bobby Edwards

Friday Feb 13

V.C. and a couple of Rex William's crew took Joe and two
other huge elephants off the lot and rode them down
Highland Avenue and up Hollywood Boulevard this
morning. Lots of media outlets and TV trucks cover the
action.

Police divert traffic for several blocks so the big-eared trio, festooned with Circus Vargas banners, can trudge up the Boulevard of Broken Dreams to the delight of children of all ages and press photographers.

Saturday Feb 14

Wild fistfight on the lot last night. Between the Hollywood towners and our Vargas brawlers. I huddle inside Cell Block 8 during the violent melee. Plenty of slugging, bottle smashing and cursing.

Sunday Feb 15

The Vargettes and a bunch of our other performers are wearing sexier, body-baring wardrobe for this L.A. stop. The TV and film stars are flocking to our evening shows along with their agents and publicity people.

Zsa Zsa Gabor turns up to ride a horse around the ring during the "Exquisite Equine Dressage" portion of the show. Child star Danielle Brisebois from "Archie Bunker's Place" sings the National Anthem.
Pint-size Herve Villechaize (Fantasy Island) strides in, all dressed in white except for wee, black cowboy boots and a buckskin, fringed cowboy vest. Tiny Tattoo poses with a towering elephant before taking his seat.
This is all duly recorded and photographed, I guess for appearances in supermarket tabloids or morning TV chat shows. Most of the other celebs just come to enjoy the popcorn and watch the lavish Circus Vargas display.

Monday Feb 16

I'm ushering celebrities to their box seats.
I recognize a bunch of them.
Connie Stevens and a couple of her actress-looking
girlfriends need help getting to their section.
I say "Hi Cricket" and she grasps my hand, giggling.
Mr. C from the "Happy Days" TV show and his wife are
next in line. His real name is Tom Bosley and he's wicked
friendly, just like on his TV show.
Escorting people to their chairs sounds like pretty easy
work. The only problem is - there are already people
sitting in those reserved seats. When I ask the squatters to
show me their ticket, they give me a dazed look and tell me
they "no speak English."
Horse has no pity for me. I can see him at the front
entrance, waving his fists and glaring at me.
Mouthing threats.
"Hurry up, Bell. Get these people into their seats before
the lights go down and the cat act starts. *Or else.*"
I race back to the front.
Celebrity guitarist/singer Charo and her guests need help
finding their seats. I guide the cuchi-cuchi girl to the
correct box and, guess what?
A family of five are already lounging in Charo's reserved
seats. A curly-haired mom with her four children.
"May I see your tickets please?" I bark, anxiously.
Of course the woman claims she doesn't understand me.
Now the lights begin to dim. Horse gives me the hairy
eyeball. I'm losing my temper.

"Lady. Get out of that chair. *Now*."
She and her kids all stare straight ahead. Not moving.
What this lovely family doesn't realize is that underneath
my civilized-looking tuxedo, I'm actually Mach Bell, the
live-wire lead singer of Thundertrain.
"Okay, honey. That's it. You had your chance."
Mach Bell is gonna raise some hell tonight.
Sitting beneath the woman's chair I spy two big sacks of
food.
The first notes of Tarzan's jungle theme ring out.
Bang. I reach down and steal the lady's groceries.
Both bags.
Startled, she looks up at me in shock. The kids begin
crying as I dump the contents of the family's shopping
bags all over the sawdust surrounding the center ring.
Momma makes a dive for her canned tomatoes.
Charo plunks her ass into the vacated chair.
I bum-rush the crying children out of the reserved box.
They scurry to mom. She's cursing me in a language I
don't understand while she scoops her dinner off the
ground.

"You're Fired" screams Horse.
His head is suddenly jammed inside my left ear.
"Get outta here Bell. Get OUT!"

After ditching my tux at wardrobe, I scoot over to the pay
wagon and collect every cent of my earnings.
I'm surprised to see Bobby Edwards standing outside the
gate. Counting his money.
"Hey what's going on?"

"Same as you. Horse just fired me."

"No shit? That's great, Bobby! How? What'd you do?"

"Actually, I didn't have to do anything.
I told Horse that if you were fired, I was leaving too, and I wanted all my money. Horse didn't like that. He told me nobody leaves with their money, unless they get fired."

"Yeah, Bobby, I know all that. So what happened?"

"Not much. I told Horse I'd pull something during the fourth act - I was all set to do it too - and he knew it. I challenged Horse...and he caved."

"But Bobby...What were you gonna do?"

"Doesn't matter, man. I got fired and I got all my money. Horse didn't want to find out what I had in mind so he just screamed at me to grab my shit and beat it."

Tuesday Feb 17

The morning after. Mach on Hollywood Boulevard 1981

Waking up in the Bowl Motel on Highland Ave.
Just down the street from the circus lot.
We got all our gear and both guitars out of Cell Block 8 last
night. I'm soaking-up a long hot shower before it's time to
hit the road again.
I got paid $238.35 in cash last night. Here on Hollywood
Boulevard we turn some of our abundant wealth into
American Express travelers checks, then we grab lunch.
Right next to Mann's Chinese Theater.
I eat a chili dog and we check out the cement hand and
footprints of the movie stars. We grab a city bus, making
our way through L.A. Past CBS Television City, onto
Wilshire, past Rodeo Drive, finally hitting the town of
Santa Monica.
We get off the bus at a grassy public park that winds along
a clifftop where the USA ends. Nothing left, except for the
beaches down below. The ocean waves to me. We clamber
down the cliff and hit the sand, right next to Santa Monica
Pier. Strum guitars, drink wine, harmonize and finally lug
our stuff up the beach two miles north. We find an
overgrown area across Pacific Coast Highway from Will
Rogers State Beach. Good place to stash our gear.
Under a secret bush.

Hike back to Santa Monica for IHOP and a drink at
Stedley's. Darkness falls over the sea as we head back to
the secret bush. We make camp on a drainage incline
beneath the Pacific Palisades. I'm in my sleeping bag.
Listening to the surf, watching the stars brighten.
Thinking about last night...and The Knops from Poland.
The "Incredible Perch Pole Perfectionists."

Bobby never told me what kind of horrible stunt he was
planning to pull during their act.

Wednesday Feb 18

Daytime temps in the 80's. Unseasonably hot.
We move our hidden campsite higher up the incline.
According to the lifeguard across the street, Goldie Hawn
lives atop the bluff just above our new campsite.

Thursday Feb 19

Hot. Scattered clouds. I'm tanner than ever before.
Hike toward Malibu. Watch surfers.

Friday Feb 20

Clouding up a bit but still sweaty hot. Writing music.
Cook lasagna over the campfire. We've been out for 40
days now.

Saturday Feb 21

Play music. Get buzzed on cheap weed from the Pier.
Walk south, down to Muscle Beach. Cook over the
campfire again. Beef and rice.

Sunday Feb 22
Once again the temperature is near 90. We walk barefoot,
north from Will Rogers Beach.

Every time we hit a rocky patch I stop to put on my "Beat Blue" sneakers.

I found these kicks in the produce department of the Yuma Arizona Alpha Beta grocery store. Not sure why sneakers get mixed-in with the produce in Yuma. We hike up to the beginnings of Malibu. Beautiful day. Bobby bought a can of Dinty Moore beef stew at the SafeWay.

We cook it up, back at the secret camp.

The Pacific view from our camp, hidden just below Goldie Hawn's mansion. Photos by Bobby Edwards

Monday Feb 23

According to my transistor radio, this is gonna be our last perfect day on the coast. Bad weather is closing in. It was sunny when I woke up. Bobby is still sleeping. I tell him I'll be down on the breakwater, with my guitar.

After two hours of jamming for some hookie-playing kids, I get restless. Bobby never shows. I cruise down the beach to the Pier. Look at bikinis and cars. There's a new, air-conditioned, three-level mall a few blocks from the Pier. Food bars, a fruit stand, Famous Amos and a shiny, clean donniker.

Tuesday Feb 24

I made it back to the campsite last night to find Bobby still
sacked out. A gray curtain is closing in on us this morning.
Right above our heads. The sun can't cut through, so we
gather up the guitars 'n' gear from beneath the secret bush
and wrap everything inside disposable ponchos. We hike
into town, find shelter and wait for the rain to begin.
Still dry.
So we wander east on Wilshire, all the way to L.A. Bobby's
foot is swelling up. He says he hurt it on the beach but he
can't remember how it happened. I'm not surprised when
he announces it's time to give up our beachcomber lifestyle
and return to New England.
I'm not ready to go home yet but my dogs are aching too.

Wednesday Feb 25

Ticket prices have shot up twenty bucks in the past few
days. We each pay $117.60 for a Trailways ticket back to
Natick/Framingham.
Incredible ride, zooming past Hollywood and downtown
Los Angeles. Feeling very melancholy watching the
Hollywood sign fade into the hills. Thinking about the
friends we left behind in the circus and on the beach.
Hollywood will always be magic to me, no matter how
much decay I see here. We hit Pasadena and the
mountains. Snow-capped mountains, hovering right over
L.A. Mind blowing. Rolling on through Palm Springs.
By the time we hit Needles, it's getting dark outside.
Good-bye California.

One way or another, I'll be back.

Thursday Feb 26

Bobby is anxious to return to Massachusetts.
I want to spend the afternoon here in Albuquerque.
We find a laundromat and wash our clothes for the first
time in 46 days.
Later, back on the bus, Bobby and I get into a rare but
terribly nasty, argument.
I want to take my time going home, he doesn't, but our
argument goes a lot deeper than that.

Finally, Bobby continues east without me.
I get off the bus in Oklahoma City.
With only $12 left in my pocket I make a rash decision and
stop in at the 23rd Street Plasma Center.
I hate to sell blood.
My mother would be ashamed if she ever found out.
I'm lying on a cot and my arm hurts and I bleed too slow.
They drain 2 pints out, spin it for plasma and return the
red blood cells into my arm. It takes two hours with a huge
needle numbing my whole forearm. The clerk hands me a
thirteen dollar check. He tells me I can cash it down the
street at Subs Etc. I buy the $1.99 special and feel a lot
better with more than twenty bucks in my pocket.
I trade my Los Angeles Magazine for an old Playboy and
talk to the elderly man who runs this used bookstore on
16th St.
Gramps wants to know about life on the road and New
Jersey and Steinway pianos. Next door, a double feature

Private Benjamin (starring my neighbor, Goldie Hawn)
and *Lord of the Rings* is playing for $1.50.
Movies start at 6 pm. I decide to come back for the show.
After that I'll catch the late bus for St. Louis.

I continue wandering around Oklahoma City, guitar case
in hand, pack strapped to my back. My boots are really
worn now, cracked clear across the soles.
Heading back to the bus depot.
In the restroom I remove the plasma bandage.
My arm looks horrible. The wound is purple and swollen.
I stare into the mirror, I don't feel so good...
Suddenly a torrent of blood gushes out of my arm, spilling
across the washroom sink. Almost immediately, I feel
dizzy. I begin to panic.
Catching my green reflection in the bathroom mirror - just
before I collapse to the floor.
Blood pools around me. Alone.
Passed out cold. On the floor of a public men's room.

I don't know how long I lay there.

Sonny. He told me his name later. A resident of Denver,
"just passing through" Oklahoma City. Imagine walking
into a bus stop crapper to take a quick leak and instead
you nearly trip over a freaky-looking dude. Out on the
tiles. Bleeding profusely all over the floor.
If something like that happened to me, I might not want to
get involved. Just pee and flee.

Grabbing a roll of paper towel, Sonny applies pressure to my forearm until I start to come around.

He props me up against a urinal. The bleeding slows down. It finally stops.

I thank Sonny for rescuing me.

He waits around for awhile, to make sure I'm okay. Nice guy. Before he splits, Sonny looks down at my guitar case and requests a song. But just as I begin to play I snap the damn D string.

An hour later, I'm back at 16th street, ready to catch the movies but locals advise me to watch myself in this neighborhood.

"Bad place to be after dark" hisses the gas station attendant. His face is battle scarred.

"Yep, he's right" chimes in the old-timer with the ragged ear.

I decide to skip the movie and retreat to the bus terminal. Walking along, I suddenly realize that just about every Oklahoma City resident passing me on this mean street is missing either a digit, an eye or a chunk of ear.

Back at Trailways, I sit and talk with a Kansas City woman for two hours until my 8:15 pm St. Louis/Chicago bus arrives. The redhead and I blab about the military, VW repair, donkeys, dogs, relatives, ghosts, Chrysler...She's on her way to Wichita Falls Texas, where her husband is in the Air Force reserves.

My luck has changed for the better, some smart-looking girls board the bus ahead of me. When I find an empty seat, I discover a wet wad of bills stuck to the floor.

Six dollars.

Hey. I made $19 today.

{ 28 }

Magnificent Four
I hit Massachusetts a couple days after Bobby. He's been worried sick about me and goes ballistic when he hears about my close call in the Oklahoma City rest room. During our final argument on the bus, I'd told Edwards I was quitting rock'n'roll for good. "I've had it, Bobby. You want to keep trying? Go ahead without me, man."

I'm not sure what else I'm gonna do. Now that I'm back East, and now that Spring is here, and now that Ric and Bobby are raring to rock. I change my mind.
We name ourselves Mag 4 because we envision the new band as a quartet. I need a guitar player to dovetail with. Someone who fits not only musically but also physically, creating the Bell/Silva look and tension my performance-style requires.
In the meantime, I run down to E.U. Wurlitzer and nab a cheap guitar.

Mag 4 premieres at the Paradise Theater on May 24th, 1981 at one of Count Viglione's rock spectaculars. John Visnaskas, a major Who fanatic and Thundertrain collector, invites Mag 4 to record a single on his indie label Pure & Easy Records.
John V is a person we take seriously.

Recording with Bobby and Ric as MAG 4. Ric Provost Archive.

We first noticed John V years ago, sitting out in the crowd
at Thundertrain shows. Sipping his drink behind a reel-to-
reel tape machine. John had the big deck set-up right next
to the empties, recording our set at The Club. He followed
us around with the tape machine for months. John dug the
out of town gigs the most. Places where I'd tell strange
stories or hurl ridiculous threats and insults from the stage
while the rest of Thundertrain cracked-up.

Visnaskas archived all his tapes and all kinds of other
Thundertrain artifacts, including the master reel from the
1978 Cape Cod Cable, Thundertrain Rat show. John
managed to rescue the footage just before (or as) the
AKtive office was being shut down for good.

John V, Bobby Edwards and Ed Buckingham mixing MAG 4.

Mag 4 is a busy band, a whirlwind. I'm writing most of the material and I can't really explain the meaning behind these new songs. Storm Brewin' and the other things I wrote last year with The Hits were, by far, the most emotional, personal stuff I've ever penned.

The Mag 4 repertoire is totally different. Science fiction, fantasy, action-adventure...lots of the tunes revolve around the band name itself, "Do the Mag" or "Rocket to the Planet M.A.G." One called "Mag 4 Go Monte Carlo" is chosen as the first single. Jim Harold gives us a Monday night residency at the Rat.

Mag Mondays.

MAG 4 at the Rat.
Photos by Tabitha Mitchell

Julia Channing rents a spare room from Ric, so I'm at his apartment a lot. His street is wired for cable TV, something I've never seen except for the HBO channel that's included in some motel rooms. It's August 1st and we're watching the premiere broadcast of MTV.
The rock music biz has gotten so fat it now has its own 24-hour TV channel. We watch all these kids running around to the beat. Privately, I realize my ship sailed years ago, Thundertrain was my shot and I blew it. Mag 4 is fun but that's all it is. I'm not staking my heart and soul on our success. We're self-contained. John V takes care of the records and we book Boston-area shows at Jacks, Jaspers, Timothy's Too and of course, the Rat.

I've lost interest in going back to the Manhattan showcase rooms. I'm done dreaming about landing a six figure advance from a major label and going national.
In fact, for the first time, I'm trying to settle-in and work a 9 to 5 job. Making deliveries and doing installations for the Music Box. When I'm not out in the van, I write repair slips and work the register down in the Service Lab. My father (and grandfather) allow me to use the company truck during the evenings to play our Mag 4 gigs.

Jaspers (379 Somerville Ave) is the venue we're playing tonight. Mag 4 usually headlines but we lucked into this slot opening for Boston favorites the Jon Butcher Axis. Butcher will pack this joint.
Just like Thundertrain used to.
I'm over by the side of the stage, quietly messing with my guitar cables. I overhear the Axis crew talking:

"Did you hear Charlie's leaving?"

"Yeah. David too."

"What's Joe gonna do?"

"Probably get back with Steven. I guess."

I'm not sure what those guys are talking about.
But I assume the "Joe and Steven" part refers to
Aerosmith. It becomes clearer as I mull it over.
I don't know much about what Joe Perry is doing these
days. Let the Music Do the Talking started playing on
WBCN around the same time as The Hits, "Storm Brewin."
My initial taste of the Joe Perry Project made a good
impression on me, I always dug Ralph Mormon's voice. I
like the band name and their sound reminds me of the
second-best live show I ever saw. The Jeff Beck Group.

Okay, yeah, and Charlie Farren is the singer on the second
record. Now it's coming back to me. I know his songs too,
East Coast West Coast and Listen to the Rock...
Wait... Charlie's leaving Joe Perry?

The Jon Butcher crew are still yakking, throwing around
names, trying to think of somebody who could take over
the Project microphone. They come up blank and I
guarantee nobody's looking my way.

{ 29 }

Joe Perry Project '82
When I show up for the audition, Danny Hargrove is smoking a butt out on the loading dock. He's the bass player from Rage and he just auditioned for Joe Perry yesterday. Danny tells me his connection came through a Project crewman named Tom Bracey.
Tom knows Hargrove is a talented, trustworthy, ambitious kid. With the ability to fit in fast. Tom urges Danny to schedule an audition. Joining Danny yesterday was Project veteran Ronnie Stewart on drums and Mr. Perry himself, leading the way on guitar.

Danny not only plays his bass at the audition, he does all the lead singing too. Power trio. Anybody got tapes?

Sure enough, Danny has been invited back.
Joe's new manager, Tim Collins, and his associate, Earthquake Morton, both think that I'd be a good fit for the Joe Perry Project.
They know I've handled crowds and long hauls before. They think I'll make a strong impression, so nobody else has been tapped to audition as lead singer, not yet anyway. I'm nervous.
I get more nervous when I arrive because as I approach the loading dock I can hear the sound of two guitars reverberating across the parking lot. Earthie told me to bring along my guitar. You know Charlie Farren - he was

the Project's lead singer before me – Charlie sings and plays guitar.

But I definitely don't want to be hired as a singing guitarist. I brought along an axe but I didn't study the guitar parts very much. I want to impress Perry with my presence and my concentration on cohesive, propulsive vocals. That's my thing. I mean, Mick Jagger can play guitar too, if he wants... But Mick shouldn't really have to do that. Let Keith take care of the riffs.

Anyway, when I get to the audition I hear this other guy playing guitar. And he sounds incredible. I'm standing in the parking lot, thinking
"Damn it, that guy is gunning for my job."
But when I get inside it turns out the other guitar player is Brad Whitford. He quit Aerosmith too.
Brad is joining-up with Joe to play a bunch of Project dates. So, during my audition, my mic is set-up in front of Ronnie Stewart, with Brad Whitford on my left and Joe Perry on my right. How intense is this?
A totally far-out jam.

Danny briefs me out on the loading dock before my audition begins. I notice he refers to Joe Perry as the "Admiral." All the JPP crew members use that same nickname when they talk about the bandleader. Once I catch on, I begin addressing Joe that way too. I never find out where or how the moniker began. Does it reach back to Joe's Aerosmith days? I seem to recall an Admiral Perry, commander of the British fleet, being written about in my 9th grade history textbooks. Maybe it stems from that.

Joe Perry Project 1982 -Brad Whitford and the Admiral.
Ward Craven Archive

The day of my call-back, Joe looks fragile. He's in sad
shape. Brad returns too and Mr. Whitford sounds even
sharper on the Project tunes than he did yesterday.
Even sharper than the Admiral.
I wander out to the washroom after our rehearsal session
ends. I'm staring at myself in the mirror when I notice the
door creaking open. In walks the Admiral. I try not to
flinch as he approaches me cautiously.
"Hey Cowboy..."
"Yeah, Joe?"
"You think you could...get me something...?"
Perry draws-in closer, talking softly. I can almost make out
his eyes, squinting through the dangling curtain of
impossibly cool hair.
"You know anybody, Mach?"

Damn it. How do I play this? I don't want to piss off my new boss. I certainly don't want to get involved in his unhealthy lifestyle either. Perry stands there, waiting for my response.

He pulls some bills out of his pocket. 80 bucks.

"Can you get me somethin'?"

Oh great. Some what?
I'm not sure how to respond. I've heard tales about this rascal and I'm guessing he's hoping for the worst.
Is he asking me to score him some junk?
Jeeesh, I don't want to come out and just say "do you mean *heroin?*" and insult the guy.

"ummm...you mean cocaine?"
"Yeah, okay... Can you get me some?"

Man, what a weird scene. Joe fukken Perry is asking Mr. Lightweight to help him score. It makes no sense.
The Admiral must know every dealer, pusher and gun runner between here and Fiji. But then it dawns on me, I bet Joe's gone back to the well too many times and his credit's dried-up. Truth is, I know a few people on the street, I can probably find something for Perry, but I'm not digging this scene in the least.
Finally, I speak.
"I know a guy."
"Good stuff?"
"Sorry man, I have no idea...but he's been in business for a while."

"When?"

"I'll try to get you something for tomorrow."

Joe shoves his cash in my hand...

He half-whispers "thanks Cowboy" as he exits.

I did what the Admiral asked me to do. I brought Joe the stuff. Thankfully, he never puts me in that awkward position again. I think my discomfort during our washroom conversation was pretty obvious.

Maybe this is another reason Earthquake suggested my name to Tim Collins. Earthie knows that I love to get wild and party my butt off, but I know when to quit - and the hard stuff is never part of my diet.

I fall back into the lead singer role quickly.

The end of Thundertrain crushed me - our flame-out twisted my head around. It left me disillusioned and ready to change my rocker ways.

The day Earthquake called me about the Joe Perry Project audition, I was in the midst of withdrawal. I was actually succeeding in tearing myself away from my chronic rock band addiction. The raging fire in my belly was being contained, the flames slowly dying.

For a brief moment there, I had turned my back on my long held goal of rocking the nation.

After years of begging, beating on doors, showcasing and starving, I'd finally had enough. Ready to throw in the towel...and that's when the phone rang and my rock'n'roll dream was resurrected overnight. But on a whole new level now...

Joe Perry Project 1982. Cowboy Mach. Photo by Manny Hernandez

The electricity of these crowds is way beyond anything I'd experienced with Thundertrain. My previous group enjoyed a lot of thrilling nights, but let's face it, the intensity generated by rockstar Joe Perry is off the charts.

In the beginning of April, Tim puts the latest model of the Joe Perry Project on the road in an ugly brown van owned by another Collins Barrasso client, Jonathan Edwards (Sunshine, Shanty) to play a handful of shows around the New York area.

We're on our way to my fourth live show with the JPP. Our first gig was at a theater in Concord, New Hampshire. Then we played a big concert club in Albany. Last night we were in New Jersey at this mammoth rock palace called Fountain Casino. Tonight we're in a much smaller venue, it probably has a legal capacity of around 400. The stage here at the Left Bank is way more compact. That means the lights will blaze brighter, our stage movements will be compressed and magnified. And the sound? Look out kids, it's gonna blow your minds.

Toys, our opening song, cracks like lightning. And we have...Lift off. The anticipation in the room is sky high and for obvious reason. Seeing Joe and Brad materialize on the stage of the neighborhood hang, rocking full force, is a dream come true for these fans. Walking onstage to such a primed crowd, already jammed against the stage and delirious before we even enter...This is totally new territory for me.

The psychology of a crowd, whether they number five thousand or just five, is a delicate wave to surf. Journeymen rockers, nobodies like me, walk onstage every night as an unknown entity. We might be carrying a ton of gear, sharp suits, expensive instruments, have a new

album out, whatever. We can be fukken Thundertrain -
and it still doesn't matter.
Not until the music starts.
Rock audiences can be stubborn.
Too loud? Too quiet? Don't recognize the song?
It just takes one impatient couple vacating their seats to
initiate a full-scale evacuation.
It's the frontman's job to break through to the jury each
and every night. To convince, command, trick, threaten, or
cajole the audience into dropping their defenses. C'mon
people, let it all hang out.

Thankfully, it only takes a single, brave, frisky seashell to
shift the entire tide and light the fuse for a super night.
But finding that missing link between the stage and the "I
dare you to impress me" audience, is sometimes a bridge
too far.

That's all gone out the window now. Everything is
different. I'm singing with Joe Perry and every kid in this
crowd is bound and determined to have a great time. No
matter what. They're here to rock their asses off, not to
judge.

Life at a Glance and Discount Dogs are next and I dig
singing these fast-paced Mormon/Perry songs. High-
energy riffage and urgent vocals. These songs would fit
into a Dead Boys or Thundertrain set at CBGB, no prob.
Kids are sitting on each others shoulders as Perry grinds
into Arrogance. Trying to sound as natural as I can, but
having trouble copying some of Charlie Farren's phrasing

from the original recording, I blend in some cues from Roger Daltrey's version of Young Man Blues (Live at Leeds, written by Mose Allison) a song with a similar hubris.

Aerosmith's Back in the Saddle is next.
I'm able to vocalize my way through this Tyler torture-test, sans Chloraseptic throat spray, due to sixteen years of windpipe conditioning.
Still, I'm glad that Mist is Rising and Heartbreak Hotel are next, because Perry sings the lead vocal on those two.
Back in the dressing room I squirt two pints of water down my throat. I'll drink more than a gallon during any given performance but I never pee. I steam it off. Back on stage I gravitate to the hottest, most blinding area of the platform I can find. If I ever feel comfortable onstage, I must be standing in the wrong place.

Rolling into Once a Rocker and Black Velvet Pants. Played back to back. I'm relieved to see and hear a strong response for this new material I helped create. Brad Whitford steps forward to major applause. He smiles at the kids before triggering Going Down. Bluesman Freddie King (Hideaway) is said to have cut the definitive version but I first heard this jam when I flipped to Side Two of the Jeff Beck Group's Orange album. I don't have the Orange record anymore so I'm not really sure what the lyrics are.

Pesky words never stop me. Steven Silva always introduces me as a song *stylist*. By that, I think Steven means, the lyrics were written simply to give me an impression of what I may or may not want to sing about.

I don't know if I'm that bad but I'll admit that coming into this game, initially as an instrumentalist, I regarded vocals as the *necessary* part of a song that lead to the *good* parts. Like the killer drum fill or the huge guitar riff.

Joe Perry Project 1982. The Admiral.

I wrote the lyrics of When Worlds Collide myself, it's up next and I get most of them right. The Admiral and Brad have turned this snake-like track into a tour de force.

Ronnie Stewart's exceptional drum solo is contained within our next selection, "Rockin' Train." Another cut from the debut Project LP, Rockin' Train sounds like something Beck could have included on Rough and Ready. My vocal is helped along by the rising voice of Hargrove on the choruses. Joe Perry sings with me on most of the choruses too. The Admiral's good at finding traditional harmony parts. But rather than follow the melodic ups & downs, Joe often sings a sustained, 7th note counterpoint vocal, very tart & tense. A signature Joe Perry harmony, heard on many Aerosmith classics.

Joe Perry Project 1982. Mark Blair Archive

Stewart's drum solo builds relentlessly - it just keeps unfolding and twisting. By the time the JPP crashes back with the refrain, the house is resounding with approval.
I Got the Rock'n'Rolls Again and Let the Music Do the Talking, the title songs from both Project albums, round out the evenings entertainment. Not sufficiently sated, the audience demands an encore.
It's interesting to watch the Admiral backstage. He allows the crowd to go on for a bit longer than I would have. The clapping and stomping seems to ebb a tiny bit...but no, Perry is right. Of course. Now it torques up again.
They begin banging on the bars and table tops, girls are screaming for Whitford & Perry.
Joe finally nods. We return to the stage.
The Admiral plugs in, grips the guitar neck, up near the 12th fret, bending the Tele-Rat strings all the way back.
Freight whistling into the opening slam of Train Kept A-Rollin.'

Next morning we check out of the Sheraton New Rochelle and after a quick breakfast, Doc wheels the van into Manhattan. Traffic is bad and I'm not sure what we're doing here in the heart of downtown New York.
After doubling back around a city block we pull to the curb. Surrounded by skyscrapers.
I don't see any music stores. Not even a packie.
What are we doing here?
Doc hustles Joe out of the van and they disappear through the stainless steel, revolving door of a serious-looking office tower. Ron Stewart is still hammering away on his practice pad. Ronnie never even looks up. A minute later,

Brad jumps out of the van and hustles down the sidewalk
in the opposite direction. Hargrove and I just sit here, we
look at each other and shrug our shoulders.

Ten minutes later Doc returns, but without the Admiral.

"He'll only be an hour or so. They were putting body make-
up on the girl"
Girl? Body make-up?
"ummm, Doc...What's going on?"

"Awww nothin.' Joe's in there posing for some pictures.
With a naked chick on a motorcycle."

"Naked chick? I don't get it, what are you talking about?"

Doc continues,
"It's for Oui Magazine. They used to be in Chicago. Owned
by Hugh Hefner. But he sold the magazine last year to
these guys here in New York.
They're trying some new things.
Naked chicks with rock stars. The AC/DC guy did one so
the Admiral figured he'd give it a shot too."

About a half hour later Whitford rejoins us and just a few
minutes after that the Admiral spins out of the revolving
door. Buttoning up his shirt.
Joe Perry hops into the shotgun seat and glances back at
us with a big grin on his face.
"That should piss-off Elyssa."

"Joe Perry. Call home. Your house is on fire."
Remember that?
A lot of us heard Mark Parenteau make the announcement
on WBCN-FM one afternoon. Maybe it was same year
Perry mangled his new Corvette and made Creem
Magazine's "Star Cars" - sitting atop the wreckage. I
followed the rise of Aerosmith intently but I began to lose
interest when they became super popular, household
names. But every so often, hearing Joe's name mentioned,
something in me stirred. Beneath my jealousy, the Admiral
was still one of my main inspirations and role models.
I don't know the story behind the Corvette crashes but I'm
pretty sure it was little Elyssa Perry herself who
mischievously set fire to the Perry household.
Joe had to go out that day. Mrs. Perry got left behind
against her wishes. Elyssa figured if the mansion caught
fire, it would probably get him back.
Joe's wife is tricky. It's getting worse by the day.

We're fortunate to have Brad on board, he's a brilliant
guitarist. And dependable. But after the first dozen gigs,
Whitford gets an offer in L.A.
A job playing with singer/actor Rex Smith.
Brad can't afford to refuse. Things get pretty dodgy for the
Joe Perry Project at this point.

Unfortunate timing. We're on the eve of a national
headlining tour. We manage to complete only six dates
when the entire trip is aborted... in a sickening way.

The Admiral suffers violent seizures two different times in a single day. First on the highway, as we van through North Carolina. Perry's face contorts. His body stiffens like a corpse with rigor mortis. The horrific episode scares the piss out of Hargrove and me.

Hours later, Joe seizes-up even worse, right in the midst of our concert. He collapses in spasms in front of a full house in Jacksonville. That's a wrap.

Tour cancelled. The Project retreats to the sidelines for two months, waiting while Joe dries out and begins re-building. Re-taking control of his life.

Strangely, it will be during this rough stretch that I grow much closer to Joe. I also get to know his unpredictably volatile wife, Elyssa, a lot better too. Everything turns out for the best because when Joe returns to the Project his strength is regained. The Admiral is back at the helm. The JP swagger has returned.

Project manager Tim Collins saved the day for Joe Perry. The Admiral had painted himself into an impossible corner. Unable to reason with his wife, coping with fatherhood for the first time, trying to salvage the Project, while trying to control, or even understand his out-of-whack physical condition. There seemed to be no escape... except to drown everything out with more booze, pills and worse.

Collins figured out an escape route.

First he separated the Perrys, putting the Admiral in a place where he could rest for awhile - before pushing ahead and helping his star client navigate a painful but necessary divorce. Tim went to work protecting what was left of Joe's possessions. The guitars in particular. Tim warded-off creditors while keeping track and fulfilling Joe's numerous court appearances...It was a long road and Tim guided the Admiral through it. How Collins found anytime leftover to manage the Joe Perry Project, I haven't a clue.

Danny and I jump for joy when the Collins Barrasso office finally issues an updated Joe Perry Project itinerary. Wow. Look at all the July shows. Topsham Fairgrounds with Joan Jett and the Blackhearts. A headline gig at Rocky Point Park. A flight to Caracas, Venezuela, headlining a massive arena for two nights. Back to America for a gig with Rick Derringer before heading to Toronto the next morning for a festival.

JOE PERRY PROJECT Cowboy & the Admiral.
Photo by James Gelletien

JOE PERRY PROJECT

July 4, 1982

Cowboy, the Admiral & Danny Hargrove

Photos by James Pappaconstantine

The next month finds Danny and me in Detroit for the first time. Debbie, her brother Dale and several other faithful Joe Perry supporters are waiting for the Project's arrival at the stage door of Harpo's Concert Theatre. The Project rocks a few other Mid West cities before continuing to the West Coast.

My head is exploding. My dream of traveling the country in a van with a rock band was never on this scale. In my fantasy it was more like Thundertrain goes West and starts from the bottom - like rock bands do. Third on the bill, on a Tuesday night, at the Coconut Teazer.

But no, I arrive here on the Coast singing lead beside a rock god. Fans are lined-up to greet us in the hotel lobby. Last time I was in Hollywood, I was leading a llama around a circus tent. My debut rock performance in L.A. is sold out and promoter Jim Rissmiller holds the Joe Perry Project over for a second night at the Reseda Country Club (18419 Sherman Way).

Following the six-city, headline tour of California it's on to the Pan America Center in New Mexico and a week of shows in Texas. Danny and I take full advantage of a short layover in the French Quarter of New Orleans before hitting Atlanta and four more cities in Florida.

JPP 1982. Mach at the Will Rogers Auditorium Fort Worth TX.

I'm just a hired hand around here. I never know how much money the Project pulls in. But keeping eight guys out on the road with eighteen hundred pounds of gear, for months at a time is expensive. Leftover cash, if there is any, is needed to keep Joe's creditors at bay.

The JPP pirate ship pulls into port just in time for the 5 pm soundcheck. We'll check the mix, grab dinner, book into the hotel, shower, play the show, party all night and pull up anchor the next day before 11 a.m. Following an evening concert, I'll be gifted with a sketch or a bandana by one fan. A photograph or a smooch from another. Joe Perry snags the hospitality bourbon and occasionally a girl or two. Danny Hargrove stuffs the rest of the liquor into his gig bag. The drummer steals the paintings off the wall and anything else that's not nailed down.
Raise the Jolly Roger. Sail on.

Joe Perry Project road crew members. These two are currently in a
federal witness protection plan and cannot be named.

The Joe Perry Project is wheels. Van wheels, truck wheels,
fighting mud, slush, blizzards, heat waves and above all,
fighting time. Gotta keep rolling.

Once we make our daily destination, Joe's fans are already
gathered, racing toward the van like children hoping to
meet Santa Claus.

Some will simply shout or slap the Admiral on the back.
Someone might have a burning question to ask, others
want a moment with Joe to offer a "thank you" for making
a positive difference in their lives.

No matter the weather, the time, or the hundreds of miles
travelled, Joe Perry listens carefully to each and every
person who waits to meet him.

The Admiral will often cover his mouth after these warm
encounters. He'll be in the dressing room or back in the
van with his hand hiding the bottom part of his face.

Joe doesn't want anybody to see him grinning so widely.

Joe Perry & Cowboy Mach Bell. Photo by Sean Feeney

{ 30 }

Joe Says a Mouthful
Buzzing along the Interstate in the van. I'm regaling Danny with my action-packed synopsis of what happened last time and how its gonna be even crazier this time. I start rattling off girls names in an animated, idiotic way. Danny Hargrove is a great audience. He eggs me on. We're both cracking up.

Meanwhile. Up in the shotgun seat, in total disregard of the crap pouring out of my trap, I see the Admiral's large head slowly begin to revolve. He owls the melon around to where Danny and I are goofing around. Fixing his deadly gaze right at me. Not amused. When Joe gives me the fish-eye like this, he totally gives me the creeps.

"Cowboy. Cut the bullshit. You and Julia are gonna get married."

Whhhaaaaat? Julia? Marriage?
(I'm only thinking this - because my mouth is flopped open, no sound emerges, I'm dumbfounded).
What the F? I've never hardly even heard of these concepts, let alone link them together...Married? Me? To Julia? A girl? Us? Married?
Why would the Admiral even suggest such a thing...

Too late. Joe Perry has spoken. Chew on that.

He only talks to me once or twice a week - and from the
way he just left me trembling - that's probably a good
thing.
A similar but different thing happens a month later.
We're in upstate New York, in the van as usual, racking up
miles to the next concert.
I can't quite recall what I was blabbing about this time.
I do have a habit of telling stories. Maybe it was how I
cured a hiccuping showgirl or the time I got a real silver
bullet from Clayton Moore when I was 5 or something like
that. Anyway, I'm yakking a mile a minute when I notice
the maned head of our world renowned lead guitarist
rotating my way.
Oh boy, look out. Here it comes again.
The Admiral usually just tells me to knock it off, y'know,
"to be cool is to be quiet" and all that.
But Joe Perry really stuns me this time.

"Cowboy. You have a lot of anger in you."

Sounds pretty simple. Right?
Nine words. I have no idea why Joe dumped his diagnosis
on me right then. I mean, my story didn't have any angry
parts. I usually cut the dark stuff out of my tales.
I'm the carefree guy around here. But..."anger in you."
Nobody has ever said anything like that to me before.
But...*damn*... Joe is dead-right.

I've blacked-out or avoided the episodes that shaped me.
The comments, the accusations. The *faggot* taunts.
But I still harbor all those memories and feelings.

Until this moment, I've been running away from it.
I've never even taken time to define my feelings, or try to
name the emotions that linger deep in my belly...Joe is
absolutely right... It's a *lot of anger.*

I thought I was smarter than this.
Am I really only realizing it now?
Almost immediately I begin to see things a whole lot
clearer. This answers a lot of questions.
My short-fuse for one thing.
But it seeps out into my music career too.
I finally comprehend one of the reasons Thundertrain
connected with the underground and especially the punk-
rock movement.
Anger can be hidden but it's palpable. Audience radars
pick up on it. Raw and authentic. For me (and most
listeners, I imagine) it's a subliminal thing, buried in the
grooves.
But for Dr. Joe Perry, my anger is *glaringly* obvious.

So I sit here in the van, wrestling with this new realization.
The Admiral shoves his Sex Pistols cassette back into the
deck. Johnny Rotten snarls with rage.
Joe is angry too.
At his ex-wife, at people around him and at himself.
Here's a song title he slipped me recently,
"I've Got Revenge in My Heart."

Back in Boston, I swing by Axis to catch the great Willie
Loco Alexander. I'm digging his show when this very
attractive blonde walks over to join me.

"You're Mach."

"Uh...yeah."

"My name's Billie. Willie told me all about you. I've been helping him out, you know, managing, doing some booking... Thanks for coming tonight, he'll be so happy you're here."

"Nice to meet you Billie. That's great you're helping out Willie. He's my favorite."

"So...Are you doing anything, Mach? Since Thundertrain?"

"Uh yeah, I've been out on the road with the Joe Perry Project, I'm the singer."

From her expression, I can tell Billie has no clue who or what I'm talking about. This happens all the time when I return to my old Kenmore Square haunts.
Lots of the people in the underground scene stopped listening to commercial radio years ago. College radio plays Mission of Burma, PIL, Killing Joke, Gang Green, the Neighborhoods and Dead Kennedys.
They don't play Joe Perry Project or Aerosmith records. I doubt many Aerosmith fans are aware of Mission of Burma or Flipper either. My singing career straddles two rock communities that co-exist - but rarely intersect.

Plenty of my Thundertrain fans from the Rat days are still right here in Boston, but when they see the Joe Perry

Project listed to play the Channel, few of them realize
Thundertrain's Mach Bell is part of that package.
As far as they're concerned, I've dropped off the map.

The Joe Perry Project returns to Blue Jay Recording in
mid-November to cut our second demo tape. This one
includes Perry/Bell compositions "Take a Walk with Me
Sally" and "When Do I Sleep."
The next night we open for Nazareth at the Civic Center in
Portland, Maine and continue on into Canada for six
shows in Ontario. Returning home on December 11, 1982,
the Project and two of our crew members get detained at
the Canadian border.

When the USA officers run our IDs through their
computer, lights begin flashing. They herd us into a small
room. Waiting until police back-up arrives. I'm extremely
nervous that it was *my* passport that sounded the alarm.

Remember that "30 days in the hole" prison sentence I
received? Way back in 1976? Well, that cloud has been
hanging over my noggin ever since. The judge in
Framingham said he'd send my case to the Cambridge
Superior Court.
Did the court date ever happen? I haven't a clue. I'm not
an easy person to track down.
I haven't owned a motor vehicle in over a decade. I haven't
had my own mailing address in years. My fan mail goes to
the Collins/Barrasso office - and before that - to the AKtive
office. Nobody ever told me about a court summons

arriving - and I certainly wasn't gonna call the judge to remind him about it.

The State Police arrive. It's not me they want. One of our new crew members has an outstanding arrest warrant. The authorities haul him away.

I still don't know if I'm totally off the hook yet... I hope the principal, the police chief and the judge decided to just "misplace" my case after their out-of-order, rush to judgement in the Framingham District courtroom failed.

I had two really exceptional years in my rock singing career. One of them was 1977 and the other is 1983.

The year begins on a rough note when most of the Project road crew either resigns or is let go. We set off on a Mid West road trip with a crew of green recruits that Tim Collins manages to corral.

In March, drummer Ron Stewart resigns.

This is a major problem. Ronnie has been with Joe since the start of the JPP back in 1979. Drummers of Ron's caliber are rare, and signing-up for duty on the Project pirate ship is a risky move. But the chance to rock across the continent alongside Joe Perry is a hard offer to pass up. We get lucky when Orchestra Luna/Berlin Airlift drummer, Joe Pet, decides to throw-in with us.

The *Do or Die Tour*. That's what Tim calls it. He sends us to the West Coast with the beginner crew and our brand new drummer. The Project's mission is to prove ourselves musically - and to stay out of trouble. Tim's mission is to locate and nail down a record deal for Joe Perry. We've been touring for over a year with no label and barely any prospects.

The tour starts off in Monterey on St. Patrick's Day '83. It rolls through California and on through Texas.

Following an arena show with Huey Lewis and the News, one of the Project crew narrowly escapes arrest. No surprise to Danny and me, we already have Zakowski pegged as a troublemaker. Things get tense as the Do or Die Tour rocks through the south.

Finally, in Tampa Bay, the wheels come off.

Zakowski is taken into police custody along with our road manager Dickman after they drunkenly trash the pool and patio areas at the waterfront Holiday Inn we're stationed in. The Bacardi 151 party happened in the Admiral's room last night, and that's where we find the boss, still breathing but conked-out. Face-down on his mattress.

{ 31 }

Once a Rocker Always a Rocker
Tim manages to land the Joe Perry Project a
record deal with MCA. We'll make an album that
includes one cover song, another written by outside
writers, and the rest penned by Joe Perry and myself.
For "Once a Rocker Always a Rocker" the Joe Perry Project
demos at least 15 original songs.

Somethin' Else, the cover, is a fast-paced rockabilly classic.
I think we added the tune to the setlist in April '83.
I don't know about the Admiral, but I was introduced to
Cochran's music through Blue Cheer (Summertime Blues)
and Humble Pie (C'mon Everybody).
Like a bunch of Eddie's songs, Somethin' Else will chart
higher in the UK than it will back home in Cochran's
hometown, Hollywood California.
Extremely nervous following the plane crash that claimed
the lives of Buddy Holly, Richie Valens and Big Bopper,
Eddie's on tour in England when the hired-car he's riding
in smashes into a light pole. Cochran's seated in the
middle of the backseat, he attempts to protect his
girlfriend, songwriter Sharon Sheeley, (Sharon co-wrote
Somethin' Else). He throws his body over hers.
Sharon survives but Eddie Cochran is ejected out the rear
passenger door. He dies the next day from brain damage.
Somethin' Else was originally released in July '59, not long
before Eddie Cochran died, on April 17, 1960 at age 21.

We perform Joe Perry's "First One's For Free" in our live sets throughout 1982.

Going over his notes, I think Joe originally titled it "The 1st One's For Free" I suspect Joe wrote this song a couple years ago. Maybe even earlier.

The number isn't a rocket ride, not like Life at a Glance or Bright Light Fright. This one unfolds at a more deliberate pace, think Mist is Rising.

A solid effort but it lacks an exciting guitar riff.

Perry's lyric is built around a drug reference, one of Joe's preferred subjects. Lots of the Admiral's song ideas are based around the use, sale or effects of narcotics.

Famous phrases with (drug-related) double-meanings are a particular favorite of his.

"Keep Your Powder Dry" "Creatures of Habit" "It's All Done With Mirrors."

Joe sings lead on this one.

Would you believe, I got a pain in my heart
Try to explain, I don't know where to start
You fall into love, As easy as can be
But I didn't know that the 1st one's for free.
It's got the feel, like a race without end
The more that you get, you just want more again

"When Worlds Collide" is another highlight of the live show. I'd just joined the Project, Brad Whitford was onboard too, when I first hear the two main riffs of this monster jam materialize in our rehearsal room. Don't know how long Joe had been devising them, but the riffs rise, growing like Jack's beanstalk, as Brad, Danny and Ronnie fall in.

I quickly begin working on lyrics to match.

Joe Perry Project performs When Worlds Collide in Lowell MA at the Commodore. Photo by Tabitha Mitchell

The form of the song is unique. I supply more of a narration than a melodic vocal line. I do, in fact, utter the words "When World's Collide," but more as a warning than as a snappy, sing-along refrain. During the formation of this tune I was under the false impression that two guitars would be required to provide the correct ambience and tension. Brad was with us when we first demoed the song in March '82, but after Brad departs, Joe delivers all the guitar lines himself, no prob.

When Do I Sleep, finds its way into the setlist during the final months of drummer Ron Stewart's tenure with the Project (Ron's final two shows are on 3/12/1983).

The lyrics and tone of the song will be totally re-vamped before it appears on the Once a Rocker LP.

In July 1982, the Project played two SRO arena concerts in Venezuela. Our collective adrenaline was rushing and the ample supply of top grade cocaine, supplied by our hostess Adriana, added to the sleepless visit to South America.

Adrianna tell me, when do I sleep?
I haven't passed-out yet, been in town for a week.

That's the original, reality-based refrain. Joe initiated the song with a catchy new riff he first played for us on October 6, 1982 while the Project was at the Cambridge Complex for three days, compiling material for the second JPP demo tape.

"They'll Never Take Me Alive" is inspired by lyrics I wrote that, in turn, were inspired by the Admiral. I spend a lot of time writing song lyrics but I have a terrible time writing about anything personal.

That's a serious drawback. I try to beat it by trying to project myself into other people's craniums.

Take Joe Perry for instance. I'll attempt to climb inside his head for awhile and try writing what I imagine his personal feeling on some situation might be. I reflect on the pressure he's currently faced with. Legal threats, emotional upheavals and general insecurity. That's where my original lyric for this one sprouted.

Hear the wind a howlin, feel the night wind blow
Into this heart of darkness, baby we will roam

430

One kiss lasts forever, one look lasts a day
Hold my hand now darlin, and I'll be on my way
Darlin' don't forsake me, They'll never take me alive
Feel my heart a poundin' Feel my temper rise
I've got a date with destiny, see the writing on the sky

I think it might've begun with the phrase, Heart of
Darkness, the title of the Joseph Conrad novel that directly
inspired Coppola's film *Apocalypse Now*, a favorite of the
Admiral's. Later, when the Project briefly holes up at the
Aerosmith Wherehouse in early 1983, I recite the lyrics for
Perry. The Admiral responds quickly, rolling out a
melancholy carpet of sound beneath my recitation.
An arpeggiated, haunting riff emerges, intertwining with
the verses. The moment of creation can sometimes take
my breath way. This was one of those times.
We eventually bring the idea to the rest of the guys. Later
we take it to White Dog recording studio in Newton where
we cut a rough demo.

"Into the Night" (aka Cries Into the Night) has a similar
origin story. My lyric began life as "Chill You to the Bone"
and like most of these tunes, I'll sing it differently and
experiment with substitute lyrics right up til the moment it
goes down on tape.
I don't know if my idea makes sense, but the "baby" who
"cries into the night" isn't just a person, it's the Admiral's
guitar.
Baby, when I lay you cross my hips
And draw your strings up tight
Baby when I lay you, Lay you down

Make you cry into the night
Baby when I string ya, sling ya up
Make you cry into the night.

The contract with MCA Records is signed on the morning of May 4th, 1983 and that same afternoon at 2 pm the Project begins pre-production work at drummer Joe Pet's "Port-a-Pet" home studio in Medford. We break for weekend shows in Wallingford CT and Hull MA and return to Pet's studio for another four days.

We're working on a bunch of ideas including Get it On (we call it "Bang a Gong"), the T. Rex song we began jamming on when Pet joined the JPP last March. Twelve years ago this Marc Bolan ditty climbed to #10 in the US and #1 in the UK. Maybe it's time for a re-make? This weekend we're booked at a beach party in Hubbardston MA with the Stompers.

Shaking the sand out of my cowboy boots, back at Port-a-Pet studio and the Admiral has news. An A&R man is flying up from MCA's Nashville office the day after tomorrow to meet with Joe. Today we're amassing more ideas for the album. Danny, Pet and Perry have discovered an instrumental groove but I'm having trouble connecting lyrics to it. We label the wordless bop, "Funky Pagans." Cries Into the Night has taken form - but evolving even faster is a slide-guitar mover we're calling Never Gonna Stop. On the 17th we make live rehearsal recordings of everything we've got and that same evening Joe meets with Leon Tsillis from the record company.

No rehearsal on the 18th. I'm at Doctor Jonas office. A visit ordered by Tim Collins. I'm a mind-over-matter guy - but it seems that even though (I think) my mind is still functioning properly, my body is reacting negatively to enormous pressure surrounding the Project and this album.

My voice is shot, I can't sleep or breath properly. Back to work the next day, after the physician gives me a vitamin injection and some magic beans. We're still in Medford, squeezed real tight in the small room with Pet's drums and the practice amps.

The newest Perry/Bell jam, "King of the Kings," is the main event today. We mess around with arrangement ideas, isolate sections, playing each part over & over again. Outsiders might find it repetitious and boring - but we love the exercise of zeroing-in on the correct execution.

The Admiral reaches into his back pocket and pulls out a cassette. We all check out a demo of "Women in Chains" for the first time. Written by Harold Tipton, Tom DeLuca and Ronnie Brooks. This doesn't sound at all like the stuff Joe and I have been writing but its a good song. Perry got the tape from the MCA rep, Leon, and he's the only label person (as far as I know) who's reached out to us, so we listen very carefully.

The Joe Perry Project returns to action this weekend in nearby Brockton MA, headlining Scotch 'n Sounds with guitarist Johnny A opening the show. On the 23rd I'm back at the Rat. Tonight it's a party for WBCN DJ turned label promoter, Maxanne Sartori.

Then we return to the Joe Pet rehearsal room.

We're met by Harry King.

I don't know how we got connected with Harry, it might have been through the record label, or Blue Jay Recording, or maybe Tim Collins.

Harry is older than us by seven or eight years and he has the indefinable but easily identifiable look of a rock musician. We run through our song ideas while King watches and listens intently. The following day, King returns but with an electric piano this time. His 88 strains Port-a-Pet studio to its maximum occupancy limit.

We rock while Harry slips chords beneath each section, identifying all the changes in each arrangement.

Black Velvet Pants and Walk With Me Sally, two of our live showstoppers, immediately lend themselves to Harry's flashy piano chops.

No wonder he fits in. Harry King has been playing since he was only four and by the time he was fifteen, King began performing live shows with a caravan of rock'n'roll legends. I'm talkin' about Dion (The Wanderer), Del Shannon (Runaway) and Chubby Checker (The Twist).

It's obvious that the Admiral and rocker Harry King are going to get along great. Neither of them talk much, they're just trying to figure out how to squeeze every drop of rock outta these songs we've assembled. We'll be going into the studio next week, but first we have more live shows to play.

Hampton Beach Casino is a huge venue on the abbreviated shoreline of New Hampshire. The rowdy, overflow crowd is all geared up for Joe Perry.

Joe Perry Project 1983. Hampton Beach Casino.
Photo by Steve Pimpis

Harry King and I are side stage, watching Randy Jackson warm up the audience. He's the lead singer/guitarist for Zebra (Who's Behind the Door?). They're on Atlantic Records with Aerosmith/Joe Perry Project producer Jack Douglas helming their debut album.

The next night we're in another seacoast village, shaking the Salem Theatre in downtown Salem MA. The town pirates and witches come from.

Onward to Bridgeton ME the next day for an afternoon, outdoor festival with NRBQ, Pousette Dart-Band, The Stompers and Bill Chinook.

And then back down to Cape Cod the very same day for an evening engagement in Mashpee MA at the Cape Channel (aka On the Rocks). We're given Monday off, but manage a final, pre-studio appearance at the Rat the following evening.

Yes. The Joe Perry Project is live at the Rat.

The last time I sang on this stage must have been a Mag 4 Monday back in '81.

Singing here in Kenmore Square opens up a floodgate of Thundertrain memories. It's an undercover, unofficial Project performance, tonight we're billed as The Pagans. That doesn't prevent hundreds of JPP diehards from showing up at good ol' 528.

Sweet Potato Magazine   July 1983

Joe Perry is doing the soundtrack for a new film called Make It. *The movie, starring Leif Garret and Sean Penn and directed by Dennis Hopper, concerns a rock band in L.A. trying to make it. Filming is scheduled to begin in December.*

Perry also has a small cameo role as a rock'n'roll journeyman who has a conversation with the up-and-comers in the back of a limousine.

What do you make of that?

Who knows where this stuff comes from, but it's press and they spelled Joe's name right...

Work on the Once a Rocker album moves swiftly. I record all my lead vocals over a ten day stretch, June 8-18.

At the console at Blue Jay Studio in Carlisle, MA is Joe Perry (left) and lead singer Mach Bell.

Sessions run long and I sometimes lose the plot as guitars blast non-stop through my headphones. At times the bass and guitar tones throw me for a loop.

Hard to describe, but after a guitar signal is processed, harmonically distorted and otherwise jacked-up, the tones can confuse my brain.

Six or seven hours into a session, re-singing my parts, trying to find the root notes, I become disoriented.

Is that the melody line Joe's playing?

What am I hearing?

Is the Bb echoing in my cans just a ghost-tone?

Some sort of psycho-acoustic red herring?

Like I said, hard to describe, but lucky for me, this is where Harry King proves to be very helpful.

On some of the really difficult vocals, say, King of the Kings, Harry comes back into the studio and grabs a seat at the piano beside me. King plays the fundamental changes of the section, and the melodic parts I'm having difficulty discerning. Engineer Michael Golub drops the Admiral's electric guitars out of my headphone mix and raises Harry's live piano. The studio piano, tuned and true, is an easier target for my exhausted ears to acclimatize to. Tape operator Meg Bryant hits the record button, I sing the tough part, sticking tight to the bell-like piano tones. Once I'm done, Meg rolls the tape back. Golub drops the piano fader, losing the piano completely, and pushes the guitar faders back up. Playback.

Now my tuneful vocal is sitting right on top.

Joe Perry Project 1983. Filming the Black Velvet Pants music video at the Strand Theater in Boston.

Once the record is in the can, the Project shoots album cover photos on Cape Cod. We tape an MTV video, to accompany Black Velvet Pants, right here in Boston. Model Billie Montgomery joins the Project for the shoot, playing her pink saxophone in the clip. We make short trips to Quebec City for a concert with Frank Marino and another to the fairgrounds in Kingston NH. The Joe Perry

Project also gets to play with Cheap Trick, Blackfoot and Krokus on 8/14, at Summer Fest '83 in Epping NH. Then its a bill with the Gregg Allman Band and the Outlaws over at Westboro Speedway on Route 9.

JOE PERRY PROJECT 1983. New England Dragway.

Photos by Michael Pellegrini

"Don't let it go to your head."
"Don't believe your own press."
Yeah, yeah, I know all that stuff.
But at the same time I have to prepare for the record
release and the thirty city tour we're about to embark on.
When we're not performing, the Project will be doing
interviews, visiting radio stations and music stores.
Getting up early to play lunchtime concerts and
autographing albums. I'd be stupid if I wasn't using this
time to mentally gird myself for the upcoming campaign.

Manager Tim is bolstering our chance of success by hiring
independent promotion people to fill gaps left by the MCA
promotion staff. Our relationship with the label has been
rocky. On the eve of our recording start-date, a big
shakeup goes down at MCA headquarters and the Project
is dropped from the roster. Joe and Tim's friend, Michael
Striar, comes to the rescue, helping fund JPP album
production while Collins figures out a way to convince new
MCA chief, Irving Azoff, to reconsider and release Once a
Rocker Always a Rocker.

The Boston Tea Party ship, docked in the harbor, is the site
of our record release party. Sipping a cool drink on the
foredeck, looking out at the city lights. Thinking back to
the Jeff Beck Group debut at the Boston Tea Party venue.
That was fifteen years ago. I was fifteen years old.
Now I'm standing on the deck of the Boston Tea Party
ship, ready to make my national radio debut. Forty-eight
hours later, Once a Rocker Always a Rocker is released
across the United States and Canada.

Of the brand new songs written for the LP, 4 Guns West, Crossfire and Never Wanna Stop are my favorites to play live. They join the regular batting order: Bang a Gong, Walk With Me Sally, Black Velvet Pants and Once a Rocker Always a Rocker.
King of the Kings and Women in Chains are sometimes left off the set lists, they're trickier to execute live. Adrianna is another that we won't play every night, I'm not sure why. It's a popular number and Danny Hargrove sings that wicked, elevated refrain at the end.

The Always a Rocker Tour is bolstered by the excellent technical crew who've come aboard since the Tampa Bay bust last April. Toby and Elwood Francis are brothers. Toby runs our house sound and younger brother Elwood is the Admiral's new guitar tech. Elwood is a cool character, he's quiet but he likes loud, uncompromising bands like Gang of Four. I don't know much about Gang of Four myself, but I nod my head in agreement, hoping Elwood will think I'm cool too. Stage manager Jay Fortune is a lanky, blonde guy, very quick to smile. New road manager, Rick, is a detail-oriented, level headed guy.

On September 23 the tour begins in the Northeast, heads up through Ontario and Quebec before hitting the Bottom Line in Manhattan and the Cleveland Agora. Once a Rocker has been added to playlists at about fifty FM stations. We're getting some good notices in the dailies and the trades. By the end of October we've pushed up through Chicago and onto Minneapolis. MTV begins playing the Black Velvet Pants video and most of our shows are packed. In November we arrive in San Francisco.

The Project, circa 1983

Ron Pownall

{ 32 }

Joe f'n Perry
Waking up at the Miyako. I flip on the bedside
radio. The dial is set to KRQR-FM - the frequency
covers the entire Sacramento Valley.
I only have to listen a few minutes before Once a Rocker
starts playing. This is a whole new feeling, having the rock
radio outlets in our corner as we roll into these big cities.
In the past few weeks we've hit Boston, Providence, New
Haven, Washington DC, Philadelphia, New York City,
Detroit, Toronto, Montreal, Cleveland, Chicago, and
Minneapolis.
Tonight we're at The Stone (412 Broadway) A deep, dark
box of a concert club, located on a hustling stretch of
Broadway that's been home to rock'n'roll shows for years.
The New York Dolls played here, so did Iggy and the
Stooges, the Tubes and even Bob Marley.
These days, a brigade of upcoming metal groups like
Anthrax and Metallica are frequent visitors.

The Project is geared up. Our pre-show tape is nearly
drowned out by the anxious crowd. Everyone is pushing
forward. Calling for Joe.
I'm stoked. I can't wait to rush out onto the stage.
That's when I feel someone tapping me on the shoulder.
Brushing up close. Talking into my ear.
It's Joe Pet, he whispers loudly,
 "Cattle Youth, what song do we open with?

My blood pressure spikes. Inside my head I'm screaming.
"For crying out loud, Pet. What is wrong with you?
You don't even remember how our damn show begins?"
I spin around in anger.
Joe Pet winks at me with a wide grin on his face.
He's just messing with me. Pissing-off the singer is way too
easy around here. It always makes him laugh.
The roar of the crowd rises. Road manager Rick pushes
past me with the Admiral. Joe steps onto the stage.
The Stone blows-up. Foot stomping, salutes and cheers.
Joe Pet zips out and vaults onto the drum riser. Slipping
behind his kit, smacking rim-shots.
The wise-guy drummer is suddenly all business.
Danny Hargrove glides out, nonchalantly flicking his
cigarette butt behind the backline as he plugs-in his Les
Paul, backwards-strung, bass guitar.
I dash to the center stage, grab the mic off its stand and
begin rattlesnake-shaking my maracas into the SM58.
The Admiral has chosen his Telecaster to begin the
festivities. It's got an added humbucker pick-up. Sounds a
lot heavier than a standard Leo Fender Tele.
The stage is still dark and our intro tape draws to a close.
Perry releases a thundering power-chord and hits the
boomerang switch on his pedal board.
Kids in the front row nearly suffer whiplash as the sound
waves ricochet back and forth across the wide stage.
Time has come today. Perry's guitar is transformed into a
train whistle and that eerie, inviting, opening wail is
answered by a super-charged whack of Joe Pet's snare
drum and BANG. Lights UP.
The engine lurches out of the station.

Delirious screams and outstretched arms span the stage as we ram straight into Train Kept A-Rollin.
Full speed ahead captain.

JOE PERRY PROJECT in San Francisco. Photo by Kyle Runge

Girls in sparkly tank-tops squeeze to the front and I shoot Hargrove the look. Kicking my boot heels into the boards I begin singing the familiar lyrics I grew up miming along with, as a 12 year-old dreamer.

I know Joe wore out the grooves of his "Having a Rave Up with the Yardbirds" record too. Just like me.

Hurtling into the lead guitar break, I glance back at the drummer. Okay, so what's on the menu tonight?

You never know with Joe Perry.

He sticks to his signature riffs like glue - but once we move into the lead guitar solos - who knows?

Before the Yardbirds, and later Aerosmith, turned this number into a rock staple, Train Kept A-Rollin' began life as a jumpin' 50's rock-a-billy tune.

Depending on his whim, Joe might attack his first solo with a more psychedelic spin. Are You Experienced?

I mean are you *really* Experienced? Or the Admiral might get twangy and rootsy for a country mile. Or he might just release a tornado of feedback and knock the crowd flat on their asses.

What's inside the Cracker Jack box tonight?

One thing's for sure, whatever Joe's selling - this crowd is buying. Finishing the opener we rock'n'roll our way straight into Eddie Cochran's classic Somethin' Else.

I know a lotta big bands, like Led Zeppelin, have covered this one too, but the Project brings Somethin' Else to the song. The lyrics are clever and I love to perform it.

Joe does some fine singing on this one. We both share my mic. The audience digs seeing the obvious bond that's grown between us.

"Joe Perry Project reporting for duty. Great to be back here at the Stone. We brought along something for ya. A new song from our new album. 4 Guns West!"
Being part of a team that's clicking is one of life's greatest pleasures. It's almost like sorcery.
The months of practice, pre-production, recording and road work have led the four of us deep into each others musical psyches.

JOE PERRY PROJECT 4 Guns West. Photo by Kyle Runge

Without a word or even a glance, we're all exactly where we have to be and doing exactly what we have to do.
Danny Hargrove feels it, even before I strain for a high note, he's already here beside me, covering.
If our jamming veers into rough territory, Joe Pet senses it. He yanks us out of the mud with his inventive rhythms.

Perry might be swinging his guitar around his head, spinning backwards one way while I'm coasting across stage the other way - but somehow we always meet up - shoulder to shoulder - for every refrain.

Bang a Gong is an easy groover and sets everybody up for the next song, Crossfire.
This one hits hard. San Francisco quakes in time to Perry's furious riff and Pet's accelerated, shifting beat.
Joe's got his silver Travis Bean guitar slung low.
Firing out notes like a nail gun.
I push myself to the limit on this one, spitting out rapid-fire lyrics until -
Perry ignites the fiery solo section. Hargrove and Pet pour musical gasoline onto the blaze. The whole city block is rocking to the hammering beat.
It's a November night outside on Broadway but the kids inside the Stone are soaked with sweat.
Crossfire comes to a sudden stop and the place bursts into cheers.

Joe Perry steps up to the mic - the crowd calls out to him. The Admiral mumbles something. He turns to Danny Hargrove and Pet. The trio rips into Break Song, an instrumental from the debut Joe Perry Project LP.

Joe's switched to his Tele-Rat for this one. The weird instrument combines a left-handed Stratocaster body with a left-handed, maple neck from a Telecaster.
The back of the guitar's body is black but the finish on the face has been ground away.

JOE PERRY PROJECT 1983. Danny Hargrove & Joe Perry.
Courtesy of the Hargrove Archive

After giving us a musical tour around the universe, the
Admiral steps up to the mic to sing the Jimi Hendrix
favorite, Red House.

When the Admiral sings Jimi's lyrics about love gone bad and "this key don't unlock the door" he speaks from his own recent, painful experience.

I gallop back onto the stage and we launch into a couple songs off the new MCA album. Women in Chains and Black Velvet Pants. The power of MTV becomes crystal clear as soon as the audience hears Joe twang the unforgettable BVP opening riff.

Next up is the part of the show where Mr. Perry introduces Danny Hargrove, Joe Pet and me to the audience. The kids kindly give each of us a nice hand. Then I take the mic from our leader, to do my Bob Hope-style intro.

"Ladies and gentlemen. It gives me great pleasure to present a young man from Boston. The man we're all here to see tonight. Right here folks. On this stage. The one, the only... Joe Fukken Perry."

The place goes bonkers as we chug into Rockin' Train. A funky, gospel-tinged mover off the first Perry solo album. An audience favorite. The song has an amped-up latin rhythm that really works with my maracas and Pet's multiple toms and timbales.

Speaking of Joe Pet, this is the song where he gets to show off his drum fireworks. No matter where we go, his solo always brings down the house.

By now the audience is drained, so we give everybody a big injection of Vitamin *R*. Once a *Rocker* Always a *Rocker*.

They love this one. Especially the young women lining the front of the stage. Glad we decided not to call it "No Time for Women."
I don't know about you but I don't wanna stop.
The Project slides into the track that closes Side Two of our new record, Never Wanna Stop.
This one starts pulsing like a voodoo conga-line dancing down your spinal cord. I recite the lyrics while Pet and Hargrove cast a spell over the crowd. The Admiral's slide guitar begins rising up. The audience gets caught in the sway. Danny, Joe and I all harmonize on the chorus.
It's the truth people - We never wanna stop. Higher and higher we climb. Perry leads us into the clouds with hypnotic, ascending bottleneck swirls...
We got time for *one more*.
Danny takes a quick drag on his Marlboro. Pet begins the build-up on his floor toms. Ladies and Gentlemen:
It's time to Let the Music Do the Talking.
Crashing to a close, the Project races off the stage while Joe's abandoned Dan Armstrong guitar cries for mercy.
A thousand stomping feet. Shouts of "Joe, come back... Please."
We return for a lightning quick version of Take a Walk with Me Sally. Solos all around.
A smashing, flashing finish.
We take a final bow and vanish. The lights come up.
The crowd staggers away in astonishment.
With only one thing left to say.
"Joe Fukken Perry."

November 18th 1983. I'm sitting in a hotel room on the
Sunset Strip, reading Project fan mail, making a few calls,
checking out the new issue of Kerrang.
Danny Hargrove swings by my room to share a funny story
from last's night's show at the Reseda Country Club.
Looking back, I guess this was the day when the shit hit
the fan. Tim Collins has flown into L.A. Meetings are going
on. Right down the hall. Behind closed doors.
I don't sense it, I have no idea anything's amiss.
The California stations are playing "Once a Rocker" the
Project video is rocking on MTV. The crowds are loving it.
Unbeknownst to the rest of us, our pirate ship has taken a
direct hit.

We're going down.

{ 33 }

Wild Bunch '84, Lita Ford, Hanoi Rocks

Crawling out of bed around noontime. It's Sunday...I think...

The last 72 hours have done a job on my head. Last night I was in New Haven, for the final Joe Perry Project show (May 12, 1984). The night before that the Project played Salisbury Beach. It really turned into scene when Brad Whitford and Steven Tyler walked out of the wings to join the Project for the set-ending jam.

Did I mention we had Aerosmith drummer Joey Kramer onboard the Project pirate ship, filling in for Joe Pet on the last three dates?

The addition of Kramer raises the stage temperature considerably.

It's a lot to think about. But I have to put all that Joe Perry Project stuff out of my mind. The Project is over.

Now I have Bruce the booking agent pushing me to hurry up with the new thing Danny Hargrove and I are trying to hustle together. It's already mid-May and according to our agent, most of the good summer slots at the big rock venues are already spoken for.

Danny and I have already talked with our JPP bandmate, drummer Joe Pet. He's tentatively committed to joining our new endeavor.

I think it was me who came up with the name "Wild Bunch" back when the JPP was touring the West Coast for the final time in March. Now all we need to do is find a replacement for Joe Perry.

This afternoon. If not sooner. *Damn.*

Two days later Danny comes to the rescue with Hal Boudreau. A slim, blonde dude with a Stratocaster. I think Hal used to play with Danny's pre-Project group, Rage. Hal might fit the bill.

But there's a dark-haired guitarist I've been watching, Glenn Otenti, from the Johnny Barnes band.

Hal and Glenn O are both about the same size. They can play and, most importantly, they both seem to have their heads screwed-on straight.

The pink palace phone is ringing. Our agent again.

"Hurry up and put a band together."

"The Gods That Rock" is the lofty title of a song Hargrove is singing for me. We don't have a rehearsal space, we're just sitting at the kitchen table in the pink palace.

Julia's Cambridge apartment. It's upstairs in a run-down
pink duplex at 354 Broadway.
Danny didn't get a chance to contribute songs to the
Project, so it's fascinating hearing his riffs and lyrics for
the first time. They're good. I've got a brand new one too.
Mine is called Back to the Front.
I have all these other Joe Perry Project songs in the works,
material for the follow-up Project album, but I don't even
want to think about that right now.
We're joined by the two guitarists, Hal and Glenn O.
We run down material, at low volume, through practice
amps.

Our hoped-for drummer, Joe Pet, pulls-out on May 31, just
a minute before I get the call. The Wild Bunch is booked to
headline The Frolics, one of New England's biggest
venues, just four weeks from now. We need to act fast.
My Thundertrain drummer, Bobby Edwards, is signed to a
production deal with his band Velocity. That means he's
on payroll and not allowed to moonlight with other bands.
I'm not looking for a part-timer anyway.
We need someone who's ready to bail out the bilge water,
raise the Jolly Roger, and set sail.
Danny agrees. We've got to keep the spirit of the Project
going. Somehow.

Johnny Barnes rescues us. He loans us his rehearsal room
in Quincy. No time to lose, we find a teenage drummer
named Louis.
Not a horrible drummer but green.

A week later (6/9) the Wild Bunch is standing in the sandpit movie location used in the great Robert Mitchum picture, *The Friends of Eddie Coyle*.

Boston's ace music photographer, Ron Pownall, is shooting the official Wild Bunch promo pictures.

WILD BUNCH '84. Glenn Otenti, Danny, Dr. Bones, Hal Boudreau, Mach. Photo by Ron Pownall

Our demo tape, Burn Thru the Night, was recorded before we even got the band together. It premieres tonight on the Carter Alan and Mark Parenteau shows over at good ol' WBCN. Normally I'd be thrilled to hear my latest song on the radio, but Burn Thru the Night was a rush job and now that we've assembled an actual group, it sounds...off.

Joe Perry is playing tonight. It's June 22nd and the reunited Aerosmith takes-off at (where else?) the Capitol Theater in Concord NH. The same place that Danny and I premiered with Joe and the Project, three years ago.

Mach Bell has a new outfit together, entitled, appropriately, The Wild Bunch. The group includes Glenn Otenti and H. Lebeau on guitars and former Joe Perry Project bassist Danny Hargrove in addition to somebody named Dr. Bones on drum — and no, it's not Mr. Bones on bones. The band is working at Sound Design Studio with Hirsh Gardner for upcoming vinyl release.

Wild Bunch premieres a week later, on June 29, 1984 at the Frolics. Joe Perry Project road manager Rick helps by digging-up my trusty JPP mic stand. He returns it to me just in time for the show. I think the aluminum tripod stand really belongs to Huey Lewis - before our rogue roadie, Zakowski, got his grubs on it.

We've worked really hard to pull this off. We lean fairly heavily on Project material, performing faithful versions of Once a Rocker, Bang a Gong, Walk With Me Sally, Black Velvet Pants and 4 Guns West. Our effort wins the approval of Project diehards scattered in the crowd.

Danny Hargrove at Frolics Ballroom.

Danny and I have both contributed several new songs to the setlist and the twin Stratocaster attack of Boudreau and Otenti seems to be gelling.

That all sounds pretty good, right? Problem is, Danny and I rocked this same ballroom just six weeks ago with the Joe Perry Project, aided by rock stars Joey Kramer, Brad Whitford and Steven Tyler.

Returning here - with the echoes of that night still echoing in the eaves - and the ghost of Joe Perry standing right here beside me on the stage...It's all too soon.

My sudden change of fortune has me on my heels. This hall was double-stuffed when the JPP played, but tonight the Wild Bunch might have a couple hundred in the house.

Obviously I'm not as popular as I used to be a few weeks ago. Amazing how quickly a large contingent of friends and followers have fallen off the map. Now when my phone rings its usually the car rental place asking for money or our agent needing something.

Oh yeah, all of a sudden I'm getting lots of these too:

"Hello"

"Hey Cowboy, How's it going?"

"Good, thanks. Hargrove and I are keeping busy. Launching our own band, the Wild Bunch."

"Cool. Hey, listen...I was wondering if you could help me score me some Aerosmith tickets for the Worcester Centrum?"

Our next Wild Bunch show is at the Roadhouse in Lynn, another room the Project recently played. So is the gig after that, at the Mohawk in Shirley.

The Mohawk stands out, mainly because we have Project lighting tech, Woody Bavota, and the Admiral's guitar tech, Elwood Francis, helping the Wild Bunch tonight.

On the 19th, Julia brings me to see her band, The Cars, down in Providence.

For the past four years Julia has been the office manager at the Cars' SyncroSound Studios, formerly Intermedia Sound. The studio where Dream On was recorded.

The Cars are surfing a tidal wave right now. Heartbeat City was just released and its already Top 10.

Frankly, now that I'm starting from scratch again, it's difficult attending shows that feature my wildly successful friends.

August is busy. After a headline show at J.J. Flash in Boston (finally, a room that the Project didn't recently play) the Wild Bunch begin auditioning for a more experienced drummer. Pausing on the 16th for Danny's birthday and the 18th for longtime Thundertrain sound man, Jon Read's, wedding.

The next show is coming up. We still can't find a drummer.

460

Lita Ford is headlining the Rat tonight, August 24th, with the Wild Bunch opening. Bobby Edwards breaks contract and fills-in on drums for the show.

Tonight is the first time I've felt at ease onstage since the Project's grand finale. With my Biggy Ratt/Thundertrain/ Hits/Mag 4/ beat brother, Bobby Edwards, laying down a thick, reassuring rhythm behind me and my JPP blood- brother, Danny Hargrove, singing and slinging his Les Paul bass guitar by my side.
Lita Ford turns 26 next month. It's been seven years since we played the Rat together. Tonight Ford fronts a power trio, they have a new record "Out for Blood" on Mercury.

September. Exactly one year ago today, the "Once a Rocker Always a Rocker" album was released. Time is flying by and I still haven't found a permanent drummer for the Wild Bunch. Recording new songs is impossible without a permanent foundation. Danny and I continue to write and rehearse with our two guitarists.

I talk to recording studio managers pretty regularly about making a Wild Bunch demo. Most of them immediately want to know if I can get Joe Perry to either play on, or produce our songs. Moving on from the Joe Perry Project is easier said than done in this little city - and speaking of that - we're playing the Channel tonight with Project drummer, Joe Pet, filling in at the drum position.

Am I moving forward? - Or regressing back in time?

MTV is playing Twisted Sister's I Wanna Rock and Van Halen's Hot For Teacher non-stop.

Thundertrain was on the right track - but no cigar.

Michael Des Barres is singing at the Paradise tonight.

His current supergroup is called Chequered Past.

After Silverhead dissolved, Des Barres went on to front Detective (Swan Song Records). He started Checkered Past around the same time Danny and I joined the Project.

Michael has managed to finally co-write a smash. It's called Obsession, but his own version is overshadowed when the pop band Animotion covers it. They score an MTV/radio hit that goes to #6 in the US.

The Wild Bunch is doing some recording at Port-a-Pet studio, the front room at Pet's place in Medford. The same room where where we prepped the Once a Rocker album.

Our former drummer likes to sit-in with the Bunch but being a family man with bills to pay, he's not up for an extended voyage aboard our leaky, creaky pirate ship.

Wild Bunch plays a Boston club called Bunratty's on October 24th and our producer, Hirsh Gardner, joins us on drums for the first time.

Hirsh sang and played with the band New England.

They made some good albums with Paul Stanley and Todd Rundgren producing.

"Never Wanna Lose Ya'" was their most popular song.

Gardner has been trying to get something off the ground with recent KISS member, Vinnie Vincent, but that's apparently stalled. So, Hirsh joins the Wild Bunch.

Gardner, a topshelf showman, immediately fills the sails of our tipsy vessel. We're back in the race.

WILD BUNCH '84. Rocking the Casbah.

Friday Nov 16th, 1984, Manchester NH.
Wild Bunch is at the Casbah opening for the Finnish
glam-band, Hanoi Rocks.
These hard-rocking boys started-out in 1979. The same
year Thundertrain was skidding to a halt. Hanoi Rocks is
touring the US for the first time, promoting a new Bob
Ezrin produced LP. It's called Two Steps From the Move.
Great vibe tonight. Neil, who owns the Casbah, is a strong
supporter of the Wild Bunch. He's known Danny and me
since we first played here with Joe Perry. Speaking of the
Project, we have JPP road manager Rick working with us
tonight.

Hirsh Gardner makes his official debut as our full-time drummer this evening and the Wild Bunch finally looks and feels like an actual band.

The overflowing party in the post-show dressing room is hard to ignore. Several members of the headline act swing by to check out the backstage Wild Bunch action. Danny Hargrove and road manager Rick keep everyone in stitches with their spell-binding Joe Perry road stories.

Each time L.A. or Hollywood is mentioned, Razzle leans forward. He's only 23 and this is his first time in America. Back in '82, Hanoi Rocks moved their base of operations from the Netherlands to London, England. That's where lead singer Michael Monroe meets a fan named Razzle. The fan ends-up joining Hanoi Rocks as drummer.

Razzle is super excited about playing on the West Coast and especially Hollywood. They're headed that way in a few weeks. After they do a few more concerts here in New England and New York.

With the Wild Bunch finally on track, it's time to cut a real demo. Over the Top, Stand Up, In My Sights, It's My Turn, Gods That Rock and Back to the Front are just a few of the original songs to choose from. It's a drizzly morning - I'm mulling everything over - still in bed.

The phone rings.

Shocking news from Los Angeles.

Razzle got killed last night (12/8) in a car wreck down in Redondo Beach. After rocking with the Wild Bunch, his band had to cancel some gigs. Because lead singer Michael Monroe mashed his ankle onstage in Syracuse NY - at a venue called USA Sam's.

So, Hanoi Rocks travels out to the West Coast where injured Monroe can continue his recuperation.

Meanwhile, the singer of Hollywood's Motley Crue invites Razzle and the rest of Hanoi Rocks out to his beach place. Everyone commences getting hammered. Vince Neil and Razzle are returning from a quick run to the packie when Neil's Pantera smacks into another car. Driver Vince survives, but Razzle - who was riding shotgun - is pronounced dead at 7:12 pm.

The pink palace hotline rings again the following week. Wild Bunch guitarist Hal Boudreau calls to inform me he's been offered a sweet gig by Gary Cherone. Playing lead guitar for The Dream (Mutha, Don't Wanna Go to School Today).

I first met Gary while in Concord NH, the night Danny Hargrove and I made our Project debuts. The Dream opened our show that night and they've been building-up steam ever since. I can't blame Hal for jumping ship.

1984 grinds to a halt and I'm sitting here in my seat at the Orpheum theater in Boston. Watching Aerosmith welcome in the New Year '85. The re-formed Aerosmith has managed to complete 65 shows this year and they're talking about going into the studio. It'll be interesting to see how that goes.

That goes double for the Wild Bunch...

{ 34 }

Paris, Wild Bunch '85
Hirsh Gardner lets the Wild Bunch rehearse in an outbuilding on his property in Braintree, a few miles south of Boston. As usual, bookings in New England taper-off as the temperature drops and snowbanks grow. That's fine. We need time to find a replacement for departed guitarist, Boudreau. Julia takes me out to dinner for my 32nd birthday but I find it hard to concentrate.
Bobby Edward's band, Velocity, is recording demos at the Ed Sullivan Theater building in New York City.
Philadelphia's Sigma Sound operates a sister studio there.
So I head down to Manhattan for a couple days, happy to cheer-on lead guitarist Johnny Press and my Thundertrain bandmate. On my return to Boston, I bid adieu to Thundertrain lead guitarist, Steven Silva.
Silva's decided to pack-up his amps and guitars and head west. I wish Steven luck out in L.A.
K-K-K-Katys, one of the venues that comprise the Kenmore Club, is currently called Celebration. Apart from the name switch, the place is unchanged from the days when Daddy Warbux, Aerosmith and Thundertrain used to play here.

Tonight the featured music is still called rock, but the current crop of bands didn't evolve from Hendrix, Steppenwolf or the Rolling Stones. I was born in the 50's and those were the kinds of groups my generation of rock musicians studied.

It was through those classic bands that I and my contemporaries discovered the seminal sounds of Chuck Berry, Bo Diddley, Howlin' Wolf, John Lee Hooker, Buddy Guy and Muddy Waters. The metal maniacs I'm listening to right now play an entirely different type of rock music.

Listen to these kids. At least a decade younger than me, weened on Van Halen and Judas Priest records. Posing on the stage, throwing horns, tongues outstretched, shredding up a storm. Whiplash guitar solos, eight finger-tips tapping at the frets, with nary a wink or a nod to Ron Wood, George Harrison or Duane Eddy. The drummer is pumping two foot pedals, rigged in tandem, to batter-the-daylights-out-of a single kick drum. Kick rolls that John Bonham and Bobby Edwards routinely toed-out on a single pedal - if they chose to.

I'm trying to follow along, but I don't understand the language, the sizzling sound of metal doesn't connect with me in a deep way. That's too bad because "metal nights" are drawing crowds to Celebration and similar venues across the land. I think the glam-rock sound of the Sunset Strip has finally invaded America (as I predicted, eleven years ago) with bands like Quiet Riot, Motley Crue and Ratt racing up the charts. Just as Thundertrain found ourselves lumped into the glitter-rock, boogie-rock and punk-rock waves of the mid-70's, the Wild Bunch is currently being sold second-hand as "metal" since it's the hot tag of the moment.

That's what I'm thinking about, as I stare into my empty gin & tonic.

My pondering is interrupted when a familiar blonde hops onto the barstool next to mine. The last time I saw Ilse she was helping-out during the making of the Joe Perry Project MTV video. That was during the summer of 1983, Black Velvet Pants was the song, and Ilse came to us through Perry's roommate, Glenda.

Ilse smiles, "Mach, I want you to meet my boyfriend, Ted."

Ted Anderson is an athletic, flashy lead guitarist/singer from Washington DC (which is also Danny Hargrove's hometown). Teddy has a hungry, modern look - he's a lot younger than us - and he can shred. So in the Spring of 1985 the Wild Bunch becomes a quartet. Metal-boy Ted joins up with hard-rockers Hirsh, Hargrove and Cowboy. Besides his guitar chops and flashy look, Teddy Anderson also owns a big, blue,"Thomas Built" school bus. I think it belonged to a traveling choir before Ted got hold of it. If you look carefully, you can still see the faded lettering across the side of the old bus "Songbirds of Our Lord."

Teddy is a big fan of Sunset Strip guitarist George Lynch. Anderson brings me to see Lynch's group, Dokken, at the Orpheum. It's a thrilling show for sure, the songs are dramatic and the wild guitar solos are impressive. Reformulating the Wild Bunch - yet again - will take a month or so, the time-off has forced me to seek a steady source of moolah.
I find a gig at Magic 106.7, Boston's FM home of...
Soft Rock.
Please don't tell anyone.

Cowboy hides. Way in the back of the listener research department, hoping nobody will discover his shame. Some days they have me entering data into a boxy, electric thing with a screen. Other days I cold-call victims, attempting to get their honest first impression of 10-second song clips from Whitney Houston, Luther Vandross and other dentist office favorites.

I'm cruising with Danny one night in March' 85 when a familiar riff begins chugging out of the car radio.

Get it On, Bang a Gong. But wait, it's not our Joe Perry Project version. And it's not Marc Bolan's original either. No, its Robert Palmer and some Duran Duran guys, calling themselves the Power Station. Over the next months, their re-make of Bang a Gong races up the charts.

JOE PERRY PROJECT   Bang a Gong

See, the Project *was* onto something when we recorded and released that same song. 18 months ago. It *was* ripe for a comeback...Too bad nobody at the record label understood it back then.

Danny and I never talk much about the struggle we're still coping with. We're both fairly intelligent guys and intellectually we've made peace with the Admiral's decision to leave the Project.

We might be able to talk our way around it, but the truth is, our souls are still chained to the mast of that proud JPP pirate ship. The Admiral still has a firm grip on our hearts.

Wild Bunch '85 debuts in Manchester NH at The Place. Hirsh Gardner pounces into the lights and scrambles up onto the drum riser, immediately launching into a showy solo that draws the entire crowd close to the stage.

At the appropriate moment, Danny strolls into the lights, driving an immense Les Paul bass riff. Teddy enters. He doubles down, turbocharging Danny's groove.

Kids are waving up to me as I appear from behind the amp-line. Maracas shaking, cowboy boots kicking-in.

The new guitarist spins forward, burning-up his fretboard as only a 23 year-old raised on Randy Rhodes cassettes, can.

The power and fresh sound of the new line-up is intense. Being an over-the-top performer myself, I require a really strong band to balance my blast-furnace approach to entertaining - and I've found it.

Tonight I command the stage.

WILD BUNCH '85 Teddy Anderson, Danny Hargrove,

Hirsh Gardner and Mach. Photo by Ilse.

Word about the re-charged, re-vamped Wild Bunch travels fast. The great gig almost makes Dan and I forget that it's been a year-to-the-day since our final Joe Perry Project performance.

The next gig is a "Metal for Meals" benefit at the Mohawk and this time I don't feel so bad about the metal label. *I* may not fit the description but my lead guitar player does. The club booker, John Coleman, is impressed with the show and the loud audience reaction. He goes to work lining-up a road trip for us.

I stop by the Channel the next night to see the Lords of the New Church. I'm happy, seeing old friend Stiv Bators again. His band seems to be doing very well.
Dead Boy, Cheetah Chrome, is here too. He's totally wasted but manages to tell me he's staying in Boston's Mission Hill at the moment. I'm bummed to see Chrome in such poor condition.
I hate to say this, but I'm having the same feeling about Bobby Edwards.
It seems like every time I see him these days he's drinking and the drinking doesn't agree with him. It causes some sort of chemical reaction that turns nice guy Bobby into a confrontational son of a gun. Things began slipping away for Bobby right after his mom died a few years ago.
She died way too early, taken by cancer.

We stack our gear in the back and find seats in the front of Teddy Anderson's blue school bus.

Ilse is now the Wild Bunch road manager and her
boyfriend, the guitarist, drives. We're doing a good 50
miles per hour (maybe a little less on the long uphill
stretches) heading to the next show.
I can finally breathe a sigh of relief.
Wheels turning. Moving up the highway. Feeling the
breeze, gazing out at passing clouds, listening to yet
another ribald road tale from Hargrove and Hirsh.
I flip open my journal and begin scribbling notes. Song
ideas, a sketch or two. This is more like it. Visualizing
tonight's crowd, thinking about what I might say or do to
get the party started...
After a good performance in Worcester at Steeple
Bumpstead, we pull into a motel. Rooming with Danny.
Falling immediately into our old post-show routines.
I feel so much more secure whenever I'm free of my daily-
orbit and back on the road.
We headline two shows at Excalibur in Portsmouth NH
and the next day it's an outdoor festival in Northwood.

WILD BUNCH '85   Northwood Festival

Teddy has brought a couple good original songs to the
Wild Bunch and Danny and I have at least an album's
worth of material. Our new Wild Bunch songs go over well
but there's always a segment of the crowd waiting to hear
the Joe Perry Project portion of the show. Danny and I
usually sing Somethin' Else, Bang a Gong and three or four
other numbers off the "Once a Rocker" album.

We circle back to Worcester for a headline show at Sir
Morgan's Cove. It's a fairly well known secret that I get
extremely pumped anytime I get to perform on a stage
Mick Jagger and the Rolling Stones once occupied.
The Rolling Stones (billed as Little Boy Blue & the
Cockroaches) played this 300 seat club on September 14,
1981, just a couple nights before the Stones '81 American
tour officially began in Philadelphia.
Eighteen hours later the Wild Bunch bus arrives back at
Boston's J.J. Flash.
On the bill tonight is Johnny Angel, one of the earliest
Thundertrain followers.
Johnny went on to sing and play guitar with Thrills which
morphed into City Thrills. Angel's latest band is another
hot Boston headliner, the Blackjacks.
Neil is happy to see Danny and me back at the Casbah the
following night.
His Manchester venue has become something of a home
for the Wild Bunch. Tonight we headline for our biggest
crowd yet.
I'm sorry to see this New England road trip end. Tonight
we're back in Boston at the Channel, opening for The
Fools, one of this area's best draws.

It feels great, hitting the stage with Hirsh, Teddy and
Danny. Took awhile, but I've found my team.

Ilse sets up a group photo session with Jodi Sinclair.
Arriving at Jodi's studio, down on Broad Street - not far
from the little rock hangout, Cantone's - I'm startled to see
Hargrove. Wait...that *is* my side-kick Danny isn't it?
My longtime bandmate strolls in, but with a whole new
look.
Head totally shaven. Except for a shark-fin mohawk,
spiked up the middle of his dome. But wait, there's more.
Danny's 'do is dyed in a fantastic rainbow of Italian ice
flavor-colors. Red Cherry, Blue Raspberry, Lemon Yellow.
Cool.
I'm still wearing my hair like I did with the Project, seeing
Danny I suddenly feel kinda old-fashioned.
Road manager Ilse whips a styling brush from her back
pocket. A couple minutes later, she's tamed my fuzz-mop
into a Flock of Seagulls-worthy masterpiece.

WILD BUNCH '85 Ted, Hirsh, Mach & Danny.
Photo by Jodi Sinclair

Shades of Palo Alto. The Wild Bunch is excited to return to Celebration in Kenmore Square tonight with the new line-up. These "metal nights" pull in an enthusiastic pack of head bangers who augment our dedicated gang of rockers. The concert starts off great, but we're only about five songs into the act when the power goes out.

Plunged into darkness, the basement club is suddenly silenced.

Emergency lamps blink on, casting a spooky glow as hundreds of pissed-off celebrants are evacuated.

All of Kenmore Square has gone dark. The absence of electric power is only the beginning of our woes - the blue bus won't start either.

Nothing stops the Wild Bunch. With the aid of a rental truck, we're able to complete the next shows, back at the Casbah in Manchester NH and here at the Rat. Meanwhile, Ilse and Ted baby the bus a few blocks over to the Fenway. Parking it out in front of their apartment.

Ilse tracks down a wandering mechanic, a guy who actually makes house calls. The ailing Thomas Built rests at the curb while the mechanic finds transmission parts.

Mama's Boys are probably the tightest rock band on Earth and I've never even heard of them - until tonight.

Three brothers from Northern Ireland.

The McManus brothers used to perform traditional Irish tunes with fiddles before switching over to the heavy stuff. Wild Bunch is back at the Casbah, and we just finished opening for these guys.

"Power and Passion" is the name of the fifth and most recent Mama's Boys album. Obvious Slade fans, these guys released a cover version of Slade's "Mama Were All Krazee Now" that made it to #54 in Billboard before getting side-swiped by Quiet Riot's chart-busting cover of the very same tune.

I laugh because in the 70's, "Mama" was a pet song of Thundertrain's. I sang that anthem just about every night for five years. It was kinda strange last year when I started hearing from my friends:

"Hey Mach, I just heard you singing on the radio."

What they were actually hearing was the Quiet Riot version of "Mama" - playing non-stop - all the way to the top.

Bret Michaels greets me outside the dressing room door at Celebration.

His band is called Paris and they're up here in Boston from Mechanicsburg PA to play "metal night" along with my Bunch. Bret is the lead singer.

I'm feeling a whole lot better now that our bus is finally rolling again. Even though this is a local show, we have the blue vehicle parked out in front. We use it as a dressing room/party overflow area.

Paris put on a high-energy show.

Bret Michaels is a dazzling frontman. The drummer, Rikki Rockett, is right on the money. Afterwards, Michaels tells me that Paris is planning a move out to California.

"Gonna try our luck on the Sunset Strip."

Playing alongside bands like Mama's Boys and Paris stirs my competitive soul, they're really good - but so is my quartet. Following a dynamite set, I toast Danny at the bar. He'll turn 27 in a couple days (8/16) and our future is bright.

{ 35 }

I Gotta Rock

I 'm also getting phone calls like this.

A friend, or a friend of a friend, calls to tell me about the seriously unfortunate ailment a cousin is suffering from - or about the roof of the important community clinic that is leaking or about to cave in.

"I know it's a lot to ask Mach, but could you possibly see if your friends Aerosmith would come over here and play a benefit performance for us?"

Getting calls like these is just a massive downer.
I feel horrible, hearing about the stricken nephew or whatever...and I don't like to disappoint people, but the whole thing is... whacked.
I have nothing to do with Aerosmith business. Those guys might consider me a friend, they might even take my call, but if I start bothering them, asking them to do favors...
I bet the Aerosmith office gets dozens of requests like this every week.

Wild Bunch was gonna rehearse today but Danny Hargrove called in sick.
That's odd. I've never known Danny to be sick before.
Tomorrow is Joe Perry's birthday. He'll turn 35.
The next day we headline at the Rat.
Danny is back. He does look sick.

Or something. I'm not sure.

On the 21st, our friend Billie Montgomery becomes Billie Perry, as she and the Admiral tie the knot.

Aerosmith continue their slow climb, Joe tells me they've nearly finished making a new album "Done With Mirrors." I remember that title well, it was one of Joe's ideas from the Project days.

The new Aerosmith record is due out on 11/4/85.

I travel to the Worcester Centrum to see Motley Crue with opener Y&T.

Theatre of Pain is the name of the tour as well as the current album. As usual with hard-rock and metal records, the first track making noise on FM is a cover of a former hit, Brownsville Station's "Smokin' in the Boys Room."

I got a really interesting call from Thundertrain's Steven Silva. He's been out in Hollywood for a few months and he just auditioned for that band - Paris.

The same guys we gigged with recently in Boston.

Steven tells me that Paris has now changed their name to Poison.

Singer Bret Michaels, drummer Rikki Rockett and bassist Bobby Dall are all still onboard, they just need a new guitar player.

Steven is pretty amped, he's made it down to the final cut. It's between three guitarists. I sure hope Silva gets it. Competing for Steven Silva's job as Poison lead guitarist is a dude named C.C. DeVille and another guy called Slash.

I'm worried about Danny Hargrove.

The kid has always been like Old Ironsides, I mean Danny can drink toe-to-toe with the Admiral and still function almost normally. Danny can stay up all night or smoke a whole bag of weed or mess around with god-knows-who-or-what and still keep his wheels on the ground.

Something has changed.

Ever since the sick-call last month.

Danny Hargrove was sky high at the Rat. Par for the course, but for first time, his disorientation was obvious. Last rehearsal I caught him muttering gibberish to himself. He was staring at the ground. Ilse has known Danny for a while and she's very concerned.

Outside of his amazing concert performances, his backstage antics and the jaw-dropping fashion choices he makes, Hargrove is an extremely private person. Discrete and guarded. Danny's rockin' train is off the tracks - and I don't really know how to address it.

Kix is touring behind Midnight Dynamite, their latest on Atlantic Records.

Singer Steve Whiteman leads this Maryland-based band.

I remember the great night we got to spend with them in Poughkeepsie a couple years ago, the night they opened for the Joe Perry Project at the Chance.

I'm catching up with Kix while I keep an eye on wandering Danny. Normally he'd be here alongside me, in the thick of the party.

But now he seems to be lost. Like he's not quite sure where he is - who he is - or what he's doing here.

Daniel Crawford Hargrove. 1985

I hope the pounding of Hirsh Gardner's drums will bring Danny back to Earth.

The Wild Bunch has built-up a solid following around Manchester and with the MTV support Kix is getting right now, the Casbah is nearly sold out.
I'm pushing really hard because its obvious Danny is barely hanging on. He's missing vocal cues, playing most of his passages perfectly but intermittently flubbing bass lines - something I've never heard him do before.

482

Teddy glances my way nervously. We press forward.
We're about halfway into Black Velvet Pants when
Hargrove seems to trip over himself, toppling to one knee.
Ilse dashes over to the side of the stage, but Danny regains
his footing, just in time to rock the final few vocal refrains.
Ted Anderson steps into the center spotlight, scratching
out the opening guitar riff to "Once a Rocker."

Kix pops out of their dressing room for this one. Anderson
plays a dead-on recreation of the Admiral's guitar line and
I rip straight into my signature Project vocal.

Once a Rocker Always a Rocker
Can you hear the beat?
Once a Rocker Always a Rocker
Now you're gonna feel the -

Danny Hargrove takes a half-step to the side…teeters
slowly…and plummets backwards. Dropping off the corner
of the Casbah stage. His big Gibson bass guitar falls along
with him. Danny plummets several feet before crashing,
heavily, to the floor.

Ilse and I run to the semi-conscious bassist. He doesn't
move for a few long seconds.

Hirsh Gardner, ever the pro, immediately distracts the
concerned crowd with a torrential cavalcade of tom rolls
and kicks that brings the crowd to their feet and brings
tonight's Wild Bunch set to a premature close.
Once the gear is collected, we load Danny into the bus.

Ilse turns to me. She doesn't really have to say anything. I know we're both thinking the same thing. The Wild Bunch has weeks of bookings, straight up ahead.
We both feel helpless.

Truth is, neither of us are on solid ground ourselves.
We spend most of our energy, time and imagination just trying to keep the wolves from our doors.
Rent, travel expenses, gear repair, phone and copier bills, agent commissions...
We don't know what's happened to Danny - but even if we did - we're not in a position to help him very much.

Back on the bus, Cambridge bound, Danny is out for the count. Ilse presses a cold compress to his forehead.
Hey, I admit it. I've fallen off stages too, after a drinking spree or similar hi-jinks.
The Project was a party-machine and Hargrove invited all the wine, women, drugs or whatever else came rolling his way. But Danny never came close to falling off a stage.
What the hell is bringing him down like this?
The thought of marching ahead with the Wild Bunch - but without Danny Hargrove - frightens me.
Rocking without Hargrove is unimaginable.

Buzzing down I-93, the skyline of Boston rising into view.

Remembering back to the summer of '68.
Watching the Jeff Beck Group in wonderment at the Boston Tea Party and hearing the Jimi Hendrix Experience at my first big show in the Carousel tent.

John Hammond Jr., Tommy Bolin, Luther Rabb,
Steppenwolf,...so many rock musicians and groups I got to
see or meet or even party with back in the sixties.
Thinking about the seventies - living with my own band,
on the road, recording, getting to perform all over the
Northeast. Experiencing first-hand the 70's glitter scene
on the Sunset Strip, rocking with Thundertrain at the
Cleveland Agora, Max's Kansas City and CBGB's.
I've been dealt some bad cards along the way.
I crushed my finger at Wood Engineering, got thrown in
jail, chased after dogs under the Circus Vargas Big Top.

But occasionally the
house dealt me a
winning card.
A Bobby Edwards or
a Danny Hargrove.
I remember Danny
standing on the
loading dock of an
anonymous-looking
warehouse in
Cambridge.
Together, we were
about to set sail on a
rock adventure of
heroic proportions.

Plucked from obscurity and thrust into the rock'n'roll
dreamscape of the Joe Perry Project.

Our days, weeks and months ahead would be a rapid - and confusing - succession of towering pinnacles, deep depressions, treacherous curves, unexpected U Turns, and full-on bliss.

He's still unconscious. On the seat behind me.

Thinking back to a warm evening on Boston Harbor.
Danny is leaning against the rail of the Tea Party Ship.
Beckoning me with a grin.
Laughter and high-hopes surround us.
Our brand new album, Once a Rocker Always a Rocker, booms across the lapping waves.

I'm so grateful for these memories.
I wouldn't change a thing.

JOE PERRY PROJECT Mach & Danny

Back in Cambridge the following day.
Danny rings me at the pink palace.
He's very apologetic about what happened last night.
Embarrassed about the whole thing - about losing it - in
front of his band, the crowd and the guys in Kix.
Hargrove sounds better now.
I cling to the hope that an overnight miracle has occurred.
My musical partner has returned!
The real Danny is back.

But my fantasy takes a nosedive as Danny continues,

JOE PERRY PROJECT '84. Danny, Mach and the Admiral.

"Listen, Cowboy...
It's time for me to step back from the Wild Bunch...
...and away from rock'n'roll.
There's something going on.
I can deal with it. But it's gonna take time."

The Wild Bunch will struggle forward,
the adventure will continue.
But I won't see Danny Hargrove again.
Not for a long, long time.

ABOUT THE AUTHOR

Cowboy Mach Bell is lead singer and co-author of
the 1983 Joe Perry Project *"Once a Rocker"* album, lead
vocalist on the 1977 Thundertrain album *"Teenage
Suicide"* and author of the 2019 book *"Once a Rocker
Always a Rocker: A Diary."* This is Cowboy's second book.
Mach lives with his wife Julia and a cat.

Special thanks to our dear, departed Lynn Ciulla.

Boston rock photographer, a supporter of underground rock'n'roll and a lifelong Rolling Stones fan.

Made in United States
North Haven, CT
14 December 2021

12797778R00297

32

RETURN TO NAZARETH

Birth minus 24 weeks

E lric sat and held the baby John as the women prepared the meal. While the other four warriors laughed and asked to hear every detail of the story surrounding John's birth, Elric only partially listened. His attention centered on the bundle in his arms.

Lacidar, unseen by the human eyes, stood beside Elric and gazed over his shoulder into the face of the newborn prophet. "It is an awesome thing to actually get to hold one," Lacidar said.

Elric glanced up at him and gave an affirming nod. He looked down at his own hands—hands that had wielded a punishing sword against the most wicked and powerful creatures in all creation for thousands of years. And now in those hands sat a frail, innocent human in his most helpless state. *I have seen thousands of babies over the years, but I've never been in a position where I got to physically hold one.*

"And," Lacidar continued, "he is already filled with the Holy Spirit." He looked at John and shook his head. "Have you ever held a prophet of the King who was filled with the Spirit from the womb?"

Elric answered with a raised eyebrow. *Oh, I do know the significance of this moment.* He smiled at the old parents bubbling around like a couple of proud young chickens. Just then, baby John tried to wrap his tiny hand around one of Elric's pinkies. Elric gazed down at him and said out loud, "What adventures are in store for you, little one?

Zacharias stopped in mid-sentence and belted out, "He is going to be a great prophet! He will prepare the way for the Lord's Messiah!" Zacharias beamed.

Elric smiled and nodded, "Yes, I believe you are right."

"Of course I'm right. This is a miracle baby, and we have a promise directly from one of the angels of God, and. . ."

Elric let the conversation drift off into the distance. *They have every right to be excited and joyful. This child will indeed play a key role for the Kingdom. But they have no idea what this will mean to them here in this life. This innocent young baby was born on the front lines of the most important spiritual battle of all time. Preparing the hearts of Israel for their coming King will be a gritty affair. There is sure to be intense opposition both in the Physical Realm and the spiritual. The Kingdom will suffer violence, and this new soldier will forcefully lead the campaign among men. Over the coming years, these happy smiles will be replaced by sorrow and unquenchable zeal. That is the way of war.*

He looked around at the proud and happy faces. He would speak nothing of the coming hardships. Let them enjoy this special time—tomorrow would deliver its fire soon enough.

With the meal preparations complete, the eight sat and enjoyed it. The light cheerful banter over the food turned more practical as the time to depart drew near. Mary excused herself to pack while the others continued eating and talking. After a short time, she reappeared in the doorway. Zacharias stood and spoke with her in private tones. Elric pretended to listen to the table conversation, but he focused on Zacharias.

"And remember," Zacharias said, "the Lord is the one who promised this Son. He will protect you and bring all things to pass. You must always believe this. What you face is not an easy task, but you have His promise. Stay strong. He will be with you."

Mary hugged Zacharias and squeezed him like she couldn't let go. "I will miss you. You have been so good to me. Thank you."

After a long embrace, Zacharias pulled her back and wiped her eyes. "The blessing has been ours," he said. "Come, let's go. You have a great adventure ahead of you."

Standing at the closed front door, Elric pulled a lightweight tunic with a hood from a small bundled sack and handed it to Mary. From the time the Lord had given him this special garment in the secret chambers of heaven, Elric wondered when he would need to use it. He recalled the King's words: "If you overshadow me with this cloak, I will blind the eyes of the enemy." This particular mission seemed like the right time to break it in.

"Mary, here is an outer coat for you to wear on the trip. The sun will be strong and the trail dusty. You would do well to keep the hood up over your head as much as possible."

"Oh, thank you, sir, but that won't be necessary."

"It is for your own protection. I would really prefer you wore it."

Mary looked over to Zacharias. Zacharias nodded.

Mary took the tunic and slipped it over her head. It fit her well. She felt the soft material between her fingers and compared it to the coarse materials she wore. She gave a sheepish teenage grin, pulled the hood forward, and rubbed it against her cheek. "Thank you," she said.

———

Four hooded horsemen emerged into the early afternoon sun, which had just passed its peak, and the men cast short shadows. They carried three bundles from the house and strapped them onto the horses. Even as they shuffled around the horses, they somehow always managed to shield their faces from any onlooking angle.

The fifth horseman appeared with someone else who also wore a hooded cloak. Zacharias and Elizabeth emerged with the baby. And then came a lieutenant of the host.

"Look," Tumur said, "the extra person in the cloak—it must be the girl."

Luchek wrung his hands. "If only we could be sure."

During the goodbyes, the girl lowered her hood, removed her veil, and kissed Zacharias and Elizabeth on each cheek.

"Can you see her?" Tumur asked.

"Only partially. I think it's the girl. And there's something else. It's hard to tell from this distance, but. . ."

"I see it, too. There's something about her spirit. Almost as though. . ."

The lead horseman quickly helped her put the hood back over her head. He scanned the area and led her around to the horses.